A QUEST FOR A SMALL FAMILY

B. L. RAINA

Commonwealth Publishers
NEW DELHI-110002
(INDIA)

Also by B.L. Raina

***Planning Family in India (Pre-Vedic to Early 1950s)**
***Social Situation in India**
***Population Policy**
***Health Science in Ancient India**
***Health Science March Through Centuries**
***World War II—Medical Services : India**
***Introduction to Malaria Problem in India (Second Edition)**
(Vedic to Early 1950s)

First Edition : 2027

ISBN 81-7169-125-0

Published by :
Commonwealth Publishers
4378/4B, Ansari Road, Gali Murari Lal
New Delhi-110002

Printed at :
Stylish Composing Agency
Bhajanpura, Delhi-110053

ACKNOWLEDGEMENTS

The author is grateful to a number of individuals and organisations who helped in preparation of this book. Many responded readily to request for information. Some gave their personal files. Others looked through part or whole of the manuscript. A very large number of persons provided information during field visits especially workers in the field, researchers and persons in all walks of life both in urban and rural areas. To all of them and the authors mentioned in "Notes and References" and publishers I offer my deepest thanks. As some of the observations are from notes made over the years since 1950s some references may have been missed. A few references are cited from other publications as they may assist in further reading.

Special gratitude is due to Mrs. Avabai Wadia for providing a number of reports giving her own contribution and contribution of Family Planning Association of India. Dr. Douglous Ensminger for giving some insights on programmes supported by him and the Ford Foundation ; Dr. Soundaram Ramchandran for her views on the main factors responsible for success of the programme in Athoor Block Gandhigram ; Mr. Valaile Chacko, Dr. Rahmathulla and her team, Mr. K.N. Sarcar, Mr. M K. Chaudhri and Mr. O. Kaul for information on "plantations" ; Mr. D. Isacc for details of family planning projects launched by the Christian Medical Association of India ; Mrs. Malika Ghosh for very kindly giving me her personal file on family planning leaders ; Mr. D.V.R. Murty for tracing and sending me rhythm study papers ; Mr. R.S. Kurup for his comments on fertility decline in Kerala; and Dr. K.C. Zacharia for the field investigation report on Kerala ; Dr. P.P. Talwar and Mr. P.S. Bhatia for their suggestions on the preliminary draft on population training and research units, Dr. Nirmal Sawhney, Dr. K. Srinivasan and Dr. P.H. Reddy for information on the India Population Projects in Uttar Pradesh and Karnataka ; Asoka Raina and Ranjit Raina for their views on communication system and role of media ; Dr. G.P. Talwar, Dr. Somnath Roy and Dr. Rabi-prasad Das for help in the preparation of the section on birth control methods.

Special thanks are due to Saraswati, Neera and Rajat Raina, and Sudha and Dhruv Kaul for assistance in a number of ways.

The views expressed are of the author and not necessarily of those who have read the book in part or whole or provided information.

B.L.R.

INTRODUCTION

The quest for improving the quality of life and birth planning appears to have begun since human beings appeared on this earth. For centuries, the major efforts were directed towards having a large family. Around early Nineteenth Century the subject to restrict the size of the family started to be discussed.

"Man is primarily an animal placed on this earth with essentially the same demands and same limitations as the other animals, even though he has developed intellectual and spiritual qualities that set him apart as human being. This is a finite globe, limited both as to its extent and composition. It is on this globe that man has to satisfy the two universal demands for standing room and food and possibilities in both respects are positively limited. In its life cycle on this earth, every living organism is directed by basic forces—the drives of hunger and sex. The unlimited potentialities of reproduction and finite possibilities of food supplies, put these two fundamental urges in direct opposition to each other. A moderate example of population increase is furnished by the oyster, who lays about 16 million eggs a year. If this rate was maintained without interference, the progeny of a single pair of oysters, their great-great-grand children, in five years would produce a mass of shells eight time the size of earth. It is a rule of nature, that the higher an organism appears on the evolutionary scale lower tends to be its birth rate, yet there is no species on earth that does not have a sufficient rate of reproduction to overflow the entire globe in a few generations, if there was nothing to stop it.... It is clear that the population of every species whatsoever must be controlled, and man is no exception. There are only two methods of control either through births or through deaths. Nature provides for the enforcement of the inevitable law of stationary population by fantastically high death rate, particularly of the new born. Man alone has the ability, which is beginning to be exercised, of controlling population growth through births".[1]

Some pesons donot subscribe to the view that the rate of growth of population in the world is a danger signal. They consider that human ability to increase resources and potential of earth and its surroundings are enormous. There are others who consider that social and economic development will moderate the population growth rate in normal course. There are still others who point to the declining birth rates in developed countries and consider "population bogy" is a creation of vested interests. Nehru, at the Sixth International Conference on Planned Parenthood, said : "There is to-day...a growing consciousness of tremendous crisis that might arise in the world with indefinitely growing population. People are frightened more particularly in Europe and America than Asia. They are frightened of the vast masses of Asia becoming vaster and vaster, of the population of India, China, South East Asia swamping all over the place. Well it is legitimate fear and we have to take that into consideration. But obviously, if the subject is approached from the point of view of Europe being overwhelmed by Asia, that is not the approach Asia would appreciate, however much there is in it...The matter have to be approached in a different way, a global way". In the Indian context he said "the first we have to consider in planning is what will be the population for which we are planning ? How much food they would require ? How much clothing ? How much housing ? How much many other things—education, health? It doesnot become a theoretical concept...if our population goes up rapidly the necessity of some kind of limitation of that growing population becomes an urgent necessity for us".[2]

Population problem is complex. In words of the report of

1. Fairchild, Henry Pratt, *Population and Peace*, The Virginia League for Planned Parenthod, Richmond 24, Virginia, cited in Raina, B.L. *Birth Control Why, When and How*, New Book Company Ltd., Bombay, 1939.
2. Nehru, Jawaharlal, Inaugural Address International Conference on Planned Parenthood, New Delhi, 1959.

the World Commission on Environment and Development, popularly known as Brudtland Report, "there are a series of ironic equations associated with population. Here are some examples. When a large proportion of infants and children die, large families are the only 'pension plan' poor families can arrange...The finite resources of our global village cannot support infinitely growing population. But we do need more people to develop the resources we have—especially trained and skilled people...Another irony is that one child added to the population of the industrial world will use at least as much globe's resources as 30 or more children to the Third World...Social support systems are essential, to persuade poor rural families they need not have so many children to guarantee a source of income when they grow older. Literate women marry later, space their children and have smaller families. No global effort to reduce population growth can be effective without major and calculated effort to foster women's right....Without more development, we cannot hope to curb the current ungovernable increase in population...The youthful population 'bulge' in the Third World means population will continue to grow over the next two or three generations, as those children reach marrying and child bearing age....Economic development reduces fertility rates. So international policies which impede Third World development—including Western protectionism and low commodity prices—have a literal and direct effect, which is counter—productive to population planning in developing nations. . Poverty alone, is not a barrier. In some areas, India's south-west Kerala State and Sri Lanka are notable examples, high literacy rates have resulted in low fertility figure, low infant mortality and high life expectancy, despite average income much lower than surrounding areas...Increasing human potential towards its ultimate capacity is our greatest challenge. That can only be accomplished in the Third World with reduced size of the families, and the freedom and power-of choice that those changes will bring to women and, thereby to there families.. .The population issue is about humans and not about numbers".[3]

---

3. World Commission on Environment and Development, *Tribute*, World Media Institute, Inc., 549 Besserer Street, Ottawa, Canada.

Family planning programmes have been in operation in a number of developing countries for a varying periods. Remarkable decline in fertility is noted in China. Many developing countries like Thailand and Mexico show a trend in fertility decline. In Singapore, where a vigorous family planning programme was launched only a few years back, the marked fertility decline has led the Government to close their family planning board and its activities.[4] The picture is not so rosy in many countries.

The population of the World will continue to grow for some generations. "If replacement were achieved as soon as 2000, a highly unlikely scenario, the world population size would not reach 9 billion. If it were delayed to 2080, world population would be close to triple to-days size"[5] "Population" issue therefore continues to be a cause of concern in world forums.

For the Twenty-first Century the Amsterdam Declaration[6] presents the following scenario:

---

4. Singapore launched, in the early 1960s, a vigorous programme to reduce fertility. The rapid socio-economic development combined with the fertility reduction programme led to decline in total fertility rate from 6.53 (1957) to 2.08 (1975) and to 1.42 (1986). Recently Government of Singapore initiated programme to increase fertility, further reinforced it in 1987 with pro-natalist incentives, including tax rebates couples with a third child, subsidy to employed mothers for each of their first three pre-school children placed in approved full day child care centres, public housing incentives, converting full time work for working mothers to part time, full pay leave for mothers to attend their sick children, etc. (Saw, S., "*Changes in fertility policy of Singapore*", IPS Occasional Paper No. 2, Times Academia Press Singapore, 1990 (*Popline*).

5. 1990 World Population Data Sheet. The Population Reference Bureau Inc,, Washington D.C.

6. From 6 to 9 November, 1989, an International Forum on Population in the Twenty-first Century was held in Amsterdam, at the initiative of the United Nations Population Fund in cooperation with the Government of Netherlands. Tho participants included ministers or officials from 79 countries, representatives of the United Nations and its specialized agencies, and of inter-governmental organizations and observers fron non-governmental organizations and from

(*Contd.*)

"...the total size of the world's population in 2025 is now expected to be 8.5 billion, some 300 million more than had been projected ;

—The World's population will continue to grow until perhaps a century from now, when it will level off at 10 billion or more".

—Yearly increament over the next 10 years will approach 97 million world wide, 94 per cent of which will be in the developing world.

—Of the 42 countries with annual growth rates of over 3 per cent 24 are located in Africa and 10 are in the Middle East ;

—By the end of the century those in the developing countries aged 0 to 25 years will number 2.6 billion, or nearly 42 per cent of the world's projected total population at that time ;

—The younger ones among this group (those aged 0 to 14 years) will largely have to depend on others for food, education, health care, clothing and shelter ; the older ones (age 15 to 24) will have to struggle to find work, especially in the cities, which are currently growing at four times the rate of those in the more developed regions (3.6 per cent per year versus 0.8 per cent) ;—By the year 2025, the proportion of the population living in

---

(*Contd.*)

academic and training institutions. "The Forum had two main objectives, *viz.* : (*a*) to delineate the major issues and needs in the implementation of population policies and programmes in the future, in consonance with the overall goals of sustainable development ; and (*b*) to adopt specific programme strategies, with due emphasis on regional perspectives, to be implemented by Governments with the support of United Nations specialized agencies and organizations, inter-governmental organizations, bilateral agencies and non-governmental organizations. "The Forum issued a statement, adopted by concensus entitled" A Better Life for future Generation : the Amsterdam Declaration.

urban areas in developing countries will reach 57 per cent, a nearly 70 per cent increase over the current proportion of 34 per cent".

The Declaration underlines that :

"At the very least, national population goals and objectives for the coming decade and beyond should include :

—A reduction in the average number of children born per women commensurate with achieving, as a minimum, the medium variant population projections of the United nations :

(*a*) A major reduction in the proportion of women and men who are not currently using reliable methods of family planning, but who want to postpone, delay, or limit child bearing ;

(*b*) A substantial reduction in very early marriage and in teenage pregnancy ;

(*c*) An increase in contraceptive prevalence in developing countries, so as to reach at least 56 per cent of women of reproductive age by the year 2000 in view of the considerable unmet needs in family planning, thereby expanding the currently estimated 326 million users-couples to 535 million user couples ;

—A reduction of the 1980 rate of infant mortality to rate of at most 50 per 1000 live births by the year 2000 in all countries and major sub groups within countries ;

—A reduction in maternal mortality from all causes, including illegal abortion, by at least 50 per cent by the year 2000, particularly in regions where this figure currently exceeds 100 per 100,000 births ;

—An increase in the average life expectancy at birth to 62 years or more for men and women in countries with high mortality by the end of the century ;

—A better geographical distribution of the population within national territories in balance with proper use of resources".

"A reconsideration of programme priorities and approaches should, in particular, be sensetive to and aware of :

—The effects of education on demographic behaviour and the critical importance for development of increasing female literacy and achieving universal enrolment of girls in primary school by the year 2000 ;

—The need to raise the social and economic value of girl children in the family, community, and national development ;

—The need to increase women's participation in decision-making and management of population policies and programmes and special programmes for economic development of women, with the aim of achieving equality of representation ;

—The need to improve coverage and quality of maternal and child health and family planning programmes wherever possible within the context of primary health care and, where circumstances make it necessary, through other approaches ;

—The health benefits of birth spacing and breastfeeding to mothers and infants, such as : the importance of spacing births two or more years apart ; the avoidance of pregnancy too early or too late in a woman's reproductive period ; and, the encouragement of breast feeding for nutritional and family planning reasons ;

—The value of information, education and communication activities in developmental work in general and population programmes in particular and the need to direct information activities to both women and men ;

—The impact of rural development and investment in regional employment opportunities for both sexes and by implication on the magnitude of rural-to-urban migration and the needs of slum dwellers ;

—The need to train adequate numbers of staff, including programme managers so as to enable them to become self sufficient in carring out expanded population programmes ;

—The close relationship between activities dealing with sexually transmitted diseases including AIDS, and maternal and child health, family planning, and population education and information ;

—The need to recognize that some problems that seriously affect developed countries are also begining to affect the developing countries, in particular in regard to international migration and to aging of populations in countries with low fertility".

The annual cost estimated by the Forum for the year 2000 is US $ 9 billion, double the expenditure estimated in 1987. The Amesterdum Forum "Call on all governments, inter-governmental and non-governmental organizations, and the private sector to take concerted steps to increase in, on regular basis, their financial commitments so as to fulfil the ongoing and emerging needs in the population fields".[7]

The global concern in the rapid rates of population growth has been shared by India for a very long time. India is committed "to promote the Welfare of the people by securing and protecting as effectively as it may a social order in which justice, social economic and political, shall inform all the institutions of National life".[8] This commitment led India to launch a Nationwide family programme as an integral part of social and economic development in early 1950s, the first Government in the world with a population policy to reduce

---

7. "The Amsterdam Declaration" cited in Demeny, Paul, ed., *Population and Development Review*, Vol. 16, No. 1, Population Council, New York, March 1990.

8. *The Constitution of India.*

the rate of growth of population.[9] The development and population policies in India are criticised from time to time—some with justification, others exaggerated or without any foundation. Progress in the field of cereal production has been spectacular. A country dependent on imports for food, is now self-sufficient and also has some to spare. Notable progress has been made in industrial field, and scientific and technological man power. Expectation of life at birth has increased from 32.1 years (1941-51) to 54.4 years (1971-81 provisional)[10] and is projected during 1986-91 to be about 60 years.[11] Per Capita income at current prices has increased from about Rs 633 (1970-71) to Rs. 2595.6 (1985-86).

Total fertility rate in urban areas declined from 4.3 (1972) to 3.1 (1986) and in rural areas from 5,4 to 4.5 in the same period. This decline is noted in all States in rural and urban areas except Bihar. The decline in total fertility rate in Kerala in 1986 was reported to be 2.3 in rural areas and 2.2 in urban areas. Couples effectively protected from having births increased from 10.4 per cent (1970-71) to 37.5 per cent (1986-87).[12]

There is also another side of the picture. The progress achieved is far from expectations. There are wide disparities between the rich and poor. About 37 per cent of the population is below the poverty line. Some estimates are higher. The reasons for such a situation are many. One of them is the shadow of rapid growth of population. This does not imply that population increase is the main cause of poverty. Nehru

9. *The First Five Year Plan*, The Planning Commission Government of India, 1952.

10. *Family Welfare Programme in India Year Book 1986-87*, Department of Family Welfare, Ministry of Health Government of India, New Delhi, 25 January, 1988.

11. Report of the Expert Committee on Population Projection in the light of 1981 Census.

12. Family Welfare Programme in India. Year Book 1986-87.

warned that such an approach would imply blaming population for the failures in socio-economic efforts. The complex inter-relationships have been indicated above. The increase in the couples effectively protected is also not reassuring. For reaching net reproduction rate of 1 by 2000, requires a level of couple protection of 60 per cent within a few years. The population of India is projected as 986.1 million (medium projection) in 2001. Poverty has various levels.

According to Malcolm Adiseshiah, "the number of poor (in India) is nearer 400 million. Of this the absolute destitute—which is the bottom 10 per cent of society-are around 50-60 million, which comprise not only the chronic indigents, but also the old, the sick, the disabled, and for this group it is not employment and opportunities of earning of income that has to be provided, but some kind of social security involving regular monthly payment......this leaves some 350 million ..—living at various levels of poverty, and for whom the employment programmes pass by, social security measures will have to be made. The poor in the rural areas are the landless labourers, who are increasingly being transformed from being wage labourers to casual labourers, the marginal farmers, the displaced villages artisans such as the blacksmith, the carpenters, the leather workers, etc.... The poor in the urban areas are the non-unionised workers in what is called the informal sector, who are the poor migrating from the rural areas and are living in slums and taking up any work at any wage or income that comes their way, such as vegetable, fruit, flowers and meat vendours, the servants in tea shops, domestic servants gardners, day labourers etc......in the rural areas the top 20 per cent own over 80 per cent of land and rural assets, where as the bottom 20 per cent have only four per cent of all rural assets. With regard to the urban rich they own all urban land and industrial assets (stocks and shares-less than one per cent of the population are share and debenture holders) and in addition they are holders of the major part of 'black' wealth and incomes which are estimated at around an annual Rs. 50,000-60,000 crores to-day, and they are the ones who stash away every year a large part of foreign exchange that is earned through exports in tax-free havens of Switzerland, St. Kitts and Virgin Islands at the rate of $ 2 billion a year, while the majority in the urban areas are either living in poverty as noted earlier or just made do with whatever they earn".[13]

The estimates of increase in population from 685.2 million in 1981 to 837.2 million by 1991 and 986.1 million by 2001 are based on several assumptions *viz.*, (*i*) increase in expectation of life at birth of males 54.1 years and females 54.7 years (1980) to 62.8 years for males and 64.2 years for females (1996-2001), reduction in the death rate from 12.7 in 1980 to 8.4 during the quinquennium 1996-2001 ; (*ii*) increase in age at marriage, reduction in incidence of widowhood due to increase in life expectancy and intensified family planning programme with improved performance, a decline in birth rate from 34.7 in in 1980 to 23.7 by 1996-2001. These assumptions mean a decline in the growth rate of population from 2.2 per cent in 1981 to about 1.5 per cent by 1995-2001.[14]

A clearer picture will emerge soon. The 1991 population census has just been completed. In any case a population near one billion by the end of the century is serious enough. In case the assumptions in respect of decline in fertility are found to be too optimistic, the 2025 population will exceed 2 billion and will be growing at even faster rate than to-day.

In whatever direction we look, whether it is health, nutrition, environment or development, the rapid rate of growth of population is a cause of a very serious concern.

The consequences of uncontrolled rate of pupulation growth are obvious : increasing unmet needs for education, health, nutrition, housing, employment, deterioration of environment, erosion of natural resources and living standards.

The populations trend shows change in age structure. The

13. Illustrated Weekly of India, 4 10 November, 1990.
14. Verma, V.S., *A Handbook of Population Statistics*, Census of India, 1981, Registrar General of India, New Delhi, 1988.

number of aged are steadily increasing. These have serious economic and social consequences.

Increasing unemployment and under-employment alone will create a large number of angry young men. In words of Willford Jenks, "There is no more explosive social compound than expectations so high and frustration so humiliating (as joblessness)". Already there are problems which threaten social harmony like religous ethnic, regional, linguistic movements. The unmet needs and aspirations could easily light the spark for social unrest.

From the above brief population scenario, it is obvious that the remaining periods of the twentieth century and the beginning of the twenty-first century are crucial for population management. Every effort must be made to moderate fertility. These efforts should include efficient management of the family planning programme, and effective ways of integration of activities related to population, environment and development. It will be fruitful to look for new approaches and strategies emerging from new developments in science and technology, innovative approaches and experience. At the sametime the experience of past and present programme and projects should be critically examined.

It is often noted that for improvement of the programme performance no further change in declared policy is required. But major change is required in the implementation of the programme, to make them more effective and efficient and to increase the pace of implementation. There is also sufficient experience by now of approaches which have succeded and which have failed. The constraints and pre requisites for success have been identified.

Indian scenario includes varied activities such as the controversial rhythm study, delivering services through clinics and out-reach paramedical workers, family planning with extension education, family planning integration with maternity child health and nutrition ; integration with social, and economic development and environment. Several strategies have been tried including determination of inhibiting and supporting factors and strategies based of action—research.[15]

The dimensions of population policy and the two-way relationships between population and socio-economic development health, education, nutrition, income, equity and others have been recognised for a very longtime. Education of women, opening new employment opportunities for them and raising age of marriage were underlined in the Third Five-Year Plan (1961-1966).[16] Their visible linkage, the stress on such linkages and development of strong policy support to integration of population, environment and development gradually took shape both in National and International scene. The experience in developing countries including India contributed to these developments.

It may be noted that there is a continuous expanding population policy base in India. The emphasis shifted "to generate motivation for adoption of a small family norm by considerably extending the base of family welfare programme apart from providing effective and efficient family planning services, the policy envisages inclusion of services to cover areas such as health especially maternal and child health, nutrition, water supply and sanitation, raising status of women, education,

---

15. The operation research or operational research approach was developed during World War (1939-45). or appreciating the need and for getting insight into a framework of the operational research in family planning programme refer to Banerji D., "Administration of Family Planning Programme" in *Management in Government*, Vol. I, 2, July-September 1969.

    The important feature of operations research is that the programme manager adopts a course of action after testing the impact of selected variables in field situation. The action research in family planning programme in India developed into testing out varied package of activities in a given population (Block, District, Horpital Post-Partum cases, Market place, etc.) to create among the people the desire to have a small family through community action supported by the professionals and the State.

16. *Third Five Year Plan*, Planning Commission, New Delhi, 1961.

employment, social justice and land reforms within the limit of family welfare programme. .. Obviously a basic shift in policy should be accompanied with a basic change in the organisation and management of the family welfare programme".[17] It will be useful to examine basic changes in organisation and management.

India especially in 1950s and 1960s became a vast laboratory for exploring ways and means to control the rapid growth of population.

This book discusses some of the observations made during this period, mainly in a historical perspective. The book is divided in two parts, *viz.*, Birth Control Methods and Selected Programmes and Projects.

Some of the important programmes like Family Planning in the Armed Forces and the formation and development of Family Planning Association of India; Statistical System Population census, birth and death registration; and the Reorganised Family Planning Programme with Extension Approach are discussed in *Planning Family in India Pre-Vedic Times to Early 1950s*, *Social Situation in India*, and *Population Policy*. Rhythm Study and a few other accounts such as demographic training and research centres included in an earlier publications have been included to complete the account.

Some questions are frequently raised like: Has vaginal contraception any place at present? Did the rhythm study make any contribution to development of family planning programme? Has it any relevance at present? How and Why changes in birth control methods were formulated? What measures were taken in search of improved methods? What are the prospects of more effective methods in the near future? How far incentives and disincentives are effective in changing behaviour to adopt a small family norm? What measures were

---

17. Bannerji, Debabar, A Critical Issue in Population Control. August 10, 1983.

taken to develop human resources for family planning programme implementation ? Was the development of "sex-less population education" a step in the right direction ? Is it desirable to enlarge the scope of population education ? What has been the experience of the programme in the organised sector ? Why the programme in India Tea Association plantations was initially a success but was later seriously eroded ? What programme approaches showed remarkable results in projects like those carried out in Southern India plantations, Gandhigram, Malur, Jamkhed ? Are education of women and age at marriage alone responsible for the Kerala success story ? How the communication system was developed and has the mix of mass and personal communication been balanced ? What is implied by "peoples participation" ; what are the constraints and essential requirements for effective peoples participation in development ?

We often hear the expression "information revolution". Is it a myth or reality ? Is the communication system well balanced ? How it can be strengthened ?

Answer to such questions are explored. An attempt is made to find leads to improve programme performance.

The determinants of successes and failures in family planning programme have been well documented in a number of publications. Some states and areas within them which require special attention also have been identified, like Bihar, Madhya Pradesh, Rajasthan, Uttar Pradesh, constituting 2/5th population of India. It is also generally recognised that the major problem is not of declared policies or commitment, but of appreciating their full dimensions and action required to fulfil them. The problem largely is of the extent, pace and quality of implementation of the programme. The aberrations related to incentives and disincentives in the family planning programme, for example, donot appear to have completely disappeared. The frequent strong support to people' participation are often not accompanied by effective action to remove constraints and detailed consideration of pre-requisites essential for such participation.

The base of family planning programme has been broadened. Have the organisational structure and management kept pace with the changes in, population policy ? A serious attempt to find answer to such questions and to examine strengths and weaknesses in the programme will be valuable. In fact continuous monitoring even of a successful programme is essential to maintain and improve its efficiency. It is hoped that this book will be of some help in such attempts.

CONTENTS

ILLUSTRATIONS

The above illustrations are reproduced from *Techniques of Conception Control* by Dr. Robert Latou Dickinson. A practical manual issued by the Planned Parenthood Federation of America Inc, Third Edition, The Williams & Wilkins, Baltimore, 1950.

PART I

Birth Control Methods

1

Birth Control Methods up to Around First Half of the 20th Century nd Developments in Vaginal Contraception

Human beings have always made attempts to plan their families. The practices adopted are rooted in their beliefs, social philosophy, social situation and percieved needs. For a very long period extending over centuries, their major efforts were directed towards having a large number of children. Their quest for a small family began around early nineteenth century. They do appear to have faced situations in earlier period also, howsoever few, to interrupt or prevent or limit the family size. We find methods to control births and to induce abortion in ancient Egypt and India, Some of the ancient practices are lingering at present in tribal communities, and folk medicine.

Petri or *Kahun Papyrus* (1850 B.C.) mentions the use of crocodile dung as vaginal pessary ; honey and soda bicarb as vaginal irrigation and gum-like vaginal inserts. The *Ebers Papyrus* (1550 B.C.) suggests use of medicated lint tampoon in which gum arabic on fermentation appears to release lactic acid. *The Berlin Papyrus* (1300 B.C.) refers to fumigation of vagina.[1] Several devices used as vaginal contraceptive have been reported from other countries such as oiled bamboo tissue paper tampoon (*Misugami*) used by prostitutes in Japan and China ; beeswax intravaginally by German-Hungarian women ; sponge soaked in diluted lemon juice by some Constantinople women ; cloth of linen rags by some Slovak women. Such devices could have been used in Pre-vedic India. It has been suggested that instead of crocodile dung the elephant dung was used in India as vaginal insert. No reliable evidence of use of such dung as a contraceptive in India is traceable. Use of clove, cinnamon, *Ajwain* and oils in contraceptive vaginal plugs, appear to have been used.

Use of herbs by tribal communities in India include those with properties to prevent conception in females. S.P. Singh and V.L. Singh has given list of 15 such plants, *viz.* :

****_Abrus precatorius_ Linn (*Ratti*)
***_Bambusa bambos_ Druce (*Bans*)
**_Boerhaavia repanda_ Willd (*Funernava*)
*_Cinnamomum camphora_ Linn (*kapur*)
*_Cassia fistula_ Linn (*Amaltas*)
****_Daucus carota_ Linn (Gajar)
***_Musa paradistaca_ Linn (*Kadali*)
***_Piper betle_ Linn (*Pan*)
*_Punica granatum_ Linn (*Anar*)
****_Peurgria tuberosa_ De (*Vidhari Khand*)
*_Semicarpus anacardium_ Linn (*Bhilawa* of cashew nut)
*_Sesbania sesban_ Linn (*Jayanti*)
****_Skimmia lauriola_ Sieb (*Nair*)
****_Ricinus communis_ Linn (*Arandi*)
*_Tamarix diuca Roxb_ (*Jhau*)

*Found with antifertility activity in female albino rats
**Root powder showed uterotonie activity
***Not studied but strong folklore claim of their antifertility property
****Frequent reference in literature.[2]

B.S. Guha, the distinguished anthropologist, investigated the antifertility properties of some drugs used by the Abhor tribes. Ranjit Roy Chaudhuri listed a number of drugs considered to have antifertility effect.[3]

Rubber Contraceptives

We find reference to use of condom in the eighteenth century. But it was the valcunization of rubber by Goodyear and Hancock in 1843-44, which enabled its general use. Friedrich Adolph Wilde, in 1838, recommended cervical cap moulded for each person. The mechanical rubber contraceptives for use by women were introduced in early 1880s by Dr. Mensinga (pseudonym. Karl Hasse or C. Hasse) in Germany and spread to Holland and then England. In USA it was hardly known until 1920, if we omit random exceptions".[4]

Chemical Contraception

The story of chemical spermicides begins with the Swiss zoologist Kolliker, who proved in 1841 that sperms are true sexual elements and noted that "many substances immobilized sperms in high and low, but not in intermediate concentrations ... he was here observing simply the effect of osmotic pressure, ... he found that the movement of sperms may be slowed down by acids and restored by alkalies showed that alkaloids have low spermicidal powers". In 1905 and 1906 comprehensive investigations on spermicides were done by Gustav Gunthur. In 1931, E. Gellhorn published the results of his investigations on effect of salts on sperms. The notable work on spermicides was started by John Baker in his laboratory in 1928, under the Birth Control Investigation Committee in England; and by C.I.B. Vogue at the Animal Breeding Research Department (later called the Institute of Animal Genetics) under general direction of Professor F.A.E. Crew, for the Committee on Maternal Health United States* between 1929-32.[5]

Change in Legislation in India on Birth Control Information

The 1877-79, Bradlaugh—Besant trial in the United King-

---

*Certain legal restrictions in the United States at that time led Voge to work tn Edinburgh.

dom had world-wide repercussions in promoting birth control movement. Lord Chief Justice Cockburn in his judgement legitimised the dissemination of information on contraception.[6] This also influenced the legal position in India. In the Indian law books a note was added that the advice on birth control was not obscene. From the legal prosecution, three times, of Professor Ragunath Dhondu Karve, it appears that the definition of obscenity in relation to advice on birth control was vague.[7] The acquital of Professor Karve on his third prosecution left no doubt in the freedom of dissemination of information on birth control in India.

Birth Control Clinics

During 1920s and 1930, we notice that the birth control devices (mostly imported) were available in a number of places in India. A birth control clinic was opened in Girgaum. In 1930, Dr. C.V. Natrajan, who had studied methods of contraception in the USA was appointed by the Government of Mysore State to guide the medical officers at the birth control clinics established in Government hospitals in Bangalore and Mysore. During 1930-1939 the places where birth control advice was available increased—in 1932 in Madras by Neo Malthus Society, in Poona by G.D. Kulkarni ; in 1935 in Bombay (two clinics one training and service clinic on Lamington Road and one in Parel near K.E.M. Hospital) by Dr. A.P. Pillay, in Karachi by Dr. Thomas, in Nagpur by Dr. S.V. Shirali, in Calcutta by Dr. S.P. Pandit ; in 1936 in Wai by Dr. Rose F. Beals ; in 1937 at Ujjain by Mr. Baburao Suryavanshi and Dr. B.L. Raina ; 1939 in Brindaban by Dr. M.A. Burchard and in Delhi in two mills by Women's League. There must be many others, which have not been reported. Well organised birth control clinics with noticeable attendance appeared after the World War II. The most notable amongst them was the centre established by the Family Planning Association of India in 1949 soon after the Association was formed. It was called Kutumb Sudhar Kendra. About the sametime an organised family planning programme was initiated in the Indian Army on the suggestion of General (now Field Marshal) K.M. Cariappa the Commander-in-Chief Indian Army. After two years preparatory phase to gain experience in August 1951, the family planning scheme extended throughout the Indian Army, as an integral part of family welfare activities.[8]

GENERAL ASSESSMENT OF ACCESSIBILITY AND ACCEPTANCE

With the exception of the Armed forces, it is difficult to assess accurately the availability of family planning services in the early 1950s in the rest of population.

In the rural areas the army personnel on leave may have introduced use of condoms. Mrs. Shakuntala Pranjpay, a close associate of Professor Karve, had been advocating cotton-pad soaked with oil. This may have been used by a few. The coitus interruptus abstinence for some periods, and some of the traditional devices may have been in use. There is evidence of practice of induced abortion.

In the urban areas sterilization operations were performed in some places.

Dr. T. Lakshminarayana and Dr. K. Mitra had surveyed the family planning clinics in the Punjab, Uttar Pradesh, Bihar, Bengal, Hyderabad and Bombay in 1953. According to their reports there were clinics attached to hospitals, child welfare centres, and clinics not working with hospitals and maternity centres by voluntary organisations and private clinics by individuals not necessarily qualified to do so and generally for profit.

The birth control methods used in them included : diaphragm and jelly, cervical cap, jelly or cream, foam tablets, pad and oil, pad and salt water, condom, rice jelly, safe period, douche, and others like trial with an Ayurvedic pill in one clinic. The diaphragm with jelly or jelly only were commonly advised and reported to be more acceptable than any other form of contraceptives. "Pad and oil, pad and salt, rice jelly, etc., were introduced by many centres, but their use was discarded after a while for one reason or the other". Advice on sterility was given at many centres and in such clinics attendance tended to be much larger than others. The average attendance was 250 only in any of the centres in a year. The standard of work of clinics under the auspicies of voluntary organisations "was in many cases high, in spite of the limitations imposed by financial stringency".[9]

General Recommendations on Birth Control Methods in 1940-50

The following extracts from an early publication on birth control methods may further give details of the methods recommended in 1940s and 1950s in India.

"Safe Periods

As the ovum is discharged about 14 days before the next menstruation it is assumed that fertilisation occurs about then or slightly later. Ogino and Knaus independently studied these processes in detail. According to the former, ovulation occurs 12 to 16 days and according to the latter 14 to 16 days before menstruation. It will be obvious that if the 12th to 16th day before the next menstruation appears is taken as the ovulation period, and two days are added before it (for the span of life of the sperm), one day after it (for the span of life of the ovum) the remaining days in the menstrual cycle shall be a safe period. To be further on the safe side it is usually recommended to add three days before and after the period of ovulation. All that is therefore required is to mark on a calendar or chart the date on which the next menstruation is due, and then to count 9 to 19 days before the period. Suppose 30th of the month is the date menstruation is due then the first ten days of the month will be safe, the next eleven days fertile and the last 8 days of the month again safe.

The problem however is not so simple as it sounds. The menstrual cycle not only differs between one women and another, but also differs in the same woman at different times. In cases where gross irregularity occurs it is practically impossible to find out when ovulation occurs. All that can be safely stated is that every woman has a safe period but it is very difficult to work it out in each case, and as a safe method of contraception it cannot be recommended. It can be suggested only to those who refuse to carry out any other method, on religious grounds, or otherwise. The risk involved and the unreliability of the method should always be explained to the couple. Complete records of the menstrual cycle for long periods (8 months to a year) are essential before the method is adopted. The dates must be carefully marked on a calender or chart for the purpose and frequently checked by the physician.*

Coitus Interruptus (Withdrawal Before Emission)

Coitus interruptus is extensively practised, but is very unreliable as a contraceptive measure. The precoital secretion during sexual excitement comes from the urethral glands of Littre and probably from Cowpers glands. In some cases, however, active sperms have been found in it. The practice of the method is reported to lead to prostatic enlargement in males, and nervous disturbances in both. Adequate figures (to enable one to form a balanced judgment) are, however, not available.

Coitus Reservatus 'Holding Back'—After Prolonged Excitement the husband avoids reaching Orgasm

Coitus reservatus, is not favoured by most of the authorities. Erroneous ideas exist in some females. Some of them consider that if they remain unconcerned during coitus and avoid reaching orgasm, pregnancy can be prevented. It is obviously not true as ovulation occurs independently of coitus.

Prolonged Lactation

Some women are relatively protected during early months of lactation. The risk however exists. Breast feeding of a child does not ensure that pregnancy cannot take place.

---

*The use of the Basal body temperature graph was also recommended as more reliable, in the first part of menstrual cycle the temperature is lower than during the latter half ; at the time of ovulation transition from lower to higher level occurs.

Pralysing or Killing the Sperms

Sperms can be killed by douches and chemicals in douches, suppositories, tablets, powder and pastes.

(*i*) **Douches.** Douches attempt to remove the semen from the vagina. Their action is more mechanical than chemical. Tap water alone can immobilize sperms in about ten seconds. If the semen is shed on or near the external os (opening in the neck of the uterus) within a few minutes sperms can swim into the neck. In any case douching should be done without losing time. The douching should be done carefully. It is essential that the solution must distend the vaginal walls to open up all the folds where sperms are likely to be hidden. If the ordinary douche-can is kept two feet above the hips and the douche is taken squatting on the floor with the labia kept compressed with thumbs and fingers around the nozzle for sometime, the vagina can be easily distended with the solution. The fingers are released to allow the water to gush out. Whirling spray syringes and bulbs are also available for the purpose. When using a bulb syringe the bulb must be compressed gently with the fingers only. If too much force is used the solution is likely to enter rhe uterus which is dangerous.

It is stated that frequent douching devitalises the vaginal flora (Doderlein's bacillus) hence it cannot be advised more than thrice a week Various substances are used mixed with water for douching for their spermicidal property. The water in each case should be warm.

(*a*) Salt Water—one table spoonful of ordinary table salt in a quart* of water.

(*b*) Soap lather—Soap suds are as good as any. One table spoonful of soap flakes** to a pint—about two glassfuls of water. It is as spermicidal as quinine and chinosol. Soap is irritating and its frequent use therefore is not recommended.

*2 Pints.

**Plain pure soap not strong soaps. $\frac{1}{4}$—$1\frac{1}{2}$ cm. soap cube in a quart of warm water.

(*c*) Alum—one teaspoonful in a pint of water. This is especially useful when parts are relaxed or when a person is suffering from 'whites' (leucorrhoea).

(*d*) Lactic acid—one teaspoonful in a quart of water.

*(*e*) Lemon juice (citric acid)—one or two table spoonfuls of lemon juice in a quart of water.

(*f*) Potassium permangnate—5 grains to a pint of water.

*(*g*) Vinegar (acetic acid)—two table spoonfuls in ½ pint of water.

(*h*) Lysol, Phenol, Mercuric chloride, Boric acid have been used. These are not recommended as concentrated solutions containing the above have caused a great deal of harm and even deaths. Douching either as a single method or combined with chemicals is not reliable.

(*ii*) **Suppositories.** These are almond shaped or cone shaped. They melt inside the vagina ahd kill the sperms. One is put high up the passage a few minutes before coitus. The woman must keep lying after insertion of a suppository, otherwise the preparation is likely to leak out of the vagina. Most of these are made in a base of cocoabutter, glycerogelatine and cocola soap : boric acid, quinine derivates, salcylic acid and phenyl mercuric acetate are the usual chemicals. Quinine and chinosol were used extensively at one time. They not only act as local irritants but the quinine absorbed sometimes causes toxic symptoms, hence their use cannot be recommended.

(*iii*) **Pastes**—Two types of pastes are usually available, simple and foaming.

These are supplied in collapsible tubes. Some provide a long nozzle which can be screwed on top of the tube. The contents are pressed out and deposited near the neck of the womb. This can be easily done while lying down in bed.

---

*Generally 20 parts of warm water and one part of lemon juice or vinegar is recommended.

It is emphasised both in the case of suppositories and pastes that reliance should be placed on a combination of these with a mechanical barrier and not on any one single method.

(*iv*) **Foaming Tablets and Powders.** Tablets are used like suppositories. The moisture of the vagina dissolves it with liberation of carbon dioxide and a spermicidal foam. Adequate moisture is necessary for dissolving the tablet and herein lies its greatest disadvantage. It is positively irritating and harmful in cases where vaginal secretion is limited. Foaming powders like tablets in the presence of moisture liberate carbon dioxide and spermicidal foam. A sponge cut into a suitable size is dipped in water. The water is squeezed out. The powder is sprinkled on both sides of the sponge. The sponge with the powder is pushed in carefully without squeezing while inserting it. Baker reports that foaming mixtures' containing tartaric acid and sodium bicarbonate in the appropriate proportion are weak spermicides and it would not be safe to rely on them for the killing of sperms in the absence of a mechanical barrier. Reports from the Planned Parenthood Federation of America show that foam powders (like Durex Foam Powder, H. K. Sponge Powder, P. S. Foam Powder, Durekol Concentrated Foam paste) have effectiveness between 80% and 90%. The diaphragm-paste method is more reliable than the sponge-powder method but the latter has the advantage of being simple and cheap. Occasional irritation is however reported by the users.

Stopping the Sperm from Entering the Uterus by Placing a Mechanical Barrier at the Neck of the Womb

Sheaths, tampons, sponges and rubber caps belong to the above group.

(*i*) **Sheaths or Condoms.** These are of two types, rubber and skin. There has been a lot of discussion for and against sheaths. These certainly have not got the disadvantages ascribed to them. It is often argued that with sheaths dulling of male sensation occurs. It may be pointed out that it is an advantage rather than a disadvantage especially for those in whom ejaculation is too precipitate. Sheaths are reliable if properly used. They should be tested before use by blowing in air and holding them before a strong light. Pin point holes can thus be easily seen. Holes can also be detected if a fully blown out sheath is slowly passed close to the face or put in water. While using a sheath about half an inch should be allowed at the blind end so that it can hold the semen. Air should be removed from this end by simply compressing it with two fingers. While withdrawing, the sheath must be steadied with two fingers. No lubricant should be applied inside as then it is likely to slip off Thin rubber sheaths should be used only once. Durable sheaths however can be cleaned with soap and water, dried and kept in french chalk and preserved for 3 months. It is a good rule to keep them unrolled. Skin sheaths are made of the peritonial covering of animal intestines. They are usually stiff and crack easily. As a precaution a suppository or paste should be used in addition to a sheath.

(*ii*) **Tampons and Sponges.** A piece of sponge or a pad of wool or cotton able to cover the cervix serves the purpose. Sponge is preferred. Absorbent cotton is likely to be compressed to a very small size. Various sizes and types are available. When selecting one it should be seen that it is of the size required. The size may have to be changed after child birth. A sponge two inches square and half an inch thick may fit a woman who has had no children, but about double the size may be required after child-birth. Oily spermicidal pastes or jellies can be used with the sponge with advantage. Olive oil has practically no spermicidal power. Vinegar solution (2 tablespoonfuls in ½ pint) or lemon juice (1 to 2 tablespoonfuls to a quart) may be used when a suitable spermicidal paste, cream, or jelly is not available.

(*iii*) **Rubber Caps.*** Rubber caps with spermicidal pastes are

---

*At present three types of rubber cervical caps are available, *viz.*, the Prentif which covers cervix only in four sizes 22, 25, 28 and 31 mm; the Dumas in five sizes from 50—75 mm; and the Vimule, a bell shaped cap in three sizes 42, 48, 54 mm; Dumas and Vimule cover cervix and part of upper vaginal vault.

the most reliable of all the contraceptives described above. Three common types are :

(*a*) Cervical caps ;

(*b*) Vault pessaries ; and

(*c*) Diaphragm pessaries.

(*a*) Cervical caps are usually available in six sizes 00, 0, ½, 1, 2, 3. They may be of rubber or metal (silver, aluminium) celluloid or plastic material. These fit on the neck of the womb independent of support from the vaginal walls. The method of insertion is however not very easy. The rubber cap is held between two fingers and inserted with the hollow side up. While removing the finger is hooked on the rim. No attempt at pulling the dome or the tag should be made as repeated pulling of the cervix may lead to displacement of the uterus. The metal, or celluloid caps are usually fitted by a doctor at the end of menstruation. The cap is taken on the right index finger just like a thimble. The finger is introduced and when it reaches the cervix then the cap is tilted and turned so that it fits over the cervix. The cap is removed by the patient before the next menstrual period begins. The cap can be partly filled by a spermicidal paste.

The cervical cap can be used only when the cervix is healthy and well formed and pointing downwards. It should also be seen that the cervical cap if used is not likely to get dislodged during coitus.

(*b*) Vault pessary is made of thick rubber at the edges, thin rubber in the centre and has a shallow dome. Its use also is limited to the cases described above. It is suitable for cases with prolapsed vagina, rectocele, and cystocele with forward pointing cervix. It is inserted by holding the sides of the cap together with hollow facing upwards. The front part is pressed backwards until it gets into the posterior fornix. The hind end easily slips into place covering the cervix on its way. It is taken out by first dislodging the cap with the thumb while in a kneeling position and then by gently pulling it out with the thumb.

(*c*) Diaphragm pessary is very popular with almost all physicians. A diaphragm pessary divides the vagina into two parts. The upper part includes the neck of the womb. Different patterns of these are available. 'Ramses' with coiled wire rim, 'Dutch' with watch spring rim and 'Matrisalus' a combination of Hodges pessary and diaphragm. The success in using the pessaries depends on selecting the right size and fitting it correctly. The correct size can be determined after a vaginal examination only. The length of the vagina is measured from the tip of the finger in the arch below the neck of the womb (the posterior fronix) to the bone in front (the symphysis pubis). The measurement is checked with diaphragm pessaries of various sizes or preferably with measuring rings. The diameter of a cap is measured in millimeters. About eighteen sizes are available in steps of 2½ mm. Sizes 70 to 80 are most commonly used. The correct size, however, is one that fits snugly without pressure on the pubic arch or posterior fornix and without any discomfort to the patient. After the diaphragm is fitted one must make sure that the finger tip cannot be passed along the anterior vaginal wall in front and that the cervix is covered. The woman must not only be taught to fit the pessary herself but also to remove it, and she should be able to appreciate the feel of her cervix with and without the pessary in position. She can fit it squatting, sitting on the edge of the bed with one foot raised, or lying in the bad rising on the left elbow. It is held with index finger hooking the rim with hollow downwards and introduced along the floor of the vagina pushing it backwards till it reaches the posterior fornix. The anterior end is finally pushed up behind the symphysis. The cervix sometimes obstructs its passage especially when it is long. The simplest way to overcome this difficulty is to pull the cap out a little and then to push it back on a downwards slope. For removal the finger is hooked under the rim and the pessary is dislodged from behind the pubis, and then pulled out steadily. Mechanical inserters are available for women with short fingers and those who are so stout that they cannot easily fit or remove a diaphragm pessary.

The Dutch cap with a watch-spring rim is especially suitable for women with lax vagina. Women with lax and sagging vaginal walls find the Matrisalus pessary very suitable and comfortable. The Matrisalus pessary has a S shaped rim ; the upturned ends of the S keep the sagging portion of the vaginal walls raised.

Caps should *always* be used with a spermicidal paste. The paste should be smeared liberally on both sides of the cap and round the rim. The pessary must not be removed immediately after coitus. It should be removed 10 hours after intercourse.

Frustrating the attempt of the fertilised ovum to settle down in the uterus

Intrauterine stems, studs, wish-bones, silver rings and intrauterine injections of irritants like iodine belong to this group. High degree of protection has been reported but serious bleeding, infection, cramps and even deaths have also occurred.

Preventing the ovum from reaching the uterus or sperm appearing in the ejaculate

The above is possible only on taking operative measures which sterilize the patient by tying and cutting the cord conveying seminal fluid from the testes in the male, or by cutting and burying the ends of the tubes which connect the ovaries with the uterus in the female.

In the male the operation is relatively simple. It consists only in picking up the structures of the cord and cutting the skin over it under proper aseptic precaution and anaesthesia. After dissecting the duct it is cut. The upper end is ligatured. The lower end is left as it is ; for if ligatured the patient usually gets pain due to retention of secretions. The skin is then sutured. There is no alteration in sexual desire, satisfaction, potency or quantity of ejaculation after operation. In females, however, sterilization is a major operation, as it means opening up the abdomen first and then tying and cutting the fallopian tubes. A modification of the same consists in burying the ampullary end of the tube under a slit in the broad ligment.

From the above brief account it will be obvious that full reliance cannot be placed on any single method alone but only on a judicious combination of a mechanical barrier and chemical spermicide. The reliable method for the wife at present* is a rubber cap and a suppository, paste or jelly. The spermicide (suppository, paste or jelly) should be applied allround the rim and above and below the cap. It is absolutely necessary that the woman gets the cap selected and fitted by a doctor with special training in conception control. She sees the doctor not only to get the correct size and type of the pessary but also to be instructed in the fitting of the pessary and its removal. It is impossible for the woman to choose a pessary herself from the market or learn how it should be fitted from written instructions in a book. The next best method to a rubber cap and paste is a rubber sheath. Spermicidal suppository, jelly or paste must be used in addition. A sponge soaked in vinegar solution is a poor substitute but a cheap one.

It must be emphasised that however vivid may be the description of a contraceptive method it lacks the information that can be gained only by personal instruction. A method suitable for a particular case can be learnt only at a standard family planning or gynaecological clinic, or from a qualified doctor who has had special training in the subject. A number of persons condemn one method or another. Some have lost complete confidence in clinical contraception. It is mainly due to faulty information, advice or instruction. Many women have been frightened by elaborate (sometime quite incorrect) descriptions of the methods. An average woman needs gentle persuasion and advice to be given to her which is harmless, convenient, and suited to the resources at her disposal. A method convenient to a rich women with the facilities of a bath room may be impossible for a poor woman in a mill 'chawl' who shares a single room with four others. Intelligence is also a factor to be taken into account. The fitting of a rubber cap may be easy for one, but for another it requires great patience and repeated personal instruction.

---

*1951.

It is essential to consider the main difficulties relating to family planning facing us in India at present.* Misleading information on the subject is surprisingly large, and public opinion is still very much divided. The creation of strong public opinion in favour of family limitation is very important. The use of contraceptives is limited to urban areas and their use is likely to be popular only amongst intelligent classes. Family planning does not imply family limitation only Infertile couples require detailed examination to find out if the condition is due to female hypoplasia, closure of tubes, cervical defects, low metabolic rate, venereal diseases, improper curettage, faulty hygiene or the like (or some disorder in the male).**

The number of doctors and nurses who can disseminate the correct information and give the necessary advice is limited. The percentage of those who are especially trained in contraceptive technique is very small indeed. For a family planning movement to be successful it is necessary to have an adequate number of doctors and nurses trained in the subject. The majority of the medical and nursing schools are adverse to their students receiving this training in their institutions.***

The high cost of contraceptives and the extreme poverty of the people (living mostly in its 700,000 villages) make the task still more difficult. It is often said that unless the people are provided with the minimum necessities of life, *i.e.*, food, education and health services, introduction of a family planning service would not be practical. We should not however be prevented by the sad social, economic and educational background from taking a step in the right direction. The great health schemes already in hand can easily include measures to

*1951.

**It was emphasised that infertility may be due to vaginal, cervical, uterine, tubal and ovarian causes in wife or various causes in husband; and wife may not be exclusively responsible. Both husband and wife require examination.

***1951.

limit families on health and economic grounds. Voluntary health organisations can create the right atmosphere.

Experience during the last few years has shown that family planning advice through birth control clinics in India is not likely to succeed at present. The few clinics in big towns are poorly attended, and the advice is likely to be given to people for whom it is not intended. The ideal place for imparting such advice seems to be a free health centre or maternity home where a trained woman doctor can give the advice, if and when necessary. The immediate task, before the family planning movement gathers momentum, is to train all the available doctors and nurses especially those employed in women's hospitals. A Provincial Government* has already taken the lead and has conducted courses for doctors in their employment. It will be desirable that the doctors detailed to train others are given facilities to tour Family Planning Clinics in the United Kingdom and America and to study the organisation and the methods employed in them. Selected candidates can also be sent to study the manufacture of various contraceptives. The most vexed problem of finding a cheap, harmless and reliable contraceptive still remains unsolved. Extensive research and intensive effort are required to enable us to produce a cheap contraceptive in this country. The market is already flooded with birth control preparations and adequate state control regarding their quality and distribution is imperative.

Facilities should be provided for those who require advice to go to a maternity home or a hospital and to be given the necessary appliances free, or at a nominal cost. It is most gratifying to note that the first government managed clinic in the world was started in Mysore State in India. It is equally encouraging to find that the Health Survey and Development Committee** had appreciated the necessity of family planning

---

*Punjab before partition of India.

**The Committee was appointed by the Government of India in October 1943 to make a broad survey of the present position in regard to health conditions and health organisation in British India and to make recommendations for future development.

for India and (amongst other things like raising the age of marriage of girls and improved standard of living) had made epoch making recommendations in their report, *viz.* :

(1) To spread 'the knowledge of birth control as far as limitations imposed by the peculiar circumstances of the country permit'.

(2) To carry out 'continuous study of population problems and genetics in which the Registrar General, Provincial Registrars, with their respective staff of the Health Department, Central and Provincial, and Departments of economics, sociology, statistics and genetics in the Universities should participate'.

(3) To give 'instructions to mothers attending maternity and child welfare centres, dispensaries, hospitals and public institutions which give medical aid to women and for whom child bearing would be injurious both to the mother and to the child'.

(4) To distribute free contraceptives to mothers for health reasons.

(5) To control the manufacture and sale of contraceptives.

(6) To assist research for the production of a safe and effective contraceptive by a grant from public funds.

Some members of the Committee considered the giving of contraceptive advice on health grounds to be justified. Others appreciated the importance of the relation of population to the economic resources of the country but felt that the active promotion by the State of contraceptive practices for economic reasons which are objected to on religious grounds are only justified if supported by public opinion.

The above recommendations, if carried out, will be no doubt a great step forward. It is hoped that the whole country will pay serious attention to the population problem facing India, and make every endeavour to encourage family planning in the whole country, and take the help science has to offer to improve the lot of scores of men, women and children".[10]

ACCEPTABILITY AND EFFECTIVENESS

Except for sterilization, there was no firm information on use effectiveness of different methods of contraception. The general assumptions placed them in the following order of use effectiveness : diaphragm and jelly or cream ; condom and jelly or cream ; condom alone ; jelly or cream alone ; foam tablets and others.

It was in late 1950s that more reliable information than before was available on acceptability and effectiveness of the available contraceptive devices in India. Dr. Sarah Israel and Dr. Melba Kamat in 1958 reported on 352 women attending (during 1954-56 and following up to 1957) two Family Planning Association of India clinics in industrial areas of Bombay. The pregnancy rate reported was 4.8 per 100 years of exposure for diaphragm and jelly and 8.9 per 100 years of exposure in case of foam tablets. In another study from sixteen clinics established between 1952-57 in Bombay, Bangalore, Bengal, Ajmer and Imphal covering 8,3 9 cases Israel and Kamat reported that 58.3 per cent accepted diaphragm and jelly, 12.3 per cent jelly alone, 25.5 per cent foam tablets and 1.4 per cent condoms ; the pregnancy rate per 100 years of exposure reported were for condom 2.6 ; diaphragm and jelly 6.1 ; jelly alone 11.0 and foam tablets 14.7.[11]

Initial Measures Relating to Birth Control Methods

Initially measures, among others, taken included : training of personnel, information, education and communication including mass and community education and instructions in specific methods of family planning, extension of family planning services including provision of birth control methods free or at subsidised rates (later all contraceptives were issued free), research, establishment of a contraceptive testing unit and issue of a list of approved contraceptives and prevention of undesirable advertisements on contraceptives for internal and external use.

Control of Objectionable Advertisements

Statutory action was taken to prevent pills and potions

which could be ineffective or harmful or both. A provision for this was made in Drugs and Magic Remedies (Objectionable Advertisement) Act 1954.

Standards for Testing

In the beginning there were no agreed international standards for the testing of contraceptives. In the United Kingdom the Family Planning Association published regularly an approved list of contraceptive products. In India, the Contraceptive Testing Unit was established at the Indian Cancer Research Centre Bombay. Davidson's modification of Baker's test was employed as one of the criteria for testing. Based on the results of the tests done and the recommendations of the Contraceptive Testing Unit, Director General Health Services issued the approved list of contraceptives. The rubber contraceptives were tested at an already existing unit. They were approved on the basis of recommendations of this unit. In 1955, the International Planned Parenthood Federation formed a sub committee for international standards for the testing of contraceptives with Dr. Margaret C.N. Jackson as Convener.

FURTHER DEVELOPMENTS AND PROSPECTS

According to the recent report of the United Nations Population Division *Trenas in Population Policy*, 123 countries containing 91.2 per cent of the World Population "offer direct support to contraceptive access".

Birth control methods described above continued to be recommended till about the first quarter of 1960. In April 1960, 200,000 copies of a pamphlet entitled *Techniques of Birth Control* was produced by the Directorate of Advertising and Visual Publicity, Ministry of Information and Broadcasting, Government of India for the Director General Health Services Ministry of Health. Its contents were mainly based on the publication from which extracts have been given earlier. The illustrations in it were reproduced from *Techniques of Contraception* by Robert L. Dickinson and his associates Emely Freret, Frances Elwyn, Herbert Hariss Williams & Wilkins

Co., Baltimore 1950. Separate pamphlets on sterilization were also issued for wide distribution among medical officers and others.

Rhythm method of control of conception, condoms, sterilization, IUD, oral contraceptives are discussed in separate chapters. Brief mention is made here of spermicides, sponges, diaphragms and cervical caps.

FOAMING CONTRACEPTIVES

The diaphragm with spermicidal cream were found effective and acceptable by the educated women in urban areas. Dr. Sushila Gore and others had demonstrated that illiterate women could be trained to use diaphragm with jelly or cream. Its acceptability in rural areas was generally considered poor. A number of arguments were put forward against their use like cost, privacy and storage. No field trials were made for their use in rural areas. Among mechanical contraceptives the use of condom only preferably with a chemical spermicide (jelly or cream) was considered suitable for the large population in India.

The foaming contraceptives available were in different forms—powders, tablets, suppositeries, and later pressurized foams. The early experiments with foam powder in a clinic in Parel Bombay was disappointing. Israel and Kamat, as mentioned earlier, had reported 14.7 pregnancy rate per 100 women years in case of foam tablets. A number of countries (including Germany, Switzerland, U.S.A. and United Kingdom) had started manufacture of foam tablets There were reports of complaints of vaginal irritation and sensation of heat by users, attributed to vagina being relatively dry. Application of saliva or water before use was suggested. The failure rates were also ascribed to inadequate instructions in use of foam tablets. The foam tablets manufactured tended to absorb moisture and raised problems of shelf life. Programme managers were therefore, not enthusiastic about large scale use of foam tablets.

Khanna Exploratory Study I

In the India-Harvard-Ludhiana Population Study in Khanna Punjab the acceptance of foam tablets was reported to be encouraging. This study was notable in many ways, the second such study on community programme for contraception and population dynamics after the 1952 rhythm study in India. In the programme on contraception five birth control methods were studied, "*viz.*, foaming vaginal tablets, rhythm, withdrawl and either contraceptive paste or salt solution on cotton pad". The foam tablets used were of three types, *viz.*, Volpar tablets of British Drug House (spermicidal agent phenyl mercuric acetate) ; Durafoam foam tablets of the Ortho Company of New York (spermicidal agent Poly-ethoxyethanols), and Fomos tablets of Fomas Laboratory of New York (spermicidal agent oxyquinoline sulfate).

The use of Fomos foaming tablets was discontinued, as its active ingredient was considered carcinogenic by the Contraceptive Testing unit Bombay, a claim which was disputed and remained controversial. The Khanna Exploratory Study I, ending March 1955 showed that of the 35 couples, 19 preferred foaming vaginal contraceptive tablets, 9 withdrawal and the remaining other various methods [12]

Baumgartner and Notestein Mission

About this time, Leona Baumgartner and Notestein visited India and submitted the report in December 1955 to the Health Minister Rajkumari Amrit Kaur. In their report, on birth control methods, it was stated that "at present, the most practical procedure would be to concentrate on stimulating the use of rhythm, coitus interruptus (separately or in combination with foam tablets). Eventually they might be supplemented by other simple methods, as experience dictates".

A strong case was made out in respect of foam tablets such as its cost, enhanced spermicidal effect of foam (formed by the reaction of tartric acid and sodium bicarborate) by spermicidal agent or agents, foam itself acting as a barrier. "A high degree of acceptance and effectiveness in uneducated and poor population" was stated to have been reported in experiments in Baltimore and Jamaica. The cost of foam tablets in vails were stated to be less than Rs. 3/- as against jelly and cream Rs. 4/- to Rs. 6/-, condom Rs. 3/- and diaphgram and jelly Rs. 10-14/- ; the estimates were based on average frequency of use of 50—60 times annually.[13]

This led to extending special support to the use of foam tablets in the Indian family planning programme. The reports of Khanna exploratory study seems to have influenced the above developments.

The trials with foam tablets especially in Khanna Study and Singur were closely watched for their acceptance and use effectiveness.

The Khanna Exploratory Study II and III

The Khanna exploratory study II, in March 1956, continued to show preference for foam tablets. "Of those accepting (contraception) two-third selected foam tablets". The acceptance for foam tablets later waned. In the Khanna Exploratory Study III, "the call on stocks of vaginal foam tablets decreased by two-third". It may be added that "the field trials of contraceptive method during Khanna Study was less successful than some others, but collateral findings brought a clearer view of significance of population pressure".[14] The reports from Singur were also unsatisfactory.

Limited Use of Foam Tablets

Foam tablets continued to be offered in the family planning programme in India, but their limitation were explained to the users. It appears that for sometime the use of foam tablets continued on a small scale in India and later their use further declined.

REVIVAL OF VAGINAL CONTRACEPTION

The introduction of IUDs and oral pills in 1960s brought

about world-wide change in the choice of contraceptive methods.

The use of diaphragm and spermicide (cream or jelly) continued in Europe and United States to a limited extent after introduction of oral pills and IUDs. In India their use virtually stopped, except in a few centres. The declared Indian family planning programme approach was called cafeteria approach, implying that while recommending effective birth control method like sterilization, IUD, oral pill a person should be offered alternatives which may be necessary under special situation faced by the individual. In practice, besides methods strongly promoted during a period, the other method made widely available (under the heading conventional contraceptive) appears to be condom[15].

There is a recent revival in vaginal contraception, both in developed and some developing countries. The technical developments, however, do not appear to be substantial.

Diaphragm

There are reports of new developments in diaphragms and cevical caps, such as "a diaphragm made of flexible plastic—like material that gradually releases nonoxynol-9 over 24 hour period".[16]

Contracap

There are also reports of a cervical cap "Contracap", "a custom-fitted cervical cap with a one-way valve to release cervical secretions and menstrual blood" reported to be acceptable but with "unacceptably high pregnancy rate".[17]

Spermicides

In case of spermicides and spermiostatic agents there have been some developments. The main contraceptive agents used in jellies, creams, foams, suppositeries and soluable film are : nonoxynol-9, Octoxynol-9 and menfegol.

The focus of new developments is on new surface acting, more effective and longer acting agents.

Contraceptive Sponge and Foam Tablet

The interest in vaginal spermicides is largely due to the simplicity of their use specially tablets and suppositories. Some developments have been reported such as in vaginal foam tablets and contraceptive sponge. The Japanese foam tablet Neo Sampoon (active ingredient menfegol), for example, was developed by Eisai Company Ltd., in 1960s and marketed in 1969. Neo Sampoon are in two shapes, disks and "life-saver-shaped loops, sold in many social marketing programmes. They have been given popular names such as "Joy" in Bangladesh and "Kamal" (lotus) in Nepal. The pregnancy rates are stated to range from 3.2 to 7.9 per 100 woman years.[18]

A 24 hour, disposal contraceptive sponge "Today" has recently attracted attention. It is like a mushroom cap, made of polyurethane containing nonoxynol-9. When inserted in vagina its concave side covers the cervix. Cumulative failure rates of its earlier design were reported to be from 13 to 28 per 100 woman in less than an year. The new design "squash ball" shaped with 30 per cent nonoxynol-9, restricted to use for not than ten times, showed in the sixth month life table pregnancy rate of 6 per 100 woman and discontinuation rate of 25 per cent. In two other comparative trials 12 month pregnancy rate ranged from 9 to 27 per 100 woman.[19]

Major donor agencies are supplying vaginal contraceptives (foaming tablets, aerosol foam, jellies and creams and diaphragms) now for a number of years. A table of deliveries from 1978 to 1982 indicates an increase (in 1000s of units) of foaming tablets from about 11,699 in 19.8 to 43,632 in 1981 and 20,163 in 1982 ; Aerosol foam containers from 155 (1 78) to 348 (1982) jellies and creams tubes from 86 (1978) to 90 (1982) and diaphragms from 11 (1978) to 36 (1982).[20] The above increase appears to reflect promotion of the products and not necessarily their acceptability.

The recent surveys (World Fertility Survey, Contraception

Prevalence surveys and others) indicate that vaginal contraceptives continue to be used although to a limited extent, in many developed and developing countries. The representative Sample Survey 1970-1982 give the following picture of the percentage of currently married women of reproductive age using vaginal contraceptive methods : Percentage conceptors using vaginal contraceptives 2 in Africa ; 1-4 in Asia and Pacific ; 1-10 in Latin America and Caribbean ; 1-6 in Middle East and North Africa ; and 1-11 in Developed countries. This data refers to the countries included in the surveys, *e.g.*, in respect of Africa the data is for Sudan (north) and Asia and Pacific for Republic of Korea, Pakistan and Phillippines only.

The data from six Latin American countries, Barbados in the Caribbean (1971), Canada (1977), U.K. (1970) and USA (1976) suggest that in the developed countries the use of diaphragms and spermicides is almost equal and in the developing countries the spermicides are used more than diaphragms.

FUTURE PROJECTIONS

Despite the low effectiveness of vaginal contraceptives compared to IUD, oral pill, sterilization, vaginal contraceptives continue to be used in different parts of the world. In both developed and developing countries, their use is being revived. This trend may be due to various factors. Some of the reasons include : the need is being felt for alternative birth control methods in situations where more effective methods are not acceptable, or not available or not within easy reach or not suitable ; and/or vaginal contraceptives have practically no side-effects and are simple to use (except diaphragm and cervical cap which require instructions by a trained person).

It is difficult to project use of vaginal contraceptives in future. The general view appears to be that use of diaphragms with spermicides will continue in developed countries. Cervical caps may also continue to be used by a small proportion of women in USA and a few in European countries. It is not unlikely that some of the improved spermicides and contraceptive sponge may also be used more than at present. On the other hand in the developing countries the use of diaphragms with jelly (and even cervical caps) may be used by a small proportion of women in urban areas especially large cities where facilities for proper advice and instructions for their use are available, but the vaginal contraceptive of choice may generally be spermicides,[21] contraceptive sponge, and simple home made contraceptives. This will depend largely on support given to them in the National family planning programme.

Research and development of *Vaginal Rings*, that can release harmones are in progress since the late 1960s and early 1970s. From the name it is obvious that they are circular in shape for insertion in vagina. They are required to be placed round the cervix, and can be inserted in the vagina and removed by the woman herself. The material for the carrier of the harmone was the same as used in contraceptive implants (NORPLANT 2). Population Council now uses another elastomer. There are two types of Vaginal Rings, *viz.*, (*a*) Low-dose Levonorgestrel Vaginal Rings, the Varlevo-20 ring which renders cervical mucus impenetrable to sperms. The ring releases 20 μg per day for at least 30 days. Another reformulated rings releasing 5 to 10 mg. progestrone daily has been developed, "after successful pharmacokinetic studies in lactating women". Population Council and World Health Organisation are conducting colloborative studies on this device.

(*b*) Vaginal rings releasing both levonorgestrel and estrogen —the ovulation preventing vaginal ring. They are left in the vagina for three weeks, then removed for a week or more to bring withdrawl bleeding.

Population Council is continuing studies on rings releasing norethindrone acetate in combination with ethynylestradiol.

The small scale trials with the ST 1435/ethynylestradiol are reported to have been successfully completed. Rings releasing ST 1435 with and without ethynyl estradiol are proposed to be tried.[22]

At the present stage, the acceptability and use-effectiveness of steroid delivering vaginal devices when used on mass scale can not be predicted.*

The above scenario points into two directions, *viz.*, (*i*) vaginal devices delivering contraceptive agents as effective as "the Pill" may be available for mass use in the future ; and (*ii*) vaginal contraceptives of the 1940s and 1950s and their recent developments have an important place in family planning programme.

An assessment of the need of various vaginal contraceptives in India is necessary to ensure their ready accessibility and free flow of supplies. This will require a number of diagnostic studies and action-research projects to get clear picture on various aspects such as prevalence of various vaginal contraceptives in India, their availability, acceptability and use effectiveness, the status of knowledge of the programme personnel on use of different vaginal contraceptives and training imparted to them, source of supply, etc. Soon after a clear picture emerges further action can be taken on their effective use, research and development and manufacture in the country.

The above measures donot require any change in general policy on contraceptive methods. The cafeteria approach is already the accepted policy in respect of birth control methods. The accessibility of all methods may not be the same. According to *Family Welfare Programme in India Year Book 1986-87.*

---

*A recent report on WHO multicentre clinical trial test of the low dose progestin-releasing vaginal ring as an effective contraceptive for women, involving 1005 women aged 19-34 years carried out at 19 centres in 13 countries during 1980-86 indicate : effectiveness comparable with oral contraceptive ; pregnancy rate increased with increasing body weight ; discontinuation of the use of the ring about 50 per cent by one year mainly due to irregular bleeding pattern ; expulsion of the ring at least once (but most continued to use it) in about 25 per cent of all users (New WHO data on a progestin-releasing vaginal ring. *Outlook*, Vol. 8, No. 2, 1990, *Popline*).

"During 1986-87, a total of 707.46 million pieces of condoms (net after deducting those supplied to vasectomised cases and free samples in fairs, etc.) including those under commercial scheme and direct to public by manufacturers, 625 diaphragms 24,582 jelly/cream tubes and 4,331 foam tablets were distributed. The number of diaphragms and spermicides is very small. The estimated number of about 10 million conventional contraceptives users, in this period could be considered mainly users of condoms. The use of a birth control method depends to appreciable extent on the promotion and ready accessibility of the method.

The cafeteria approach has four main elements : (*i*) decision of the couple to have a small family ; (*ii*) accessibility of all harmless and effective birth control methods, (*iii*) communication of degree of effectiveness, advantages and disadvantages of each method with special emphasis on effective methods for a couple ; and (*iv*) the final decision by the couple themselves, *i.e.*, the family planning educator gives advice for an appropriate contraceptive method at a given time, the action of the couple is based on "well-informed consent" and their well considered decision.

2

The Rhythm Study[23]

The first study on a birth control method undertaken by the Government of India was on "safe periods". It has often been maligned and ridiculed as a study on "the Coloured Beads". In fact "the coloured beads" were hardly used. They were rarely found round the neck of women but were reported in some cases adorning the neck of their cattle. The questions at present are : Did the rhythm study make any contribution to our knowledge related to the development of the family planning programme ; and has it any relevance at present ?

Background

It may help to recall some aspects the general environment before and during the period the rhythm study was conducted in India. In early 950s, there was only one large organised group among whom the family planning services were available—the Indian Army. Field Marshal (then General) K.M. Cariappa, the Commander-in-Chief Indian Army had pioneered the family planning programme in the Army in 1949 as an integral part of family health and welfare scheme. In rest of the country the voluntary organisations, especially the Family Planning Association of India, under the dynamic leadership of Lady Dhanvanthi Rama Rao, were attempting to spread the message of family planning in India and to establish services wherever possible. Their activities were limited to urban areas.

A very small number of persons were using chemical and mechanical contraceptives. In some hospitals, sterilization operations were being done for females. One of the major problems was to find a birth control method which can be used by people in rural areas. Shakuntala Pranjpya was advising cotton pad soaked with oil for village women. In practice the use of such pads was insignificant.

The population policy of the Government was still in the process of formulation. While the urgent need to stabilize the rate of growth of population to suit the resources of the country was accepted, there was no concensus on methods to be adopted. There was a strong lobby of conscientious objectors to artificial methods of birth control. The conversation of Lady Dhanvanthi Rama Rao with the Chief Minister, Bombay State, Sri Morarji Desai illustrates the intensity of attitudes of conscientious objectors. She writes : "On one occasion he (Chief Minister Bombay State) told me, he would ban (her) work if he could, but I smiled and said it was fortunate for me that he could not do so".[24] It may be added that the approach of Sri Morarji Desai becomes clear from his recent letter on the subject. He said : "It is well known that personally I do believe in doing it (birth control) by self control. But I have no doubt that self control is difficult for the vast majority as very few believe in it and even out of them very few can practice it successfully. Government cannot successfully preach self control as it is not possible for most people and it has to help people by propaganda and provision of proper methods as population control is vital for the country. I did not hesitate to provide funds for the purpose as Finance Minister (Government of India)".[25] Health Minister, Rajkumari Amrit Kaur, was very much opposed to artificial methods of birth control. Initially, she even opposed the discussion of family planning programme by a separate panel of Planning Commission as prelude to drafting the First Five Year Plan. Even after she agreed to discussion on family planning "she still had her reservations, for she insisted that no contraceptives should be used".[26] The Population Growth and Family Planning Committee April 1951 had recommended that "the State should provide facilities for sterilization or giving advice on contraception on medical grounds" and "such help, and advice should not be withheld from others who seek and need it on social and economic grounds". Dr. Shushila Nayyar, a member of the committee in a separate statement to the Committee report had observed, "...There is a large section of the population which is opposed to contraceptives on moral, religious and other grounds. The utmost that can be asked of the State is that it should not interfere with any social agency which wishes to undertake (family planning) activities...The State should not undertake population control through furtherance of contraceptives".[27]

Since Ogino[28] and Herman Knaus[29], in 1930s had demonstrated that ovulation generally takes place about 14 days before the next menstruation a great deal of interest had been created in safe period method—a method acceptable for use in India to Rajkumari Amrit Kaur and other conscientious objectors. Rajkumari requested the Director General World Health Organisation for services of a consultant.

There were encouraging reports on safe period (ryhthm) method from the United States of America by Dr. John Rock in Boston and Dr. Abrahm Stone in New York. These studies showed that safe period method was effective among couples who followed the method carefully and regularly. These studies, however, related to urban population of a developed country with social, cultural and economic situation different to India. There were a number of unanswered questions such as : How safe is the Safe Period ? Will this method be accepted by the Indian couples ? Are the menstrual cycles regular enough in Indian women to determine easily fertile and non-fertile periods particularly in villages ? How easily can a village woman learn the calculations involved in the use of the safe period method ? Is it possible to simplify the method of calculation of safe period ? How faithfully can an average couple practice the abstinence required in the use of safe periods? How much reduction in birth rate can be achieved by the use of safe period methods ? The general feeling among advocates of a vigorous family planning programme was that any exercise to find answers to such questions would be delaying provision of effective methods already available to the people. At the same time, there was no scientific evidence to reject a pilot project on Safe Period.

In this debate Prime Minister Nehru provided a sobering influence. He emphasised that the growth of population could be limited by "various ways including (social and economic development) and birth control".[30] This led to some change in views of Rajkumari. Dr. Abrahm Stone, who was assigned the post of the WHO consultant to advise on pilot study in family planning states that Chisholm* in his letter to him stated that "the study is to concern itself with rhythm method of birth control .. the Indian Government is definitely for the moment unwilling to consider any other type of family planning in India".[31]

Various Known Methods of Safe Periods

Study on one of the methods on safe periods could only be suggested by Stone. Brief mention of various methods on safe periods may help in appreciation further of the choice of method for the study in India. The conception takes place when ovum and sperm unite. If couples have sexual union during the period ovum and sperm in the female genital tract are incapable of union, conception will not take place. The calculation of "safe period" thus depends on the determination of the time when sperm and ovum are not capable of union. It is generally assumed that ovum is released from the ovary 14-16 days before the onset of the next menstruations, the ovum can be fertilized upto about 24 hours after its release from the ovary and the sperm after it enters the female genital tract is able to fertilise the ovum for about 48 hours. Ovum remains in the tube connecting the ovary with uterus (the fallapion tubes) for about 3 days before they begin to decay. "According to William Collins, under favourable conditions sperm may be capable to fertilization two days and on rare occasions for longer periods.[32]

---

*Dr. Brock Chisholm, Director General World Health Organisation.

RHYTHM METHODS[33]

The different methods for determining the time of release of ovum to calculate safe period have been evolved, *viz.* : (*i*) the calender method ; (*ii*) the Basal Body Temperatures ; (*iii*) the changes in Cervical Mucus method ; and (*iv*) the method using multiple indices to determine safe period called sympto-thermal method.

The Calender Method

The Calender Method is the oldest. The length of cycles are observed over six to twelve months. The average fertile period is calculated on the basis of longest aad shortest cycle. The estimate of beginning of fertile period is generally arrived at by subtracting 18 days from the shortest period of her previous 6-12 menstrual cycles and of the end of fertile period by subtracting 11 days from the longest cycle.[34] For example if the shortest cycle is 24 days and longest 34 days, the sixth to twenty-third days will be fertile and the rest safe period.

Basal Body Temperature

The Basal Body Temperature (BBT) method is based on the observation that "waking temperature of a normal fertile woman changes during the various stages of menstrual cycle. There is a slight increase (between 0.4 to 0 8°F) in BBT which "begins one or two days after ovulation, responding to rising levels of the harmone progestrone... 3 days wait after the temperature rise is intended to assure that the ovum is no longer fertilizable. Only about 10 days after 3-days wait and before menstruation are considered definitely infertile". The woman is required to take Basal Body Temperature (by mouth, or vagina or rectum ; rectal temperature is most accurate) daily with great care at the same time after 3-5 hours uninterrupted sleep using special BBT thermometers. Taking temperature by mouth is the usual practice.

The interpretation of BBT chart requires considerable care, as it can change not only due to illness but also from changes in regular pattern of behaviour ; emotional factors and even in the normal course.

The Changes in Cervical Mucus

There is an interplay of harmones during the menstrual cycle. One of the harmones is estrogen. The change in cervical mucus occur in response to changes in levels of estrogen. The woman with dry vagina starts feeling "moistness" and "wetness". In the beginning of rise, in estrogen level the secretion becomes "sparse and sticky" (moistness in felt). At the time of release of ovum nears, abundant lubricative mucus occurs giving feeling of wetness. John Billings, who developed the method, insists that the woman must learn to study mucus itself to identify the peak symptom, which is the last day of wet, slippery mucus after which mucus thickness disappears. The fertile period may extend to last 4 days after the peak symptom. The woman has to learn the presence and quality of cervical mucus occuring normally in menstrual cycle and also due to infection.

The Sympto-Thermal Method (STM)

This is a combination of methods. There are symptoms which some women feel during ovulation such as abdominal pain, tenderness of breast, changes in general mood, changes in cervical mucus. These symptoms may not be easy to detect. The example of variation of STM may be continuation of Calender and BBT or BBT and cervical mucus changes.

Choice of Rhythm Method in the Pilot Rhythm Study in India

At the time rhythm study was started in India, it was known that in a healthy fertile female the cervical secretion varies with the stage of menstrual cycle. But the safe period method based on these changes was not well developed at that time. The choice of the method was thus limited to the calender and BBT methods. The latter was considered difficult for women to follow; the available choice therefore was the calender method.

Coloured Beads

Stone, worked in India from October 24 to December 16. 1951. He visited a number of cities and some rural areas—

Bangalore, Bombay, Calcutta, Delhi, Hyderabad, Lucknow, Madras, Nagpur, Simla and nearby villages in some places. He discussed the family planning in general and the proposed project in particular with varied groups—officials and non-officials, physicians and social workers, lay and professional, administrators and field workers.[36] During his discussions the major problem repeatedly mentioned was the difficulty in keeping record of menstrual cycle and making calculations for safe periods by women in villages. A woman physician in Delhi suggested use of beads. Stone constructed a string of 28 beads—green beads to indicate non-fertile days, red beads for fertile days and orange beads for rest of the days of menstrual cycle (the actual days of menstrual flow). On the basis of menstrual cycle of an individual woman the physician or health worker could string in a thread different coloured beads for the woman concerned. The woman could then be instructed to move one bead daily from one side of the string to the other, beginning with the first day of menstrual flow. The beads used were those sold in Janpath, New Delhi, by Nepalese vendors, reported to be favourites (considered dainty) by European and American women. A simple device was incorporated in the string to prevent the beads slipping back.

Pilot Rhythm Studies

Finally two studies on rhythm method were carried out—one in Ramanagram (Karnataka) and another in New Delhi. The World Health Organisation provided two field workers Mary Langford (Mary Taylor after marriage) and Margaret Snyder. They assisted in the day-to-day carrying out of the rhythm studies. The United Nations made available the services of C. Chandrasekaran and Sten A. Wahlund for advice and evaluation of the studies. R. Vasantini was appointed officer-in-charge of the Ramanagram study. Jayashri Katju (Rehman after marriage) was in charge of New Delhi Study. Each had a team of female and male social workers, a technical assistant and clerk-cum-typist.

The major areas of the studies were evaluation of the

rhythm methods in terms of : (*i*) acceptability by the population served ; (*ii*) effectiveness in reducing the number of pregnancies among those who undertake to use it ; and (*iii*) effectiveness in reducing the birth rate of the population served.

The two studies were carried out from May 1952 to March 1955. The studies were so designed as to provide information on : (*a*) basic data on the general characteristics of the population and amenities in each household—their sex, age, relationship to head of the household, marital status, education, employment characteristic and the pregnancy histories of the woman who was or had been married and on births and deaths which occured to the residents of the household between 7 April 1951 and 6 April 1952 ; (*b*) attitude towards birth control and use of birth control methods (no reference to rhythm method was made during attitude survey) ; (*c*) cultural factors affecting family size and related matters ; and (*d*) biological factors directly pertaining to the application of the rhythm method such as the menstrual cycle pattern among the woman in the population studied and other bio-statistics relating to menstruation and pregnancy.

Two ad-hoc studies were also conducted—one on how women recognised colours, if they know the days of week, how they reckoned the days, weeks and months and what counting system was used. Two case histories were taken relating to interruption of pregnancy.[36]

Differences in the Studies

The two studies differed in a number of aspect : (*a*) Ramanagram study included rural population in 14 villages and 19 contiguous hamlets in the experimental area and 16 villages in control area. Each (experimental and control areas had a population of about 8027). The New Delhi study was carried out in urban population of Lodi Colony in seventeen blocks of Type B accommodation, each block of about 72 apartments. Each apartment had two rooms with kitchen and toilet facilities intended for Government employees with basic salary exceeding Rs. 80/- per month but not exceeding Rs. 325/- per month. As it was difficult to select another group similar to experimental area. The New Delhi study had no control population ; (*b*) the families were close to the staff conducting the study in Lodi Colony unlike Ramanagram where they were scattered in 14 villages and 19 hamlets. The proximity of women to the clinic in Lodi Colony facilitated timely contact with them and maintaining relatively more accurate data on menstrual cycles ; (*c*) Lody Colony, New Delhi, couples were using some birth control methods, whereas Ramanagram couples were not familiar with modern methods of birth control ; (*d*) the attitude survey was carried out amongst both husbands and wives in the Ramanagram area, but amongst wives only in Lodi Colony ; and (*e*) In New Delhi wives were given calender cards. In Ramanagram "over half the number of wives received the beads when they received their first rhythm advice. Their husbands were either given the calender card or oral instructions....In many respects the beads and the calender card proved to be more of a hindrance than a help. Both the women who accepted the beads and the men who accepted the calender cards have claimed to be too busy to check them daily. Most of the couples resorted to weekly checking. The beads were soon rejected by women.

The objections to the beads were : (*i*) they were not attractive ; no one would wear them ; (*ii*) they were magical—a silver clip would have been more acceptable than the copper one ; (*iii*) if handled during the days of menstruation, they would become polluted ; and (*iv*) during certain religious festival days they were unclean and should not remain in the house "on several occassions they were returned to the worker for safe-keeping".

OBSERVATIONS MADE DURING THE STUDIES

Menstrual Cycle

Variations in menstrual cycle, as expected, were noticed. The Lodi Colony data, which is relatively more accurate than Ramanagram showed that :

(*a*) The menstrual cycle in about 80 per cent of women ranged between 24 and 34 days. Occasionally these women gave a high or low value for menstrual cycle ;

(*b*) In about 8 per cent of women the menstrual cycle was either less than an average of 24 days or more than an average of 34 days ; and

(*c*) In about 12 per cent of women the regular feature of menstrual cycles was their extreme irregularity, although the average of their cycle length were between 24 and 34 days.

Social and Cultural Practices

The sex-union survey showed that village population abstain (from coitus) for at least 8 days after the onset of menstruation. In some cases this avoidence extended for 12 to 15 days. The coitus was also avoided on religious days. Such abstinence was reported by 50 per cent of women interviewed in Ramanagram. The number of days of such abstinence mentioned by some individuals extended to 120 days per year.

Menstruation and Pregnancy

The menstruation was resumed within a year after the termination of pregnancy in less than half the number of women. The menstruation was delayed to over 20 months in about 25 per cent of cases due to the practice of prolonged breast feeding (lactation amenorrhea). About 80 per cent of women in Ramanagram breast fed their children. The breast feeding period continued for 2 years or more. This practice in Lodi Colony was for shorter period.

Induced Interruption of Pregnancy

There was evidence that some women were anxious to limit their number of children. The delay in onset of menstruation caused them great anxiety. They resorted to interrupt pregnancy. The abortificients taken by mouth reported included jaggery mixed with gingelly seeds or bamboo leaves, or unripe papaya paste, turmeric powder and mustard. There were reports of insertion of "a stick with a green paste" into the cervix, and some oral concotion given by a local woman and some medicines from some itinerant vendors.

Attitude Towards Birth Control

In Ramanagram area 75 per cent of husband or wife or both wanted to learn a birth control method (818 couples out of 1089 interviewed). In Lodi Colony the women in favour of birth control was almost the same—76% (of the 1274 women 65 were already using a birth control method and 898 wanted to learn a method). The degree for desire to learn a method increased with size of the family and age (less among young women and those nearing the end of the reproductive life than those in the intermediate age group). The average number of children born to women wanting to learn a method in Ramanagram was about 4 and to those not wanting to learn a method was about 2. This number was less in Lodi Colony, about 3 among women who wanted to learn a method. A significant feature was that "unwillingness to learn a method for religious reasons was extremely rare".[37]

Developments in Rhythm Method

In the beginning of the study advice on rhythm method was given to women who fulfilled the following conditions: (*i*) Women should have recorded her menstrual cycle for 8-12 months; (*ii*) no cycle should be more than 40 days; (*iii*) no cycle should be less than 20 days; and (*iv*) difference between shortest and longest cycle should not exceed 9 days. The woman fulfilling these requirements had to work out safe period in the following manner: Counting backwards from the date of expected onset as worked out on the basis of the longest cycle recorded 12th to 19th days both inclusive as fertile days; Similarly counting backwards from the date of expected onset of menstruation on the basis of shortest cycle 12 to 10th days both inclusive also as fertile days; The rest of the days was safe period.

This required observation of about 8-12 consecutive menstrual cycles. Only highly motivated and disciplined couples could abstain completely for such a long period. A number of women became pregnant before the actual study could commence. It became necessary to evolve rules by which advice could be given by observing after a few cycles. A method of giving advice by observing one cycle only was evolved.

A formula was also be developed for mass application by which fertile days could be determined without observing any menstrual cycle, called the "Omnibus rule". This was based on the information of menstrual cycles collected among women in the Rhythm Study. The omnibus rule required abstinence starting from the eighth day of the cycle and extending up to the twenty-second day of the cycle both days inclusive. The Omnibus rule, however, could not be studied ; as the project was terminated before the trial of omnibus rule could commence.

Acceptability of Rhythm Method

The number of couples given rhythm method advice were 264 in the Lodi Colony and 191 in Ramanagram. In 28 per cent of couples followed rhythm method, but 17 per cent only used it regularly. In Lody Colony, number of couples using rhythm method regularly was still lower about 10 per cent. But 41 per cent continued the use of rhythm method with other methods. About 8 per cent of couples only "retained some interest in the rhythm method for atleast a year". The major factor against the use of rhythm method was long period of abstinence.

Effectiveness of Rhythm Method

The analysis of data collected in both Lody Colony and Ramanagram showed that "the rhythm method if used regularly is likely to reduce the pregnancy rate to about one-half of what it would be without the use of any method at all". Rhythm method teaching, was unable to bring about a significant reduction of birth rate in the community, as the percentage of women who used regularly was small.

Criticism of Stone Mission

Some adverse reactions to Stone Mission may also be of

interest—one widely observed in India and another unexpectedly noted in the World Health Organisation. The criticism in India was on recommending the safe period method. It will be obvious that as a WHO consultant with a specified mandate he could not give advice except on safe period. In fact in his personal capacity he made suggestions for a country-wide family planning services for India including: education of doctors and medical students in techniques of conception control; clinical services in maternity homes and hospitals for all who wanted to plan their families, and research on contraceptive measures and study of social environs and the popular reaction to contraception.[38] He showed films on 'Biology of Conception' and 'Contraceptive techniques' in several places. His suggestions led to the Indian Council of Medical Research to establish a committee on research in human reproduction. In the year following his visit as a WHO consultant, he sent a detailed memorandum on implementation of family planning programme to the Secretary, Ministry of Health along with enclosures on how to establish a planned parenthood centre, a review and preview on research in contraception, survey sheet for opinion polls on birth control, etc. The studies on rhythm method were by no means infructuous. They led to greater understanding of use effectiveness of the method than before. These projects provided the first experience in the field of discussing family planning with couples in urban and rural communities, an experience which gave several leads to programme operation. Appreciable data on cultural factors, biostatics relating to manstrual cycles and pregnancy, sex behaviour, knowledge, attitudes and practices related to family planning and fertility were made available. The ground was prepared for further studies and training in these areas. The WHO Mission for initiating these studies attracted world-wide attention to population issues and the need for launching family planning programme and perhaps stimulated other developing countries with similar problems to take action. According to Stone, the most important aspect of his mission was that "for the first time a consultant of WHO was travelling through the country under auspices of the Government......and was free to discuss frankly and fully the problem of population control and the implication of family planning for the welfare of the individual, the family and the Nation", "To me", he said, "this indicated an important step in the social history of India. It might also serve as an impetus to other Nations with similar problems to initiate and develop population planning programmes in their own countries".[39]

The reaction in WHO was of a quite different nature. There was strong protest in the Committee on Programme and Budget against provision of consultant services for family planning to India. A resolution by Italy, Belgium and Lebanon against WHO support for family planning was expected to be adopted creating a very embarassing and traumatic situation influencing unity in WHO. Dr. Laxmaswami Mudaliar and Dr. C.G. Pandit suggested postponement of the discussion. Dr. Wickremsinghes' (Ceylon) suggestion to withdraw conflicting resolution was finally agreed. Subsequently, Belgium representative Dr. Van de Calseyde insisted on recording his interpretation on the views of the Committee in plenary session of the World Health Assembly May 1952. Director General WHO Brock Chisholm diplomatically assured that "he would take the wishes of member states into account whether or not they were expressed in formal resolution".[40] This illustrates the international climate relating to birth control at that time.

Relevance of Safe Period at Present

A few facts emerging from the rhythm study in India may be recalled while considering relevance of safe period method at present, now called *Notural Family Planning* (*NFP*) :

(*i*) The method was effective among those who used regularly ;

(*ii*) The long period of abstinence made its general use difficult ;

(*iii*) The use effectiveness is far below other methods like voluntary sterilization, IUD, Pills, diaphragm with spermicide ;

(*iv*) There are conscientious objectors to artificial birth control methods in India ; their number is relatively small ; and

(*v*) The Catholic Church is against any method other than Natural Family Planning. This has been reiterated in the Papal encyclical *Humane Vitae.*

There has been considerable advance in new techniques of Natural Family Planning. The reported use effectiveness of the cervical mucus method "range from a low of 0.4 pregnancies per 100 women years to a high of 39.7". A WHO study in few countries including India indicates a pregnancy rate of 20.0 per 100 women-years.[41] In India by 1980 there were about 60 local NFP centres all affiliated with the Catholic Organisation Estimates of the number of users served by these program ranges from 18000 to 100,000.[42] "Most scientifically accepted studies have shown NFP failure rates ranging from 11 to 35 per cent a year.[43]

The available evidence[44] leads one to conclude that despite the limitation of Natural Family Planning, serious consideration could be given for its further study and inclusion in the National Family Welfare programme, for those who refuse the use of other methods. Conceptually, it is included in the Indian programme, but in fact those delivering the services generally do not have adequate knowledge about the method.

There are several problems which may arise in actually implementation of the above suggestion. The number of cases seeking Natural Family Planning method in a given population are expected to be small. A separate trained person for giving NFP advice may not be feasible. The existing health personnel will need adequate training to give advice on NFP. They may not be interested, let alone dedicated to NFP. The cervical mucus or sympto-thermal method may be too difficult to follow by women. Moreover, the NFP centres are very few in the country and are not within easy reach of the people. The development of any referal system may not be generally possible.

The limited available information shows that the period of training of trainers and women in NFP vary. In a WHO study "relatively well educated lay volunteers in a few developing countries and two developed countries were trained to teach periodic abstinence techniques, fertility awareness and psycho-social aspects in a course that averaged almost 50 hours".[45] "In two Indian programmes by Catholic nuns, couples learn the cervical method in four visits and subsequently are visited every week or every other week and in another non-literate couples may need instructions for as along a year, literate couples for about three months".[46]

It seems further studies involving the present family planning programme personnel in NFP including their training will be necessary to get a clearer picture of programme issues.

It may be that generally the Calender Method will be easy to follow by the people in the villages. Before reintroducing it, the so-called "Omnibus Calender Method" suggested in the 1950s in the report on the Rhythm Study and/or some other simple effective method could be given trial among conscientious objectors.

In areas where NFP centres are operating regular referal system can be developed even at present—Family Welfare Centres referring those cases who do not accept any other method to NFP centres and NFP centres referring to Family Welfare Centres cases who desire to follow methods other than those available at NFP Centres.

The declared policy in India is to offer all available methods of birth-control. There are reasons to believe that some of those who started the use of rhythm/Natural Family Planning method, after unsuccessful experience adopted more effective methods. There are also reports that some combine Natural Family Planning with other methods of contraception. The major problem in Natural Family Planning is long periods of abstinence from inter-course. The focus of research on NFP therefore, is for upgrading knowledge on early predictions and detection of the fertile period. Reports are being received on new possibilities for identifying the fertile period such as through testing saliva to detect ovulation and a paper test tapes to measure alkaline phosphatase level in saliva which rise in the pre-ovulation phase of the normal menstrual cycle".[47] There is thus a case of persuing research in this field. Discovery of a simple, and acceptable method of early detection and prediction of the time of ovulation with greater precision will be a great advance in methods to control fertility and infertility.

3

Condom

The Name

The origin of the word condom is uncertain. In Latin there is a word *condus* meaning to collect, to preserve, to protect. A Persian origin is mentioned—*kendu* or *kondu*, the word used for a long vessel made of animal intestines for storage of corn or grain. Its origin in literature on venereology is often traced to a proper name—Condom a physician (or a courtier) of Charles II (1660-1685). It is also said that Dr. Condom or Mr. Condom is stated to have invented for his monarch a device to prevent births of illegitimate children. There is no firm evidence to support this story.[48]

In India the condom manufactured in the Public Sector is called Nirodh meaning control, check in Sanskrit. The private manufacturers sell condoms under their own brand names.

The Inventor

In the absence of any firm evidence, about the inventor of the condom, it may be justifiable to assume that the unknown inventor was probably a worker in a medieval slaughterhouse as mentioned by Himes, who by accident got the idea of using membranes of some animals to cover the penis to protect against getting sexually transmitted diseases. He perhaps used such a cover with success and spread the information to others.[49]

Usage, Material and Forms

We find the early Egyptians and a number of peoples (males and females) in remote ages used some material to cover their reproductive organs. Sheaths over penis have been noticed in early Egyptian art. It may be surmised that they were used for protection against injury or diseases (not from sexual contact). These are speculations. The material used to cover sexual parts were perhaps used as decoration or status symbol or just simple modesty.

It is doubtful that they were used for modesty, as there is ample evidence in ancient sculpture and art that the people in ancient times had no inhibitions about exposing sexual parts.

No reference to sheaths for protection against venereal diseases is traceable in ancient medical texts in India. Reproductive organs, however, are classified among those which require special care. It may be added that the description of syphilis in Sanskrit works in India appeared for the first time in the sixteenth century in *Bhava Prakash* and the disease was called *Ferangi Roga* (the disease of the foreigner) or the Portugese disease.[50]

The earliest published description of condom is given in *De morbo gallico* by the Italian anatomist Fallopius published in 1564. It is described as a linen sheath to put on the glans, after washing the genitals, for prevention of syphilis. During the seventeenth and eighteenth centuries the references to use of condoms increase, the material used changed from linen to coeces of animals, covering the penis and not only glans. Its use mainly for protection of veneral diseases and its association with houses of ill fame continued for a long time.

The next step was emergence of rubber condoms. In 1843-44 Goodyear and Hancock developed the vulcanization of rubber, which by the early 1900s facilitated large scale availability of condoms. In 1930s further major development took place. The manufacture of condom from liquid latex (concentrated and stabilised rubber tree sap) commenced.[61]

The use of liquid latex concentrates, the developments in manufacturing processes, electronic testing to detect pinholes and standards of testing at the manufacturing plant level and the Government level contributed to improvement in the quality of condoms.

Around mid 1900s the use of condoms for control of births increased. A number of forms of condoms gradually appeared in the market—plain, with a teat (reservoir) at the end, smooth, textured, coloured, natural, dry and lubricated. The estimated number of condom users in the world in 1982 reported was 40 million couples.[62]

There are recent reports on development of female condoms. These are still in trial stage. A report by Sakondhavat and Potter on their use of US made WPc-333 female condom by "high risk female sex workers" in 20 massage parlours in Khon-Kaen Thailand indicate that "2/3 of the volunteers reported no aversion to the female condon, 1/3 disliked it". These volunteers were provided unlubricated female condoms, lubricants and male condoms, the decision to use male or female condom was left to the volunteers. In the 32 per cents of episodes of vaginal intercourse use of female condoms was reported, of these in S cases male condom was also used, the male condom was used in 35 per cent of episodes. The objections to female condoms by volunteers included big size, use of lubricant messy and inconvenient, less comfortable and difficulty in insertion. This study is being repeated.[63] The word condom for the present means male condoms.

In India, like other countries, condom have been in use for a very long time. It may be conjectured that the use of condom in India may have been introduced by the *Ferangi* foreigners. The wider use of rubber condoms, as indicated above, began in the 1900s. The members of the Indian armed forces on leave and retirement may have introduced condoms in the rural areas.

The condoms in the early years were imported in India for sale in the market. There imports was reported to be increasing since 1958.

There was hesitation, in the begining, to advocate the use of condom on mass scale for birth control. A number of reasons were advanced for not including use of condom in the official family planning programme such as condoms would not be acceptable by the couples because rubber decreases sensitivity during coitus, there would be difficulties of storage and disposal, they were likely to break and would have minimal use-effectiveness. The bias against use of condoms was mainly due to pre-concieved ideas about their acceptability and effectiveness and perhaps also association of condom with prevention of sexually transmitted diseases. The trial of foam tablets dominated the field trials. It was with some persuation that condoms were included in comparative trials.

Soon after the condoms were made available along with other contraceptives, the doubts about their acceptability were removed. K.T. Chitre, for example in his report on the use of contraceptive methods in Maharashtra during 1958-62 stated that of all the cases registered in rural and urban centres in Maharashtra acceptability of condoms in rural areas increased from 8.24 per cent (1958) to 46.6 per cent (1962) and in urban areas from 8.79 per cent (1958) to 34.1 per cent (1962). During the same period use of foam tablets declined appreciably both in rural and urban areas.[54] The condoms were reported to be not only acceptable, but the effectiveness of good quality condom when properly used with spermicidal cream was appreciable.

The condoms in India were and are made available through a number of channels. They can be freely purchased in the market. They are available to eligible couples free of charge at hospitals, dispensaries, maternity and child health centres and family welfare centres in the urban areas and Primary Health Centres and Subcentres in the rural areas. The Village Health Guides serve as Depot Holders and sell them at subsidised rates.

and retain the proceeds from sale as their incentive. The condoms are also widely available through social marketing.

The estimated number of condom users in India is about 10 million. As stated earlier, "during 1986-87, a total of 707.46 million pieces of condoms (net after deducting those supplied to vasectomised cases and free samples at fares, etc.), including those under commercial scheme and direct sales to public by manufacturers". The distribution of diaphragms, foam tablets and jelly/creams during this period was 625,4331 and 24582 respectively. It may noted that condoms figures predominantly among distribution of Conventional contraceptives. The condoms are procured from manufacturers in Private sector (M/s. London Rubber Co. Madras and M/s. LORCUM Bombay) and Public sector (Hindustan Latex Ltd. Trivandrum).[56]

Manufacture of Condoms in India

It was estimated that since 1958, the imports of condoms were doubling each year. The estimated landed cost in 1964 was US$ 625,000 There were indications that for 536 million pieces of condoms which might be required in 1966, foreign exchange required could be US$ 3,380,000. There was thus urgency in starting indigenous production of condoms.

The first advice received in respect of indigenous production of condoms was discouraging. It was stated that the indigenous rubber was not suitable for production of good quality condoms. The Chairman, Rubber Board, however, assured that not only the indigenous rubber was of good quality but sufficient supplies of suitable latex could be made available in Kerala. With assurance of availability of suitable latex in the country, the ways to make India self-sufficient in requirements of condoms were explored.

A serious controversy on their production in private or public sector commenced. The production was initially commenced in private sector. By March 1964, licences were issued to manufacture about 335 million pieces to private agencies.

The condoms produced did not meet the standards laid down by Ministry of Health and Family Planning. The Ministry was severly criticised for rigid quality control standards. The quality control standards were, in fact, based on accepted international standards. By March 1964, only one company with annual manufacturing capacity of 4 million pieces, was approved. A private company in Madras (with collaboration with London Rubber Company of England), with manufacturing capacity of 57.5 million pieces a year was expected to produce condoms of the required quality. It was faced with difficulties of maintaining quality. Some of the small companies did not proceed beyond getting the licenses. Some of those who imported machines did not start operations 'after almost one year of effort'. In one case it was reported that the Company 'could not find any one who knew how to set it (the machine) up, let alone operate it' after more than one year. The private companies had some genuine grievances such as the long time taken to procure manufacturing licenses and foreign exchange (in one case reported to be two years). After a company was ready to start production, it was reported that more than six months were required for approval of the product. It was also anticipated that the indigenous manufacturers might be faced with consumer preference for well established foreign brands and hard competition in price of indigenous condoms compared to imported products. Imported contraceptives were free of duty, where as local manufacturers were required to pay excise duty on almost all of the required raw materials. It was apparent that important reasons for inability of private sector to utilise their license and to produce condoms of required quality in early years included : delays in approval at various stages, unsatisfactory quality of equipment, lack of technical know-how and inability of small companies to bear costs involved in delays before their plants could start production. The delays estimated in production appeared to range from two and a half to four years, including complying Government requirements at various stages, exploring and obtaining equipment and know-how from a well-guarded industry, building plant and machinery and training personnel. The production of condoms in public sector was considered.

In February 1964, a team of Ford Foundation Consultants visited India and submitted their report on Manufacture of Male Contraceptives in India, in the following month. The capacity of the private sector to meet the growing demand was found deficient.[56] In 1966, it was decided to start manufacture of condoms in the Public Sector and at the same time to encourage their production in the Private Sector.

Ministry of Health and Family Planning considered the recommendations of the Ford Foundation Team and other offers of equipment and transfer of technology. Japanese offer was most favourable. Kirpa Narain, a far-sighted and remarkable person, mainly negotiated the offer of the Japanese most modern automatic plant with capacity of producing 144 million pieces per year, using high grade latex from Kerala rubber plantations. The contract with the Japanese firm provided for orientation and familiarisation in Japan with modern methods of condom manufacture, installation of the factory by the Japanese technicians and Indian Engineers and technologists, provision for two units each with manufacturing capacity of 144 million pieces. The agreement included not only the transfer of technology known at that time but also continued transfer of research and development in Japan in the future for some years.

On April 5, 1969, the Hindustan Latex Ltd. (HLL) was inaugurated by the Governor of Kerala in Trivandrum. Thus commenced the production of high quality of condoms, comparable with the best produced anywhere in the world, in the Public Sector in India and their use on mass scale. The condoms produced by HLL were called NIRODH.

The production of high quality condoms in the Public Sector stimulated efforts to modernise the equipment in the Private Sector. The Private Sector also made progress and pioneered production of other varieties of condoms such as lubricated condoms.

The increasing demand, as anticipated, led to commissioning of the second unit of HLL. HLL has further expanded the production capacity and has further updated its technology. Two new plants have been added, one in Trivandrum and another in Belgaum. The HLL collaboration with Japanese Company, in these efforts has continued. Okamoto Riken Gomu Co. Ltd. and Mitsui & Co. are the collaborators. The two major developments are reducing the thickness of Nirodh from 0.06-0.07 to 0.03-0.04 mm and multi-coloured lubricated condoms. The demand for multi-colour lubricated condoms is estimated to be 60 million pieces yearly. The HLL hopes to capture major share of the market. Hindustan Latex Ltd. during 1989-90 produced 589.40 million pieces of condoms. The company has declared a dividend of 3.5 per cent in the same year, with sales to the level of Rs. 2,482 lakhs, exports Rs. 151 lakhs and profits (before tax) of Rs. 357 lakhs.[67]

The sales of Nirodh under social marketing in India during August 1990 was 87.12 million pieces.[68] Two brands of Nirodh Dry and lubricated are available for sometime. A thinner variety Super De Luxe is also now available.

SOCIAL MARKETING OF CONDOMS

With availability of condoms in the required quantity, it was possible to make them available through Family Welfare Planning centres, sub-centres. local bodies, voluntary organisations and Public Sector undertakings. These outlets were around 50,000. These were supplemented by depot holder scheme which included selected persons in villages holding stock of condoms and also selected post offices in remote areas. Even with this innovation, the channels of supplies were limited. There was no experience of using commercial channels. Meerut study by the National Institute of Family Planning New Delhi provided valuable leads. It was basically a study on family planning communication.

Earlier B.B.S. Bhatia, D.C. Dubey and A.K. Devgan had demonstrated in a study in Alwar District that the printed word can cross the illiteracy barrier. The massages and education material mailed to village leaders and addressed to them by name were generally distributed by them to literate villagers who invariably discussed them with illiterate villagers. The direct mailing was found to be inexpensive and effective.[59] This experience was incorporated in Meerut Study. The Meerut study besides mailing of printed materials to the 1310 village Pradhans included newspaper inserts, news letters and cinema slides to assess the result of a low-keyed family planning information programme, and a system of condom distribution at subsidised rates through existing commercial channels. Small stores and shops selling daily necessities were selected to stock Nirodh. Condoms (Nirodh) were given free to the commercial organisation. The commercial organisations sold them to retailers at 10 paise for three. The retailers sold to customer at 15 paise for three. The number of outlets selling Nirodh in Meerut District study rose from about 50 to 562 within three months. In terms of actual sales by the end of 1966, monthly sales rose from 50 gross to 300 gross. A level of 600 gross per month was reached in two years.[60] It was anticipated that this figure could easily be increased to 1000 gross per month if a regular supply of Nirodh was maintained. The Meerut Study was mainly developed by R.R. Blake, supported by the team of National Family Planning Institute and the very enthusiastic local commercial organiser in Meerut. The study demonstrated that condoms sold at a price a common man can afford (*i.e.*, subsidised by the government or any donor agency) through commercial channels can augment considerably the use of condoms.

The major impetus to social marketing of condoms was given by Health Secretary Govind Narain. He invited representatives of leading consumer goods organisations to discuss the involvement of their vast network of salesmen, sub-distributors, stockists, wholesalers and retailers in distribution of condoms in the country. Ajit Haksar of the ITC took prominent part in this discussion. This meeting led to the involvement of six of the largest and most experienced consumer goods organisations in the Private Sector in condom distribution extending to the smallest village. The condoms were made available at 15 paise for 3 as conveniently as tea, soap or cigarettes.

The full utilisation of the commercial network was promoted through establishment of a marketing organisation, sale and publicity campaign and research studies. D.R. Gupta was appointed the marketing executive directly under the Secretary Health and Family Planning in the Family Planning Department. He developed the marketing organisation in record time. The organisation monitored field sales, advertising operations, analysed consumer and trade behaviour and attitudes and evaluated programme performance. The scheme was launched late in 1968 and covered the whole country within about one year. Wide scale use was made of Press, Radio, Film, Point of Purchase material and later television (when television facilities were made available). Ministry of Information and Broadcasting took an active part in these developments. Initially, some people were opposed to the use of mass media for condoms. In fact such a step was unthinkable in 1950s. The Meerut Study had demonstrated that the hesitation of the people to purchase condoms openly disappears soon after they are openly displayed and advertised. The experience of nationwide publicity campaign corroborated this experience. Besides promoting sales the publicity campaign of condoms dispelled the 'hush-hush' attitude of the people in their purchase and gave respectability to their use. The number of outlets increased from about 45,000 in 1969 to 2,00,000 in early 1972. By 1980 twelve large consumer goods manufacturing companies, seven in Private Sector and five in Public Sector were making available condoms at a subsidised rate of 25 paise per packet of three pieces. The total outlets had increased to about 3,00,000 by 1986-87.

The year 1986-87 recorded a sale of 227.76 million pieces under social marketing. In addition the manufacturers sold 51.88 million pieces under their own brand names. In 1981, a special pack of six condoms was made available through Health Guides and Multipurpose Health workers. They could sell it for Rs. 0.50 and retain the proceeds from their sales as incentives. The Department of Family Welfare provides assistance to the Marketing Companies at 3 paisa per piece sold. Marketing companies also contribute one paisa per piece from their own sources and promote the national family planning programme "Dry Nirodh" are sold at a price of 25 paisa for three condoms and lubricated Nirodh called Deluxe Nirodh at price of Rs. 1/- for 5 pieces, and the third type (thinner lubricated and coloured called Super Deluxe) expected be sold at price Rs. 2/- for 4 pieces. The consumer goods manufacturing companies distributing Nirodh include : Arsan Match Company, Bharat Petrolium, Brooke Bond, Hindustan Lever Ltd., Hindustan Petroleum, IDPL, Indian Oil, ITC, Smith Stanistreet, Pharmaceuticals, Tata Oil Mills and Union Carbide. The condom has moved far in the family planning programme—from distribution through family planning and health centres and depot holders in the community to subsidised retail sales through consumer goods outlets. The lead given by a small group of researchers in Meerut in social marketing have given rich dividends.

Social marketing of contraceptives is now an important part of family planning programme in many developing countries like Bangladesh, Sri Lanka, Nepal, Jamaica, Maxico, Colombia, El Salvador, Egypt, Ghana. Distinctive brand names like Nirodh culturally acceptable in India are also given, *e.g.*, RAJA in Bangladesh, CONDOR in El Salvador DHAAL in Nepal.[61]

USE-EFFECTIVENESS

The reports of use-effectiveness of condoms widely vary. The pregnancy rate per 100 couple years reported in a British study (1976) ranged from 0.8 to 6.8; in the World Fertility Survey data for Colombia, Costa Rica, the Dominian Republic, Panama and Peru 7 for women age 30 or above and 17 for women under age 30[62] ; and in India (studies 1952-1966) ranged from about 3 to 26.[63]

A careful examination of reports indicate that use effectiveness depends mainly on the quality of the condom, the correctness of use, and the regular continuous use during every coitus. The variation in the pregnancy rates among users of condom under 30 years and 30 years and above show that the older couples are more careful in use of condom than younger couples. The effectiveness of condom further increases if used with a contraceptive cream, jelly or paste. Recently the promotion of use of condoms for prevention of AIDS has been intensified.

The strong support for the use of condom is well illustrated by the National Condom Week launched on August 13, 1990 in the United Kingdom, for the third year in succession to increase personal and social acceptance of the condom and to educate people to practice safe sex. The week was coordinated by the British Safety Council. The women were urged to buy and carry condom themselves and not rely on their partners. James Tye is reported to have said : "Casual sex is risky and until a vaccine is available using condom could save your life. "Tony Belfield of the United Kingdom Family Planning Association is reported in *The Independent*" saying condoms are very safe and rarely split if used correctly".[64]

4

Sterilization

The sterilization operations, mainly among females were being performed in some hospitals in India for a long time. The sub-committee of Health Panel Planning Commission, in April 1951 recommended provision of facilities for sterilization, along with advice on contraceptives on medical social and economic grounds. Health Minister Rajkumari Amrit Kaur was strongly opposed to it. The First Five Year Plan document while launching the policy on family planning did not refer to surgical methods of birth control on social and economic grounds. There was, however, no statement against sterilization method in the Plan document. In 1958, Tamil Nadu took the initiative to introduce sterilization operations in males and females as their official policy, on the basis of the Planning Commission Health Panel Sub-Committee recommendations and watched the reaction".[65] Maharashtra soon followed the Tamil Nadu policy. Gradually, the sterilization operations facilities were introduced on increasing scale as one of the important methods of birth control in almost all States. The number of operations increased from about 800 in 1956 to 40,000 in 1959.

The Government of India finally decided to extend financial support for the sterilization operation as one of the methods of birth control. But before announcing the official support and offering financial assistance to sterilization programme a number of aspects regarding it had to be resolved such as the legal position, the form of informed consent, the extent of financial and other support, the logistics of equipment and material, training of personnel, the measures needed for information and education of the people, the reporting system and monitoring.

There was no case on record in India in which legal action was taken against a surgeon performing sterilization operation or against the person undergoing the operation. The case of Bravery *Vs.* Bravery in 1954 in England had raise some doubts on launching sterilization programme without legal protection. In the case of Bravery *Vs.* Bravery the wife had put forward the husbands vasectomy as ground of divorce. The majority judgement in this case was that voluntary sterilization was legal. But one judge had considered the operation "potentially injurious to public interest".[66]

The Family Planning Research and Programme Committee, in 1954, had reviewed the situation and especially noted the view of Phillip Weintraub that "The Swedish Sterilization law and its application show that there was merit in the legal regulation of sterilization for every one legally qualified for it ; it offers protection to the physician who otherwise would act at his own risk or would refuse to act at all". The crucial question was whether sterilization operation was "physical injury", a mutilation of part of an organ or function. The Ministry of Law advised that no legal provisions were necessary, as voluntary sterilization was not considered to cause physical injury as it was for the benefit of the person concerned. Ministry of Health decided to go ahead with the sterilization programme and laid down regulatory measures with special emphasis on on informed consent of both husband and wife.

The method, for all practical purposes, being irreversible and therefore a terminal method, it was considered that for ensuring marital harmony both husband and wife should consult each other before deciding the adoption of sterilization method. The regulatory measures, therefore, included written consent of both husband and wife. Ministry of Health letter of 20 April 1960. offering 100% central assistance for sterilization facilities specifically stated that "sterilization should be voluntary with consent of the couple and following consideration should be taken into account in effecting sterilization: (*a*) the number of living children and their sex ; (*b*) the ages of husband and wife ; (*c*) socio-economic prospects of the couple ; (*d*) emotional and mental attitudes ; and (*e*) their preparedness for permanent birth limitation." Great stress was laid on giving the couple opportunity to consider all aspects related to operation before making final decision. Ministry of Health letter to State Government emphasised that "no sterilization should be done in a hurry. The couples should be given ample time to think over the effects of sterilization and to decide whether the husband or the wife should best have it".[67]

The 100 per cent Central assistance included provision of facilities throughout the country for (*a*) strengthening the staff of teaching medical institutions for training of doctors in the techniques of male and female sterilization operations and care.* (*b*) strengthening the staff of hospitals initially upto District level and later upto Tehsil/Taluk and Primary Health Centre level for performing sterilization operations.

These facilities included provision of staff, arrangements for visiting teams where ever required especially from teaching institutions wherever possible ; equipment required and at later stage provision of additional beds. Guidelines for sterilization operations were prepared by Dr. Shrodker (female sterilization) and Dr. Phadke for male sterilization.

The lack of,-or deficiencies in the health infrastructure and long distances of health centres from people, posed serious problems in reaching them, especially in remote parts of the country. In the Armed Forces mobile medical units including specialised units had been used for a very long time. Eye

*Besides the medical officers of State Government, local bodies and voluntary organisation, private medical practitioners could also avail of this facility.

camps among civilian population also had been used successfully. Feasibility of sterilization camps was, therefore, discussed. Maharashtra State took the lead in demonstrating that sterilization camps for males could be arranged without much difficulty. Dr. Chitre developed a plan of operation of such camps. There was in the beginning hesitation in arranging sterilization camps for females, as tubectomy involved opening the abdomen and keeping the woman for a few days in bed. Dr. M.D. Sehgal in Gujarat ventured to arrange a tubectomy camp. He reported that with proper organisation and care, tubectomy operations could be performed with same safety as in a static hospitals. Vasectomy and tubectomy camps soon became popular throughout the country.

The Reorganised Programme 1962-63 laid emphasis on holding small sterilization camps with careful preparation and follow-up of each case. It was observed that sterilization camps both for males and females were not only convenient and safe, but also facilitated mobilisation of adequate surgical services at a time and place desired by the people wanting such a service and camp situation provided important group psychological support. A notable innovation was made by very energetic innovative and vocal young doctor Pai in Bombay—the sterilization units at railway stations.

The Government of India extended 100 per cent assistance for holding such camps as widely as possible throughout the country. A new dimension to camp approach appeared in 1970s—the Mass Sterilization Camps. The first two mass camps were held in the Ernakulum District in Kerala in November-December 1970 and July 1971 under the dynamic leadership of S. Krishna Kumar. Over 60,000 operations were performed.[68] The Mass Sterilization camps had three main features in programme operation, *viz.*, a forceful leadership of the administrative head of the area, a widescale mobilisation of administrative and technical resources, and provision of monetary compensation higher than usually given. The extraordinary number of operations performed in these camps gave high hopes of this strategy. The example of Kerala was followed in several districts in other States, during 1971-73. Over two million acceptors of vasectomies were reported during 1972-73.

The enthusiasm for Mass Sterilization Camp approach did not last long. When this approach was used Nation-wide several weaknesses emerged, mainly in selection of cases, their preparation through sustained educational process, the quality of service and follow-up. After reviewing the situation, in 1973, the sterilization programme reverted to old approach, *i.e.*, sterilization operations to be performed in static units and in mini-camps which provide manageable opportunities for education ensuring well informed consent, proper selection of cases, suitable arrangements for operation and proper care during the operation and adequate follow-up.

In June 1975, a national emergency was declared. The sterilization programme with strong support of Sanjay Gandhi achieved a very high level of performance during this period. The declared official policy was sterilization on voluntary basis. But there were reports of excesses on a number of places. There were also reports of fear among field workers for not fulfilling their quotas of sterilization operations. Such reports were highly politicized and contributed to the defeat of the ruling party in 1977 elections.

A serious erosion of family planning programme followed the change in the Government, especially the sterilization programme. The programme was rehabilitated when Congress-I again came to power in 1980. The traumatic experience during the Emergency and after appears to have contributed to revival of a rationalized approach to sterilization programme.

The technique of sterilization in female is not so simple as sterilzation in males. Experimental studies were initiated on tubal occlusion by chemicals such as quinacrine and silastic, use of bands or clips on tubes, fulguration, plugs and improvement of older methods. Professor B. Rakshit was the first researcher in India on chemical blocking of fallopian tubes[69] and also later to use liquid plastics in humans.[70] Since 1960, minilaprotomy (popularly called minilap) and laproscopy have made female sterilization simple, quick and safe. The former requires a small incision of less than 3 cm. gently pulling the tubes to this incision, blocking the tubes and returning them back to abdomen, in the latter case laproscope is inserted in the abdomen. In both cases the sterilization procedure takes 10-20 minute and patient is allowed to go home after a few hours.[71] This method has been recommended nation-wide. In a few cases only the newly developed methods are considered unsuitable, for example obese patients. The improvement in female sterilization technology increased the number of women offering for sterilization. The 1986-87 Year Book reported 4.22 million tubectomy operations. The technique-wise break-up is available for 3.33 million. Of these 41.2 per cent were done by laproscopic technique.[72]

Introduction of new technique poses its own problems. It is reported that the failure rates in USA are 0.2-0.4%. In India these rates are relatively higher especially in rural areas. This underlines the importance of training and rigid quality control of materials used.

Reversal

The early experience had shown that cases demanding to reverse the operation in circumstances like death of children or re-marriage were few, guesses put it one in a million. However, it was expected that if reversal techniques are developed sterilization would be more acceptable. Efforts were made to develop techniques of vasectomy reversal. The husband's frozen semen storage was also discussed, which would not require surgical procehdures. Other attempts included intra-vasal contraceptive device. Dr. P.S. Jhaver a young innovative surgeon at Indore had developed a vas occlusion clip, but did not receive much support in India. Later his work started being noticed when experimentation was done with US collaborators.[73]

In 1960s, encouraging reports on reversal operation techniques developed by investigators in Bombay were received and greater understanding of difficulties associated with such operations also emerged. Government of India supported the establishment of centres for reversal operations in a few selected places. The vas anastomosis has a long history beginning around 1900. But the technique developed in 1960s were much advanced involving mucosa to mucosa anastomosis. A number of problems were reported such as suitability of cases, technique adopted in initial vasectomy operation, skilled man-power, ready availability of material required for operation, etc.

The attempts for reversal of sterilization operation in the female has been more difficult than in case of male sterilization, Dr. V.N. Shirodker was the early pioneer in developing reversal technique. Similar developments were reported in other countries. Sterilization techniques used in case of males like clips, bands, plugs, chemicals, cautry were tried in case of female sterilization. Wolfgang Walz in Federal Republic of Germany had reported the use of operating microscope in 1959. This led to further development of micro-surgery. The reversal method that has largely survived is micro-surgical technique. The success with this technique has been reported to be almost double in 1980s as compared to 1960s, about 60 per cent success.[74]

Sterilization now is the worlds most popular family planning method. "Some 100 million couples around the world rely on surgical sterilization to prevent pregnancy as of 1985. The highest levels are seen in Puorto Rico, where 46 per cent of married women of reproductive age are protected by sterilization and in the US where the level is 39 per cent, including women who have had hysterectomies".[75]

In March 1987, of the estimated 132.6 million eligible couples in India, 49.70 million were effectively protected; of this number 27.9 per cent were protected by sterilization. In the beginning of the sterilization programme proportion of male sterilizations was higher than female sterilization. A swing took place in this proportion. In 1986-87 the proportion of the tubectomies to total sterilizations was 83.9 per cent. There is a strong case to promote vasectomy, a simpler method.

5

Intra Uterine Contraceptive Device

The use of IUD was reported by the Arabs and the Turks—pebbles into uterus of their camel to prevent conception. Ibna Sena (Avicenna) had referred to contraceptive pessaries around the 11th Century. The use of studs and stem pessaries in the cervix were reported in the 19th Century. Such cervical devices appear to have been used in some places till recently.* In 1909, Richard Richter, a German physician, designed an intra-uterine device using a flexible ring of silkworm gut. In 1925 K. Pust used almost a similar device with a tail and a button fixed at the end of the tail to facilitate its removal. Late in 1920s a spiral of silver ring (Grafenburg ring) attracted international attention. But their use was very limited and was widely discouraged by the medical profession. In 1934 Tenrei Ota of Japan designed a gold plated silver intra-uterine ring. In 1959, Oppenheimer of Israel and Ishihama of Japan reported favourable results with IUDs. Several investigators by this time were experimenting on IUDs of different designs and material. The view from outright rejection of IUDs was gradually changing to assessing harmlessness of various devices developed including

*A sample of such a device was given to the author in one of the Caribbean Islands in 1970s.

plastic device (the Margulies Coil and Lippes Loop). The data presented at the International Conference convened by the Population Council in 1962 in New York led to the view that a stage was reached to evaluate in some depth the use of some of the IUDs. A cooperative Statistical Programme under Christopher Tietze was launched to evaluate the various sizes of Lippes Loop (A, B, C and D), the Margulies spiral, Birnburg Bows (large and small) and several others including steel rings.*

IUD Programme Launched in India 1965

The Population Council New York held another conference on IUDs in 1964. Several experts from India attended this conference. Reports of investigators from different countries were favourable in respect of Lippes Loop. Ministry of Health requested the Indian Council of Medical Research (ICMR) to examine the desirability of using IUDs in India. The ICMR recommended the use of Lippes Loop. Ministry of Health approved its use in the Nation-wide family planning programme in 1965.[76] The Central Family Planning Institute, New Delhi organised a seminar in 1966 to discuss various aspects of IUDs in the National Programme.[77] The major impetus for use of the IUDs in India was given by the United Nations Advisory Mission in February 1965. The Mission recommended that three courses of action should be taken simultaneously : "the loop programme should be launched energetically in selected areas in the country ; the sterilization programme should be intensified ; and the use of condoms should be promoted particularly through commercial and other channels".

IUD Manufacture in India

A factory for manufacture of the Lippes Loop was started in Kanpur with the mould made available by the Population Council.

*About this time Sheldon Segal arrived in India to establish a reproductive biology laboratory at the All India Institute of Medical Sciences New Delhi. He brought a few IUD devices. A very controlled trials on IUDs by a few carefully selected gynaecologists and obstetricians was started in India.

Review of IUDs

In 1963, a seminar was jointly organised by the ICMR and CFPI to review clinical and laboratory research in the country.[78] The reassurance in effectiveness and harmlessness was further provided by the decision of the United States Food and Drug Administration in 1968 and the reports of the Scientific Group meetings of the World Health Organisation held in 1966, 1968 and 1971.[79] The IUDs were considered at that time a major technological break-through. A large scale IUD programme was thus developed in India. Clinical Services were provided through static and mobile units. Private medical practitioners were involved. Scholarships to medical students especially women were introduced. A Central Family Planning Corps of medical officers especially women, primarily for IUD work was formed. Large scale training programmes for insertion of IUDs and education programme were launched. At a later stage, Auxilliary Nurse mid-wives after training in selected Primary Health Centres were allowed to insert IUDs.

1973 Study in IUD in India

After initial favourable response, the number of IUD acceptors began to decline. In the beginning, such results were attributed to inadequate preparation of cases, rumours and lack of follow-up of each case. The IUD training programme was therefore revised. Arrangements were made for prompt treatment of complications. The education programme was intensified. Still IUDs available at that time could not be rehabilitated.

A study in 1973 showed that about 46 per cent complained of bleeding. 26.2 per cent vaginal white discharge, and 27.7 per cent abdominal pain. The pelvic inflamatory diseases were found in about 1 per cent of cases.* In about 71 per cent of cases removal of IUD was reported to be due to prolonged and heavy bleeding during menstrual period. The favourable aspects of IUD users were, lower age and parity of acceptors

*Much higher incidence of PID was reported in developed countries, presumably due to free sex relationship with several mates.

than among sterilization acceptors. A trend of decline in both age and parity among IUD acceptors was also observed. Over three-fourth of IUD acceptors were in the age group 25-34 years and gradually increased number of acceptors were coming from lower socio-economic group.[80] It soon became obvious that IUD available was not living to its expectations. It appeared that intrauterine device as such would be acceptable if some further development was made to eliminate side effects.

Development of Different Types of IUDs

There were two major reviews on IUDs, *viz.*, one in 1973 a workshop sponsored by the Battelle Memorial Institute in Scattle and another in 1974, the Third International Conference in Cairo, sponsored by the Population Council. The focus now is on the new generation IUDs (the bio-active and medicated devices) to deal with problems of side-effects. They are mainly copper wire wrapped round the plastic devices, or steroids or other agents incorporated devices. The evaluation of the IUDs besides the Population Council and its International Committee on Contraceptive Research is done by International Fertility Programme, the United Kingdom IUD Research Programme of Exter University, World Health Organisation and centres in other countries.

Since Jack Lippes and Margulies had introduced in 1960s intrauterine devices, a number of devices have been developed Saf T-coil by Ralph R. Robinson in 1965 ; Cu-7, or Gravigard by Jaime Zipper and Harvey Abramson in 1974 ; Copper T-200 or Gyne T by Howard Tatum and Jaime Zipper in 1972 ; TCu-220 and TCu-380 Ag by Population Council; Multiload cu 250, or Multiload-D 250 by W.A.A. van Os in 1974 ; Nova T Cu-200 and 200 Ag by Ahti Kosonen and Tapani Luukkainen in 1979 ; Progestasert interauterine (progesterone) Contraceptive System by Alza Corporation USA in 1976 ; Uterine Therapeutic System by Alza Corporation ; Chinese ring and Chinese Shanghai V (People's Republic of China) ; Dana Super (Czechoslovakia) ; Ohta Ring (Japan) ; Soonawala by R.P. Soonawala in 1972 ; Modified Lippes Loop (Lippes Loop D coated with *ethylene* vineyl acetate carrying trasylol, a protease *inhibitor* to reduce bleeding) International Fertility Research Programme.*

The heavy menstrual bleeding in some cases using IUDs has been a cause of serious concern especially among aneamic women in developing countries. World Health Organisation had recommended use of TCu-220 in cases where women experience bleeding with Lippes Loop. The studies by the Population Council on TCu-200, TCu-220 and TCu-380 show lower pregnancy rates with TCu-220 and TCu-380. This is attributed to copper wire only on vertical arm of TCu-200; and copper sleeves on both vertical and transverse arms in case of TCu-220 and TCu-380, *i.e.*, copper sleeve on transverse arms rest in the fundus of the uterus. The Population Council is concentrating on TCu-380 as it is stated to be somewhat easier to manufacture and has slightly better performance than TCu-220. The TCu-380 Ag carries two sleeves of solid copper on the crossbar and coil of copper wire, with a core of silver around the stem. The silver core is intended to lengthening effective life of the device (silver keeps the copper from fragmenting). A variation of silver-cored copper wire device is Nova T. Progestasert (Alza Corporation) approved by USFDA contains a reservoir of 38 mg. of progesterone in silicone oil. The trials on progestin releasing intrauterine devices by the Population Council and the World Health Organisation and on IUDs containing antifibrinolytic substances by the International Fertility Research Programme are in progress. Biodegradable chromic sutures affixed to the upper horizontal bar of the IUD inserted in post-abortion and post-partum cases to reduce incidence of expulsions are being tried. Research on improvement of IUDs continue.[81]

In 1989, Copper T 380 Ag IUD was approved by the FDA for sale as a six year method. A very high effectiveness has been reported for Copper T 380 Ag—six year cumulative pregnancy rate with continuous use 1.2 per 100 woman years of use.[82]

---

*They do not include several devices extensively tested but no longer manufactured like the Dalkon Shield, the Gynekoil, the Majzlin Spring. urther developments and the list of widely used IUDs as in March 1988 are given in the following pages.

Mode of Action

The mode of action of the IUDs has been a subject of debate. In the early 1960s, the view generally held was that IUD sets in changes in the endometrium which are not hospitable to nidation of fertilised ovum. Therefore some labelled it as an abortificient. Sivin calls it as a "social myth". He observes that IUDs act as contraceptive by diminishing the number of sperms that reach the oviduct and incapacitates them, and all studies show that primary mode of IUD action appears to be interference with fertilization rather than with implantation.[83]

Effectiveness

The pregnancy rates with most devices are reported to range from 1.0 to 3.0 per 100 women per year. The pregnancy rates for TCu-380 A, TCu-380 Ag. TCu-220 C, and MLCu-375* are reported to be less than one per 100 women per year.[84] In a major World Health Organisation study the cumulative pregnancy rate with TCu-380 is 1.4 per 100 women and for TCu-220C 4.5 per 100 women reported.[85]

Care in the Use of IUDs

The IUDs are not suitable for all cases. A careful screening of cases is essential. It is obvious that great care should be taken during insertion and each case should be followed up with equal care.

The IUD should not be advised in cases of active or recent genital infection, or with history of more than once pelvic inflamatory disease, or abnormal cervical smear, abnormal vaginal bleeding or other signs of genital cancer, or

*TCu-380 A is T shaped device made of polyethylene with barium added for visibility by X Rays and 314 mm^2 copper wire on vertical stem, two 33 mm^2 solid copper sleeves on each transverse arm. The wire in the TCu-380 Ag has a silver core. In TCu-220C there is 220 mm^2 copper in seven copper sleeves two on the arm and five on the stem. The Multiload-375 (MLCu-375) is also of polyethylene but with two flexible arms with spurs and has 375 mm^2 copper wire available in three sizes.

pregnant women. There are other contraindications such as repeated genital infections, history of ectopic pregnancy, anaemia, fibroids and other tumours and conditions that alter the shape of the uterus or cervix, painful or long menstrual periods, and when parents wants children. Some of these require individual evaluation. Two words given in *Population Reports* Counselling Guide J-36 December 1987 may be helpful to remember important elements in family planning counselling. *viz.*, GATHER and PAINS. Six points in GATHER ARE : *G*reet Client ; *A*sk client about themselves ; *T*ell clients about family planning methods (all available methods, how they work, advantages disadvantages, side effects, etc.) ; *H*elp clients choose a method (method suited to a clients need, effectiveness, risks benfits, etc., the dicision based on the *informed* chöice of the client) Explain how to use the IUD. *R*eturn for follow up.

The word PAINS may help the IUD user the warning signs of pelvic infection or pregnancy. *P*eriod late (pregnancy), abnormal spotting or bleeding. *A*bdominal pain, pain with intercourse. *I*nfection (such as gonorrhea) abnormal discharge. *N*ot feeling well, fever, chill. *S*tring missing, shorter or longer.[86]

Widely Used IUDs

About 85 million women are using IUDs in the World*. As of March 1988, the widely used intrauterine devices include : TCu-380A, TCu-380 Ag, TCu-380 Slimline (TCu-380 S) ; TCu-200, TCu-200Band TCu-200 Ag ; Nova T Lippes Loop MLCu-250 and MLCu-375 TUCu-220 C. Progestasert Intrauterine Progestrone Contraceptive System Chinese IUDs—stringless single coil stainless steel ring most widely used ; Newly developed uterine cavity shaped steel ring, double coiled stainless ring, Shanghai V-200 made of silicone plastic on a wire frame with 200 mm copper wire, and.[87]

Increasing Use of IUD in India

Cu 'T' and Lippes Loop both are being used in India.

---

*1987 estimate, *Population Reports*, B. 5, March 1988.

During 1986-87, about 4 million IUD insertions were performed, about 96 per cent Cu T. The services of Auxilliary Nurse Midwife for insertion of Cu 'T' are now being utilised. It is stipulated that only experienced and properly selected ANMs who have rendered a minimum of five years service may be trained in the insertion of Cu T at 'A' type teaching and non-teaching Post-Partum institutions including District hospitals ; only those ANMs may be certified as trained who have successfully done at least 25 Cu 'T' insertions ; the facilities should be extended only to the selected sub-centres which have got the proper physical facilities and equipment. An increasing trend in IUD acceptors and further decline in mean age of acceptors are reported.

The problem of eliminating all the side effects especially bleeding has still to be solved. The search for bio-active and medicated IUDs to overcome side effects continues.

6

The Oral Contraceptives

Indigenous Herbs

The family planning programme in India from its very inception showed interest in contraception in two fields, *viz.*, indigenous herbs and other substances reported to have anti-fertility effect and in physiological control of conception. The position in respect of the former, as in 1959 was : (*a*) Pharmocology Department Lucknow University tested *Mallotus phillipppensis* (Kambila) ; *Punica granatum* (Anar) ; *Chenopodium album* (Bathwa) ; *Taxus baccata* (Talis) *Patram ossypium herbaceum* (Kapas) , *Carum carui* (Siahvira) ; *Soanum xanthocarpum* (Bhatkatraia) ; *Vitex ag us castus* (Shambhuluk abija) and *Daemia extensa* (Phalkantaka). *Anar* and *Kambila* only showed some effect on fertility on rats and guinepigs when administered in crude form ; (*b*) The Institute of Post-graduate Medical Education and Research Calcutta was investigating anti-fertility effect of cirantin ; (*c*) The Contraceptive Testing Centre at the Cancer Research Centre Bombay tested Hibuscus betelnuts impregnated with latex in the trunk of banana and on seeds of caricapapaya ; (*d*) The Director Tribal Bihar Research Institute had been issued a grant from Ministry of Health for study of herbs reported to be in use for control of conception by the Abor tribals* ; (*e*) S.N. Sanyal was conti-

*Reference to herbs used by the tribal communities is made earlier in Chapter 1.

nuing investigation on meta-xylohydroquinone. This investigation is traceable to 1935, when Professor N.C. Nag of Sir J.C. Bose Research Institute Calcutta in collaboration with Dr. Pyne observed that feeding of rats on *Pisum-sativum (Matar dal)* makes them temporarily sterile. Sanyal, in 1950, obtained similar results from injection of oil extracted from the seeds of *Mattar dal* and also through oral administration of Meta-xylo-hydroquinone said to be present in the oil. This investigation was later continued at the All India Institute of Hygiene and Public Health Calcutta under a Technical Committee including the Director of the Institute as Chairman, and Drs. C. Chandrasekharan, Mukta Sen, S.N. Sanyal, S. Ghosh and B.K. Aiket as members. The tentative conclusions reached were : administration of about 300-400 mgs. of Meta-xylo-hydroquinone on the 16th and 21st day after onset of menstruation reduced pregnancy rate by about 50 per cent and as far as could be ascertained, constant use of the drug for a period of about 6-7 months didn't produce any toxic effects.[88]

In 1965 the Indian Council of Medical Research set up a committee togather information on plants in India reported to prevent conception. Ranjit Roy Chaudhury, convenor of this committee, listed 321 plants, of these fifteen plants were tested, *viz.*, *Abroma augusta*, *Abrus prooatoria*, *Ananas comosus*, *Carica papaya*, *Dondrooalamuj structus*, *Glorisa superba*, *Cossypium herbacum*, *Mocholta champaoa*, *Polygonum hydripiper*, *Randia dometurum*, *Rubus bark*, *Somacarpus anacardum*, *Taxus baccata*, *Aristolichta tagla* and *Utaria logopoidaos*. Only bark of Rubus was found effective.[89] The tests were not done for all the parameters. The method of administration of the plant product and the use of specific parts of the plant are likely to influence results. It was also argued by some observers that the results of tests carried out in different experimental animals need not necessarily be applicable to human beings. This calls for extension of investigations in primates and further extension to humans. It seems that testing of indigenous products claimed to have anti-fertility property was not persued vigorously.

Physiological control of conception by hormones taken by mouth overshadowed the investigations on indigenous plant material.

STEROIDS

Beard, as early as 1897, suggested that corpus luteum was responsible for suppression of ovulation during pregnancy. He was partly correct. In 1898, Zoohkko lent further support to this view. He demonstrated that removal of retained corpus luteum in cows led to prompt resumption of aestrus. In 1914, Pearl noted that injection of mamalion corpus luteum extract decreased egg production in cows. These observations were followed by reports notably of Smith in 1920, Halberlandt in 1921 and Parkes in 1929 that either the presence of corpus luteum or administration of corpus luteum extract prevented the induction of ovulation in experimental animals. In 1934, Makepeace isolated progestrone. In 1937 Makepeace and his associates and in 1939, Astwood and Fovold demonstrated its ovulation inhibiting action in rats and rabbits. In 1932, Hartman suggested the use of a preparation of oestrogen (amniotin a preparation from bovine amniotic fluid) to inhibit ovulation in order to relieve dysmenorrhoea. By 1937, it became known that progestrone, estrogen and testosterone, could inhibit ovulation. In the 1930s diosgenin was isolated from sweet potatoes or yam by Japanese scientists. In 1941, Marker started work on synthesis of steroids using diosgenin as the starting point and later offered his finding to commercial organisation in Mexico which became the Syntex Corporation. In 1954, Djerassi and his coworkers developed a new method of synthesis of orally very active progestogen and synthesized Norethisterone. Soon after the potential of steroid drugs for inhibition of ovulation and fertility control was widely recognised. In 1956, Gregory Pincus, and his associates developed "the Pill" with 19-norsteroids and a combination of progestogen and oestrogen was used in human trials "The Pill" composed of Norethynodrel and Mestranol was marketed laterly by the Searle Company under trade name Enovid.[90]

By 1950s the news of "great breakthrough" in contraceptive

technology through physiological control of conception and clinical trials in Peurto-Rico reached India. It was not till late 1959 that the discussion on introduction of the Pill in the family planning programme in India was seriously considered by those responsible for directing the family planning programme in the country. The opportunity for discussion, between clinicians, researchers and programme managers in India and Pincus, Rock and others with first hand experience with the use of "the Pill", was provided by the Family Planning Association of India and the International Planned Parenthood Federation during the Sixth International Conference on Planned Parenthood in February 1959 in New Delhi. The paper by Rock, Garcia and Pincus on two clinical studies on Oral Contraceptive, followed by the paper on "Field Trials with Norethynodrel as an oral contraceptive by Pincus, Rock and Garcia and discussions on them were of considerable interest. Main conclusion in the second paper was that: "norethynodrel taken in a dose of 10 mg. alongwith 0.15 mg. of ethinyl estradiol in a single daily tablet (popularly called the Pill) from days 5 through 24 of the menstrual cycle acts an effective contraceptive", Reference was made to various menstrual cycle phenomena in women taking "the Pill", *i.e.*, bleeding, side reactions like vomiting, nausea, dizzinness, headache and gastralgia ; such reactions were considered by Pincus to be largely psychogenic ; and results of other investigations, *e.g.*, two liver function tests indicated normal liver function, and follow-up on 86 subjects showed that subsequent fertility was not effected by taking the Pill. There was difference of opinion on a few points (not related to effectiveness of the Pill), *e.g.*, Professor R.B. Greenblatt felt that breakthrough bleeding was far more than 14 per cent, some patients discontinued the use of these drugs who have nervous tensions the premenstrual syndrome and "it is well to take notice that administration of 19 norsteroids to pregnant women has resulted in slight increase in genetical anamolies of the new born female child". Edward T. Tyler Medical Director, Los Angeles Planned Parenthood Centre where the study was started, a year after the commencement of the study in Puerto Rico, disagreed that gastro-intestinal reactions were largely psychogenic. He also believed that "acceptability of this method as compared to the acceptability of other methods is definitely lower because of the side effects" and "24 per cent of (his) patients who had side effects and discontinued oral method did so because of gastro-intestinal reactions".[91] In an informal discussion with the Director Family Planning, Pincus presented a strong case for a large scale trials on "the Pill" in India. There was no doubt in the effectiveness of the pill. But at the same time there were a number of unanswered questions such as the effect of "the Pill" on lactation and amount of the drug in the milk, on anaemic women in view of the high incidence of breakthrough bleeding and other side effects like nausea and vomiting, and other possible effects due to long use of steroids. It was expected that the Indian women (like those at Los Angeles clinic) will be very disturbed "if they do not bleed on schedule or if they bleed at a time they don't expect". The dose was considered to be high. Pincus had already made studies on the effects of halving and quartering the daily dose. There was a strong feeling that daily dose could be further reduced. There was serious apprehension among programme managers in India that introduction of "the Pill" at that stage for field trials among large number of women many of whom may be anaemic could effect their health and also the credibility of the programme due to its side-eff.cts and pose problems when the dosage schedule is stabilised and the pill forms a part of contraceptive methods of Indian family planning programme. Ministry of Health and Welfare in Japan* had not approved the use of the Pill. It was felt that hasty action might prove counter-productive. India waited for further information from researchers in the country and abroad. This view was not shared by several groups of people. Pressures were brought from various levels to introduce "the Pill" in the Indian programme. Criticism of Government approach was voiced in the Press. The Pill manufacturers started supporting financially some gynaecologists and obstetricians in the country to conduct clinical trials.

*According to reports, Ministry of Health and Welfare Japan has not yet approved the oral contraceptives.

A manufacturer helped a tea plantation in Assam to carry out trials among tea plantation labour, with disappointing results (women were unable to take pills regularly and the trial was discontinued, perhaps due to side effects). India kept a close watch on research and developments and waited for appropriate time to introduce "the Pill" in the National Programme.

Further research showed that the initial hormones in "the Pill" was very much higher than necessary for suppression of ovulation. The dosage of both progestogen and oestrogen were later markedly reduced. The very low dosage tended to increase the failure rate, especially when the woman missed taking the tablets. A number of formulations and schedules were developed to meet this and other problems. Ths progestogen was reduced from the initial 10 mg. to 1 mg. or less and estrogen from 0.15 mg. to 0.03 mg.

Side effects diminished. The combination Pill (progestogen cum estrogen was reported to have pregnancy rates of less than 0.2 per cent, far lower than IUD. Gradually the picture of absolute contraindications for the use of "the Pill" became clearer such as past history of thromboembolic disorders ; liver disease or jaundice, diabetes mellitus ; cancer of breast, cervix or uterus, organic heart disease, undiagnosed vaginal bleeding. Other contraindications were recognised such as migraine, epilepsy, allergy, skin disorders especially eczema, blood conditions like anaemia, hypertension. This facilitated screening of cases and keeping watch on any developments in cases using "the Pill". Recent reports show that "risks associated with oral contraceptives use are largely confined to women over age 35 and specially to women over 35 who smoke. The risk of younger women is very small" and benefits of regular use outweigh risks. Although "the Pill" aggravates malignant condition, there is no evidence that cancer of genital tract or breast can be caused by contraceptive steroids. The quantity of milk secretion is reduced in oral contraceptive users. Generally advice given is not to use "the Pill" for at least six months after delivery. Small amounts of steroids are secreted in the milk. Although its effect on the new born is not very clear, the use of Pill should be avoided and another method of contraception can be used. A wide range of combination of progestogen and estrogen are now available. Initially low dose formulation can be used. Subsequent change can be done according to side effects. The progestin only pill (the mini pill) may be suitable in a limited number of cases.[92]

Oral Pill Project in India

With sufficient research data available, the Indian Council of Medical Research had given clearance for conducting large scale clinical trials in 1967. In August 1967, Ministry of Health initiated a pilot project to study various aspects of oral pills under field conditions in selected clinics throughout the country. By mid-1969 in over 200 clinics 12,000 pill acceptors were participating in "the Pill" Project. The project covered bio-medical, bio-social and demographic aspects. The findings showed : The women in the pilot project were a modernised group of women. younger in age, with fewer children, better education and higher income than acceptors of IUD. But the rate of drop outs among them was almost twice of IUD acceptors by the end of 12 months of use". The pill acceptors were mostly urban residents and almost two-third of them had previous contraceptive experience" "including 12 per cent Pill users from other sources". One-third of the Pill acceptors did not report any medical complaints....about one.fourth reported nausea, vomiting and dizziness as the most brother-some complaint. The next in order were the ones associated with menstrual disorders (10 per cent). The net cumulative discontinuation rates at the end of 6, 12 and 18 months of use were 46, 61 and 73 per cent respectively". The maximum rate of discontinuation was during the first three months. Relatively higher continuation rates were observed among women in younger age groups, with fewer live births, with better education with either no previous contraceptive experience or experience of IUD. Wife's education had the strongest influence among all variable".[93]

ORAL PILL IN INDIAN FAMILY PLANNING PROGRAMME

Despite some discouraging features like high discontinuation rates and side effects, it was considered that there are several favourable factors relating "to Pill" acceptors in the Pilot Project, and a stage is reached to include the pill in the National programme. "The Pill" recommended, in July 1967, was composed of ethynodiol diacetate 1 mg. and mestranol 0.1 mg. (Ovulen). The use of the Pill in the National Programme initially was for those who could not or did not like to use IUDs.

The effectiveness of "the Pill" was beyond any controversy. The major anxiety was about their side effects. Both oestrogen and progestogens appeared to be involved with the adverse of effects.[94] It was gradually realised that not only reduction of dosage was necessary to improve the safety, but also some modifications in them and their combinations in "the Pill".[95]

The studies on modifications led to some of the following changes :

(*i*) Change in the oestrogen. In most of the Pills now the mestranol has been replaced by ethynyl oestradiol ;

(*ii*) Change in progestogens. Some progestogens and androgenic receptors seem to have affinity between them. Androgenic progestrones cause decreased sex hormone binding globolin and high density lipoprotein level. The latter is an important determinant of thombo-embolic episodes. The chemical structure determines the endrogenic activity. Synthetic progestogens are 170 COH progesterone and 19 Nortestosterone derivatives. Among the former are Pregnanes and the latter Estranes such as Norethisterone and Gonanes, such as Norgestrel, desogestrel, gestrodene. The Pregnanes, which have no adrogenic activity are seldom used in the Combined "Pills" except for cyproterone acetate as little adrogenic activity is required for cycle control The gonanes and estranes share the structural features, but the former in addition is characterised by an ethylgroup in a specific position. Gonanes include the most effective new progestogen, such as desogestrel, gestodene, levonorgestrel norgestimate.

(iii) Reduction in oestrogen and progestogen content. Oestrogen below 0.03 mg. appears to cause problem of break through bleeding and cycle control. Progestogen in many Pills now has been reduced to 1.0 mg. or 0.5 mg. Further overall reduction in total intake of Progestogen per cycle has been reported by imitating the harmonal pattern of menstrual cycle, *e.g.*, in the Triphasic Pills in the early part (1-6 days) low dose combination (Progestogen 0 05 mg.+oestrogen 0.03 mg.), in the mid cycle slight increase 7-11 days (Progestogen .075 mg+oestrogen .075 mg.) and later part 12-22 high progestogen and low oestrogen (Progestogen (0.125 mg.+oestrogen 0.040 mg).[96]

The above developments are reflected in the changes in the choice of "the Pill" in Indian family play programme. The first replacement was in the "The Pill" composed of norgestrel 0.5 mg. and ethynylestradiol of 0.05 mg. (ovral). At present two formulation are in use, *viz.*, MALA-D [Norgestrel 0.05 mg.+Ethynyloestradiol 0.03 mg.] and MALA-N [Norethistrone 1.00 mg.+ethynyloestradiol 0.03 mg.].

"The Pills" were made available at Family Welfare Planning Centres at all District Headquarters, CGHS, Defence, Railways, ESI and other centres and a few Primary Health Centres where adequate supervision could be exercised. By 1974 all urban centres and those Primary Health Centres where adequate supervision and follow-up were possible were distributing the pills. In 1977, the oral pill programme was further extended to all Primary Health Centres with doctors.

The difference in opinion regarding management of the Pill distribution continued. Some emphasised that "the Pills" should be distributed freely across the counter by pharmacists and para-medical personnel. It was argued that in most developing countries the risks of pregnancy was far more than the risk of taking "the Pill". There were others who did not entirely agree with this view. They believed and still believe that already known information about Pills and limitation of knowledge of long term effect of Pills, demands that a woman before taking the Pill should be examined by a physician who should take detailed history of the woman, carry out general physical examination including breast and pelvis, cervical exfoliative cytology and examine "the pill user" at intervals of about six months.

Some countries in Asia like Thailand began allowing paramedical personnel to issue pills. Ministry of Health and Family Welfare in India after careful examination of all aspects of the problem, decided to give oral contraceptive to eligible couples through certain category of para-medical personnel such as Public Health Nurses, Lady Health Visitors, Graduate Nurses and those Auxilliary Nurse Midewives who are posted in a Sub-Centre regularly visited by doctors. Further safe-guards were also stipulated, especially the insistence that the above mentioned category of paramedical personnel can distribute the oral contraceptive on the condition that the acceptor must be examined by a doctor within three months of acceptance of "the Pill".

The ICMR recommended to allow village Health Guides to distribute oral pills subject to examination of pill acceptors within three months by a doctor and to use within parameters of carefully prepared guidelines. The Ministry of Health requested to begin with four States (Andhra Pradesh, Haryana, Uttar Pradesh and West Bengal) to allow Village Health Guides to distribute pills. The pills for use under the programme as stated earlier are :

(*i*) Norethisterone 1.0 mg.+Ethynyloestradiol 0.03 mg. (called MALA-N) ; and

(*ii*) D-Noregestrel 0.05 mg.+Ethynyl estradiol 0.03 mg. (called MALA-D).

Iron tablets are also given for seven days in both cases. On the basis of experience in these four States on the use of the two types of pills, the scheme of allowing Village Health Guides is proposed to be extended in other States.[97]

"The Pill" programme in India has been relatively slow. This may be due to the inability of woman taking oral pills regularly. The problem is not simple.

A study on motivational components of two groups (continuers and discontinuer of the oral pill) of women attending the family welfare clinic of the National Institute of Health and Family Welfare New Delhi indicated : Continuous pill users were "very cautious, fear-organized, systematic, planned, and controlled with no inhibition or repression of sexual desire and willingness to express the need for affection as well as to help others in their need for love and affection". The discontinuers showed casualness, poor control over their behaviour or their frustration due to unsatisfied needs especially pertaining to sex, love and affection, resulting in persistent tensions and conflicts.[98]

There appears to be validity in the assumption that a method found popular and successful in one culture might not be successful in another culture to the same extent. Research on methods of birth control and type of "Pill" most suitable to different group of women thus assumes great importance.

It is estimated that during 1986 87 about 18 lakh women were using oral contraceptives in India. Besides commercial outlets, as of March 1987, there were 23,775 centres in India from where "the Pills" were available (20,901 Primary Health Centres in the rural areas, 2,853 in urban areas and 21 others (rural/urban breakup not available). The Social marketing scheme, provides distribution of MALA-D (Dl Norgestrel 0.50 mg.+Ethynyl Estradiol 0.03 mg.) package of 28 tablets (21 oral pills+7 placebos) for Rs. 2/- per packet, on the prescription of Registered Medical Practitioners.[99] The estimate of user of "the Pill" worldwide is about 120 million women.

7

Medical Termination of Pregnancy

The spectacular reduction in birth rates in Japan through legalized abortions had attracted world-wide attention. Many associated with family planning programme in India were keen to get the termination of pregnancy legalized in India. The subject was however highly sensitive. When Sushila Gore once referred to it in an official meeting, the suggestion was summarily rejected.

The opinion in favour of legalization of abortion began to gather support not so much as a method of birth control but to control the reported increase in the number of illegal abortions which seriously effected the health and life of the women resorting to abortion. On the 25th August 1961, the Central Family Planning Board (CFPB) expressed anxiety on such an increasing trend. The CFBP recommended that the subject should be examined in detail by a committee.

On the 29th September 1964, Ministry of Health constituted a committee 'To study the questions of Legalization of Abortion in all its Aspects'.[100] Shantilal Shah, Minister of Health, Law and Judiciary Maharashtra was appointed Chairman of the Committee. Shantilal Shah with his unique background of law, health administration and public affairs guided the deliberations of this committee with great understanding and skill, ensuring widest possible discussions and consultations. A detailed questionnaire was circulated to all Ministries, State Governments, Members of Planning Commission, Parliament, State Assemblies, Central and State Welfare Boards, Central and State Family Planning Boards, Medical, social, legal, political and religious organisations. The committee toured the country to discuss the subject with a large number of persons reflecting views of different influential groups and experts, and examined in depth the laws prevalent at the time in other countries and legal position and research data available in India. The committee was anxious to avoid undue controversies and present an objective scientific and generally acceptable recommendations. This exercise inevitably took time.

In December 1966, the report of the committee was submitted to the Ministry of Health. The recommendations in the report included : the existing law "should be liberalized to allow termination of pregnancy by a qualified medical practitioner acting in good faith not only for saving the pregnant women's life, but also (*a*) when continuation of pregnancy would involve serious risk to life, or grave injury to health, whether physical or mental of the pregnant woman, whether before, at or after birth; or (*b*) when there was a substantial risk that if the child is born it would suffer from such physical or mental abnormalities as to be seriously handicapped in life ; or (*c*) when pregnancy results from rape, intercourse with unmarried girl under age of 16 years or intercourse with mentally defective woman." The reports from Japan had indicated that there was high incidence of repeated induced termination of pregnancy. In order to avoid the dangers inherent in repeated abortions, the committee recommended that "in case of woman who is not fit to bear the strain of further pregnancies the medical practitioner should advise the woman and/or her husband to undergo voluntary sterilization". The committee further recommended that "the idea of small family norm achieved through control of conception should be vigorously promoted ; readily accessible services for family planning should be extended and family life education to develop healthy and responsible attitude towards sex, marriage and parenthood should be promoted".[101]

The Government approval of the Shantilal Shah Committee took a long time—almost five years, presumably due to anxiety to reach National concensus and to avoid any backlash from strong objectors of legalization of abortion. The Medical Termination of pregnancy (MTP) Act 1971, was finally passed by the Parliament and became effective on 1st April 1972. It was almost on the lines suggested by the Shantilal Shah Committee. It was emphasised that the Act was not for promoting family planning, but it was a social legislation with focus on health of women to prevent sickness and deaths due to illegal abortions. The Act did become an important supplement to family planning programme. The Act specifically mentioned that "where any pregnancy occurs as a result of failure of any device or method used by married woman or her husband for the purpose of limiting the number of children the anguish caused by such unwanted pregnancy may be presumed to constitute a grave injury to mental health of the pregnant woman".[102] The Government of India was required to make rules by notification to carry out provisions of the Act. The rules were notified on 19th February, 1972.

Rules and regulations framed initially were modified in October 1975 to eliminate time consuming process and to make services more readily available.

One problem in providing MTP services on wide scale was limitations of trained personnel. A training programme for various categories of doctors was launched including those serving in medical colleges, District hospitals, Primary Health Centres, voluntary organisation institutions and private medical practitioners. By end of March 1983 over 10,000 doctors were trained. This number includes over 3,.00 doctors from Primary Health Centres. About 5820 institutions were providing MTP services at the end of March 1987. The number of MTP cases gradually increased—the number during 1986 87 was 584,218. The percentage of MTP cases with sterilization during 1985-86 is reported to be 30.3 per cent, based on information received from most States and Union Territories.[103] Total number MTP cases from April 1972 to March 1987 was 5.22 million.

Reasons for termination during 1985-86 are stated to be danger to life 9.6% grave injury to physical health 18%, grave injury to mental health 11.4, rape 2.0%, and others 59%, The age group 20-34 years formed the large group among MTP cases—26% (20.24 years), 33% (25-29 years), and 23.1% (30-34 years). The duration of pregnancy was within 12 weeks of pregnany in about 85.8% of MTP cases and 12-20 weeks in about 14.2% of cases.

A large number of illegal abortions still continue. It is estimated that deaths due to abortion and puerperal sepsis account for one-fifth of total maternal deaths, in India. A large number suffer from due to illegal abortions. Shantilal Shah Committee in 1966 had estimated 4 million induced abortions for a population of 500 million. There are no National statistics available for illegal abortions. The figure at present may be around 6 million yearly. The reasons for this may be many, such as lack of adequate services (such as lack of readily accessible and personalised attention, privacy) for legal abortion and management of abortion complications ; hesitation of women to go to public hospitals and clinics for termination of the pregnancy, inadequate contraceptives services and failure of contraception. It is also felt that information on legal abortion is not yet widely known in rural areas and still there are misconceptions on the procedure and complications of MTP.

Estimates of number of abortions world-wide were reported a few years back as 40 million, half illegal. This calls for vigorous efforts to prevent contraceptive failures, to extend services for legal abortions and to improve management of illegal abortions.

8

Genesis of Reproduction Research in Family Planning Programme in India and A Look in the Future

The so called "knowledge explosion in the field of science and technology does not seem to have extended to biology of human reproduction. There are many gaps in our knowledge on human reproduction and endorocrinology. It is not suggested that no progress has been made in this field or births cannot be controlled by already available methods. At the same time there is great need for better methods than now available.

The Committee on Population Growth and Family Planning of the Planning Commission, in 1951 recommended that the State should through financial and otherwise assist in establishment of research and information centre organised for "collection, study and dissemination (of knowledge) based on scientifically tested experience in our country and abroad in respect of all aspects of family limitation and countering illeffects of incorrect information and (carry out) research necessary for the development of inexpensive, safe and efficacious (birth control) methods".

In 1952, the scope of research was enlarged and included research on physiology of reproduction and biological aspects.

In December 1952 Abrahm Stone suggested establishment of a central scientific body to deal with various medical aspects of human reproduction. C.G. Pandit initiated the discussion on this suggestion at the meeting of the Indian Council of Medical Research (ICMR) Scientific Board. The Board approved the appointment of a Committee including experienced persons in one or more aspects of research including a physiologist, a physician, an endrocrinologist, a gynaecologist, a pharmacologist, a biochemist, a geneticist, a psychologist, an anthropologist, a demographer, the Registrar General of India and the Secretary ICMR (later called Director and still after Director General). The areas of research suggested were : clinical studies of contraceptives and their evaluation, research on indigenous methods, production of contraceptive material with support of the Council of Scientific and Industrial Research, research on new methods, and research on sex and reproduction problems.

In 1956, an advisory committee (called Advisory Committee on Physiology of Human Reproduction) was formed with V.R. Khanolker as Chairman. The composition of the committee was not as suggested at the ICMR Board meeting. The members of the committee in the early years included a Professor of physiology, (B.K. Anand), Professor of Gynaecology and Obstetrics, (Miss P.K. Malkani), Director of Central Drug Research Institute Lucknow, (B. Mukherjee) and Dy. Director Indian Cancer Research Centre Bombay (K.J. Ranadive). For close collaboration with Ministry of Health and to maintain organic unity with other research advisory committees the Director Family Planning served as member-Secretary of the committee. International agencies also gradually started taking greater interest in research on human reproduction notably the Population Council, New York and the World Health Organisation.

The major push to build Nation-wide network of research in human reproduction in India was given by Sheldon Segal in research 1962. The research plan on human reproduction in the family planning programme evolved, on his advice included five major areas : (*i*) to look for support of experienced researchers and institutions; (*ii*) to develop centres for reproductive biology research around them ; (*iii*) to train promising young persons ; (*iv*) to provide such support as needed by individual scientists ; and (*v*) to conduct urgent comparable collaborative studies.

Segal had considerable experience in organising bio medical research and great insights in priority research areas. In 1957, a bio-medical laboratory of the Population Council had started functioning under his overall guidance at the Rockefeller Institute, New York with financial support of the Rockeffeller Brothers Fund, with the specific purpose to explore "ways of supporting research on the effectiveness, safety and cost of various methods of birth control". After two years, in 1959 unanswered questions in fertility research were reviewed by leading investigators at an International Symposium sponsored by the Population Council and Planned Parenthood Federation of America. This led to better identification of research areas. Sheldon Segal was the motive force, behind these activities. He took leave of absence from his post of Director Population Council's Bio-Medical Division to work in India as Ford Foundation Consultant primarily to assist in setting up the laboratory for human reproduction (now the Department of Reproduction Biology) at the All India Institute of Medical Sciences in New Delhi. His most valuable contribution, however, was in assisting in the development of bio-medical research centres in about twelve places throughout the country including institutions like Central Research Drug Research Institute Lucknow, Institute of Research in Reproduction Bombay, University of Delhi, All India Institute Medical Sciences, New Delhi, Zoology Department University of Delhi.

A LOOK IN THE FUTURE

It is difficult to predict the future developments in contraceptive technology. We can, however, explore from the past and current experience and studies and likely developments in future contraceptive technology.

The discussion in the preceeding pages on past and present experience suggests that we have to rely on the present methods of birth control for a long time. This calls for support to further developments of the already available methods, along with developments in new technologies.

Natural Family Planning Methods

The rhythm study in Ramanagram and Lodi Colony New Delhi and subsequent studies underline the fact that major problem in the practice of rhythm method has been the difficulty in prediction and detection of the precise time of ovulation, consequently long period of abstinence required for users of safe period methods. A number of studies on potential indices of the fertile period (such as enzymes and steroids in saliva, vaginal secretions, and urine, changes in temperatures) indicate development of improved reliable and simple methods to predict and detect beginning and the end of fertile period.

Barrier Methods

Among the barrier methods male condoms continue to be an effective, safe, and reversible method, when used properly and regularly Over the years its quality has been considerably improved. Some developments may be expected to suit the needs of users such as sizes, thickness, texture, colour, lubricants. Stricter quality controls are likely to ensure their safety. Major efforts may be devoted to their proper and regular use through information, education and communication ; and development of ways to promote their wider use including improvement in social marketing.

Female condom is still in development stage and offers another alternate method, which may be used by the women.

The use of condom, besides a birth control method, plays an important role in two other areas, *viz.*, (*a*) the well known effective method to prevent sexually transmitted diseases especially now against AIDS ; and (*b*) not so well known method to reduce sperm anti-body—related infertility. Some women produce anti-bodies to sperms, when the sperms come in contact with their cervical tissues. In a study, the use of condom for 60 days to six months, followed by unprotected intercourse during ovulation period, of the five women three became pregnant.[104] Further studies may give clearer picture.

The major developments in vaginal contraceptives are medicated Vaginal rings carrying steroids, *e.g.*, Vaginal rings with natural hormone progesterone, designed for breastfeeding women ; progesterone releasing rings presently tested by the World Health Organisation and Population Council ; and Population Council studies on several rings delivering both progestins and oestrogens.

Intra-Uterine Devices

Improved copper-bearing and Progestin-releasing intrauterine devices are expected to be available. In the former category Copper T 380 Ag is reported to have a high degree of effectiveness.

The progestin releasing intrauterine devices, especially developed to combat heavy bleeding faced some problems. The device introduced by the World Health Organisation releasing levonorgestrel was discontinued "because of an unacceptably high incidence of ectopic pregnancy". The device introduced by the Population Council with levonorgestrel was reported to have high effectiveness (0.1 to 0.3 pregnancies per 100 women years), but in 1987 the elastomer used in the manufacture of hormone releasing reservoir was reported to cause liver cancer in rodents when given in many thousand times the human dose for prolonged periods,[105] which required further toxicity studies. Further developments indicate that the device may be available earlier than anticipated in 1987. "In December 1988, an advisory committee on the safety of the levonorgestrel-releasing IUD (developed by the Population Council) concluded that this device is expected to provide a safe method of Birth Control".[106]

Sterilization

The future developments in sterilization may be mainly to improve techniques for reversible sterilization and non-surgical methods.

The Pill

The research efforts are likely to be directed to find a progestogen which is most effective with least androgenic effect, and slow release formulations. The developments in the latter case will be a notable advance, as it will provide a slow sustained constant rate of release of the steroid and also lower dose of the steroid may be possible. Research in the development of microspheres and other formulations are in progress.[107] A non-hormonal pill may be available.

Post-Coital Pill

There are occasions when the coitus is unprotected for various reasons such as mechanical method used has failed, or unpremeditated intercourse or rape. In a World Health Organisation multicentre trial the use of levonogestrel 0.75 mg. appears to be effective alternative to high dose oestrogen or oestrogen progestogen combinations in post-coital contraception.[108] Reports from China indicate that Norethisterone 5 mg. (called vacation Pill) is effective with few side effects.[109]

Termination of Pregnancy

In 1966 reports of Sultan M.M. Karim on the role of prostoglandins attracted attention.

It is now well established that during the second trimester prostoglandin are very effective.

Antiprogestins (RU. 486) have also been found capable of interrupting pregnancy.

The sequential combination of an antiprogestin (RU 486) and low dose of synthetic prostaglandin in menstrual regulation and termination of early pregnancy have shown success. Further studies are in progress.

Almost complete abortion has been reported by lower dose intramuscular or intravaginal administration of prostoglandin analogues that cause little or no side effects to women pre-treated with anti-progestin RU 486.[110]

These reports indicate the possibility of simplifying techniques of menstrual regulation and induced abortion ; making it self-administered proceedure under medical supervision.

Injectables

The two injectables, *viz.*, DMPA (Depo-medroxy-progesteroneacetate) and NET-EN (Norethisterone enthate) have been in use in several countries for some years. A single injection remains active for 3 and 2 months respectively. They are not in general use in India mainly because of their side effects such as irregular bleeding, slow return of fertility, amenorrhoea and other reported adverse effects. It is reported that the menstrual disturbances are mainly due to drugs not being released at a constant rate. The number of users of injectables in the world are estimated to be about 6 million, *i.e.*, some prefer injectables despite their side effects.[111]

The developments in injectables include : the synthesis of newer steroids with better or zero order release rate profile, increasing frequency of injections with smaller doses of steroids, combining with natural oestrogens and using new delivery systems. The new delivery system involves the delivery of one or more hormones in a small biodegradable polymer envelope or support matrix in the form of the microspheres (polymeric particles) and microcapsules (contained in the core of the particle). The protection against pregnancy may extend for one or three or six months depending on amount of daily release of hormone. Promising results are reported with two hormones, *viz.*, norethindrone and norgestimate used in microspheres. "A 3-month dose injectable norethindrone microsphere usually contains particles consisting of 50 per cent hormone and ranging in size from 0.6 to 0.1 mm. in diameter".[112] Further studies are in progress.

Sub-dermal Implants and Transdermal Patch

In the late 1960s, the Population Council began work on sub dermal levonorgestrel-releasing non-biodegradable implants and soon after started collaborative studies in Austria, Brazil, Chile, Finland, India, Italy and the USA. Since then a number of delivery systems have been develop —Norplant six-capsules, and Norplant 2, two rods (hormone in both levonorgestrel) ; one rod (hormone ST-1435) and one rod (hormone 3-keto desogestrel).[113]

As of March 1990, "Norplant has been approved for marketing of family planning programme use in 13 countries". The Norplant 2 "implants are believed to be more uniform, exhibit superior release rates and have a longer effective use period*".[114] Biodegradable implants also are being tested. They include Capronor, levonorgestrel in an ethyl oleate vehicle contained in a biodegradable capsule made of the polymer tube (E-caprolactone) and Norethindrone and small amount of cholestrol pellets.[115]

There are possibilities of transdermal administration of hormones**.

Antifertility Vaccine

Anti-fertility vaccines for both males and females are being developed. Among vaccines for females, the anti-hCG vaccine has attracted much attention. In the early 1970s, in New Delhi, G.P. Talwar succeeded in raising anti-bodies to the beta—sub unit of the human chorionic gonadotrophic hormone (hCG) by injecting the beta-sub unit conjugated with tetanus toxoid. The biological effects of hCG are neutralized by the antibodies so generated. These findings were followed by clinical trials in a few women. The result showed significant rise of anti-

---

*A monography by Doria, B.T., and Greenslade, F.C.; *Norplant Contraceptive Sub-dermal Implant : Managerial Guideline* (provisional version) 1990 has been published by WHO Programme of Maternal and Child Health Including Family. WHO, Geneva.

**Studies on Transdermal steroidal harmonal patch by Cygnus Research Corporation and Family Health International have been reported.

bodies to hCG, as well as to tetanus toxoid No toxic effects were reported. With the assistance of the Population Council and the International Committee of Contraception Research, clinical trials were carried out in women in different countries. The result showed significant anti-body response in several cases, but also insignificant response in some. The question of increasing immunogenecity and standardisation to avoid batch by batch variation have arisen. Attempts have been directed to add a suitable adjuvent to conjugate in order to generate a sustained anti-body response. Other vaccines for females are also being investigated. National Institute of Immunology, New Delhi is actively engaged in these developments. The development of anti-fertility vaccine, which can prevent pregnancy without altering the pattern of menstrual cycle, is awaited.

Among the vaccines for males, two are reported to be promising. The one is designed to elicit antibodies that will neutralize biological effect of luteinizing hormone releasing hormone (LHRH). The Centre for Biomedical research Population Council Cooperatively with National Institute of Immunology New Delhi and the National Institute of Child Health and Development in the United States are actively engaged in developing fertility vaccines for males. The libido is effected and LH-RH analogues have to be supplemented with long acting endrogens.

The other is aimed at counteracting the Follicle Stimulating Hormone (FSH). N.R. Moudgal and his group at the Indian Institute of Science Bangalore have demonstrated that FSH has an obligatory role in regulating the testicular function and fertility in adult bonnet monkeys using specific antiserum to FSH. They have also shown that administration of highly purified ovine testicular inhibin resulted in significant decrease in total sperm count, without any significant change in serum testoterone levels, *i.e.*, no reduction in libido. Further developments are awaited.

Research on other vaccines are being done such as anti-trophoblast vaccine and anti-sperm vaccine.[116]

Studies on active immunization with Ovine FSH as means of rendering male bonnet monkeys infertile are also continuing at the National Institute of Family Welfare New Delhi.[117]

Research on male fertility regulation is being done also in a number of other fields such as the use of Nal-Glu—LHRH antagonist, 19-NT-HPP (Anadur), STS-557.

World Health Organisation programmes include investigations on interfering with the peneterating ability and or motility of the sperm without blocking spermetaogenesis, *i.e.*, methods to bring about qualitative changes in the sperm. It is expected to take long time before the investigations reach clinical trial stage. The major problem in research on male contraception is the limitation in the knowledge of the human reproduction especially the male reproductive system, and issues like safety, reversibility, suitable targets for fertility interference.

Plants for Fertility Regulation

The one seed that has been widely discussed is cotton seed, the source of Gossypol. It has been demonstrated that gossypol reduces sperm count in several species of animals and humans. This raised the hope of a male contraceptive pill. The clinical trails showed high degree of irreversibility when treatment continues for more than two years, hypokalaemia and episode of neuromuscular disorders. In one study a significant decline in plasma potassium was noted. Gossypol is not likely to be used until a new generation, Gossypol or analogues are available which show no side effects in approved animal toxicological studies.

A number of plant products are being tested such as a pure compound of pseudolaric acid root of *Tripterygium wilfordi* in China, *Murraya paniculata* in Hongkong, isolate from *Pseudolarix kaempferi* in Shanghai and London.[118]

A very large number of plants, including those used by tribals in India as mentioned earlier have been listed to have antifertility property. Some have been tested. Tests on them in all parameters have not been done. It appears the tests on pla .t products in India have not been given sufficient attention. With growing interest in plants, it may be expected that plant products reported to have properties to control fertility will be systematically listed, screened and tested.

Behavioural Sciences Research

Development of safe and effective birth control methods is obviously not enough. They must be accepted and used properly and continuously. The problems of poor acceptance of contraceptives or a specific contraceptive, their inadequate use and high discontinuation rate when used in a country or a part of a country or a group of persons pose serious challenges. Research to meet successfully such challenges becomes essential. The behaviour of human beings is rooted in a complex matrix of biological and behavioural sciences. Their are gaps in our knowledge of both. A remarkable inventory of 1045 findings from the scientific study of human behaviour is given by Bernard Berelson and Gary A. Steiner in their book *Human Behaviour*.[119] It underlines the valuable contribution of behavioural sciences in understanding human beings and their behaviour. There are wide gaps in our knowledge of human behaviour. There are wider gaps in the knowledge of reproductive behaviour including those related to acceptance of a method of birth control and their continuous use. Some studies have been made on attitudes towards use of methods since early 1950s. Such studies began in Mysore and Khanna. Several studies were done on knowledge, attitude and practice (KAP). Later focus shifted to evaluation of the programme and consequently greater weightage to fertility studies. Recently interest in developing strategies to improve acceptance of birth control methods and reduce their discontinuance has increased. The attention has been focussed on health services research, and motivational, social and other factors. Studies like motivational components of continuous users and discontinuers by M. Kapoor and A.K. Ghosh mentioned, early on, are few. The need for supporting a wide ranging behaviour research science is essential.

Self Control

In every society there are norms of sexual activity in and outside marriage. Traditionally sexual union with spouse only is permissible, and sexual relationship outside marriage are condemned. Controlled sex union within marriage and self control was advocated by groups of people in many cultures. The promoters of family planning programmes rejected the idea of "self control" for the simple reason that an average person will not find it possible to practice it.

The norms of sexual relationships in several cultures have changed recently. Marriages appear to be developing as a practice of "just a young man and a woman living togather". Some change partners, often with justification, frequently. Promiscuity appears to be increasing. The society in cultures where promiscuity is on appreciable scale seems to ignore it or does not take much notice. Recently the support for "Self Control", is re-emerging. This is not for any moral reasons. The concept of morality differs in different cultures, places and times, *e.g.*, childless widow having intercourse with brother of her dead husband to have a child, polygamy, cousin marriage or temporary marriage may be moral in one culture at one time and not in another culture or time in the same cultural group. The support to "self control" is re-emerging for a very practical reason—to prevent the spread of a lethal disease which has so far no cure, the Acquired—Immuno—Deficiency—Syndrome (AIDS), a disease which damages the defences of the body against other diseases. The problems of AIDS is so serious that the World AIDS Day was observed on December 1, 1990. The World Health Organisation estimates that 8-10 million people have been infected with HIV infection.[120] Number of children born with AIDS virus and children who will be orphoned are on the increase. In India the estimated number of AIDS infected persons is 50,000. This is considered an underestimate. AIDS spreads through sexual intercourse, and also by infected blood or blood products, unsterilized needless or syringes, and infected mothers passing the disease to their unborn and newborn children. The foremost preventive measure is *safe-sex, sex between faithful partners (i.e., through stamping out promiscuous sex behaviour)*, besides use of condom when in doubt, safety of blood, blood products and injection needles, syringes, avoiding pregnancy by women with AIDS. A vigorous educational campaign on prevention of AIDS along-with with wider issue of "Self Control" is essential. Promiscuity, irresponsible sexual behaviour or need to use "The vacation Pill" may not be eliminated but may be substantially reduced through educational campaign.

Need for Massive Support for Research and Development

There is an urgent need to develop a simple, safe, effective and long-acting method(s) to control births and their acceptance and use. The gaps in our knowledge of human reproduction and behaviour stated above are many, despite significant progress made in recent years. Behavioural science itself is relatively new. In words of Howell, "possibly with the exception of the phenomena of human consciousness, there is no fact of life that excites more interest and seems to offer greater difficulties in arriving at any definitive conclusion than the functions of reproduction".

The problem of population, environment and development has to be dealt urgently and cogently. There are several determinants of uncontrolled fertility. Among them a simple safe, effective and acceptible birth control method is an important one.

Massive support is required for fertility research, both basic and applied, in human reproduction, contraception, biomedicine, in behavioural research, and programme operation.

The population problem has ceased to be of serious concern for a single country or group of countries variously called the Third World, the South, the developing countries, the underdeveloped countries. For sometime now the scientific community and other thoughtful people have been advocating international coordinated research efforts. The resource mobilisation has been tardy. The quantum of resources needed for research have been far more than made available (in 1968 the research needs were estimated by Oscar Harkevy and Anna Southam as US $150 million, and estimated available support was about US $50 million).[121]

Several questions arise, such as : What should be the priorities ? What should be the relative inputs in basic and applied research ? What should be the mechanism to promote, develop disseminate the findings and coordinate research ? Should a single international centre for research or several centres be developed ? Where such centre(s) be located ? What measures are necessary for promoting scientific manpower development ? How to establish continuous communication between researchers ?

Study of human beings, as stated early on, has a number of facets. The areas of research, inevitably, are placed in different groups like behavioural sciences, bio-medicine. There is thus a trend that scientists of a group of discipline talk only to each other. There are occasions when such discussion may be necessary. But there is increasing need to discuss problems of human reproduction in multidisciplinary forums.

At the International level, the agency that can influence global action is the United Nations. A multidisciplinary group can be formed consisting of experts from United Nation and its agencies and research institutions in Government and Non-Government Organisations and selected experts. Such a group, asssisted by sub-groups can identify research needs in a long term broad perspective, make recommendations on research priorities and suggest the estimated financial needs.

A consortium of aid giving agencies can make it possible to provide financial resources for research. The resources can flow to the existing organisational structures International and National, *e.g.*, the resources for bio-medical research can flow to the World Health Organisation who in its turn identify problems and agencies capable of conducting research in different countries.

At national level, a National Committee with experts in

various disciplines, with sub-committee of experts in specific activities may be one of the mechanisms that can be considered for assessing National priorities, making recommendation for support to individuals, organisations and institution and ensuring coordination. The word "coordination" is simple, and often underlined. But in practice, it poses problems. Many seem to be happy in coordinating other people's programme, but not their own with others. A coordination group which establishes strong linkages and keeps every one concerned informed is generally successful.

Fruitful results are expected through developing and strengthening, existing institutes Nodal Regional institutes, task forces for specific priority research, support to experienced researchers and institutions, trans-disciplinary research, building research capabilities and promoting research in Universities, support to individual scientists, training young persons, facilities for training to promising young persons in the country and abroad. The location of major research centres should be in areas where the problems are, so that the researchers have a continuous realistic feel of the situation and impact of their efforts. There are many areas that have an important bearing on research, such as continuous supply of scientists and technicians, suitable employment opportunities, satisfactory working conditions and opportunities to improve their knowledge and skills. Senior scientists have a special responsibility for creating successive generation of science leadership. In case a competent person has an innovative idea and there is no post available for such a person in an institute, he or she should find a place in a newly created post and the project built round him or her.

The entire mechanism of promoting research should be flexible. Great advances in human history have been made by individuals often working in isolated and obscure places. It may also be added that research now requires sophisticated tools and a scientist should not be expected to give his b.st without provision of such tools.

We are familiar with remarkable results when the researcher breaks out of conventional barriers of his of her own discipline.

The young scientists with competence, enthusiasm and dedication in developing countries sometime find themselves in an environment not conducive to research or lack of adequate facilities in projects or temporary research support or in situations when the work is interrupted because lack of chemicals, or spare parts or an item which has to be imported.

Research by its very nature takes time to produce results, and its results are unpredictable. A researcher or a research team may not produce a single paper for some years and may come out with a brief paper announcing an outstanding discovery. Nine projects out of ten after a longtime and appreciable investment may give no fruitful results; but the benefits from the tenth project may be many times the investment in all the ten projects.

The question of basic and applied research has ceased to be controversial. The basic research of to-day is the applied research of tomorrow.

Research ultimately is for the people. Effective ways should be developed further to keep them informed, interested and involved. There is only one condition, *i.e.*, the researchers should exercise self-discipline. The temptation to pass information of success prematurely or to dramatise their efforts should be resisted, as it may lead to undue expectations, impatience to get results, confusion and loss of credibility of scientific endeavours.

An attempt is made above to underline the urgent need for mobilization of adequate resources for research and develop a fast moving flexible mechanism, International and National, to persue both basic and applied research. The scientific community has a special responsibility for focusing attention of the people on the fact that the research inputs are required for our very survival.

PART II

Selected Programmes & Projects

9

Incentives and Disincentives

In the 1950s, Madras State (now Tamil Nadu) experimented with incentives to motivators (canvassers) and persons offering for vasectomy. This led to large number of cases volunteering for sterilization. Some malpractices were reported. It was reported that the cases were brought by canvassers even from the neighbouring State of Andhra Pradesh.

Some years later, in a plantation in Southern India it was observed that doubling the monetary incentives did not increase the number of persons volunteering for sterilization. Exhortations for large monetary incentives, however, continued both by responsible persons in India and abroad.

The arguments in favour of incentives centered round mainly on two assumptions, *viz.*, the educational and extension approach would take a very long time to establish a small family norm and in a largely illiterate and poverty ridden societies monitary incentives could achieve dramatic results. This view was further reinforced by exhortations of some international experts.

In the late 1950s and 1960s, the programme managers and social scientists strongly felt that behavioural change could be brought about by making people themselves feeling the need of small family size for their own good and generating a inner urge among people to plan their families through educational process and any offer of incentives would shift the focus from a rational path to add extraneous factors which might erode the programme. Large allocations suggested for incentives could instead be utilised for educational activities which might take time to show results, but the results would be enduring.

The introduction of incentives were resisted for some time. After prolonged discussion it was conceded that loss of wages for daily wage earners might become a barrier to fulfill desires to undergo sterilization operation. Provision was therefore made to compensate for the loss of wages in cases of sterilization operation and IUD insertion. When the decision to make payments to those who volunteered for sterilization operation or IUD insertion was taken, it was emphasised that such payments were to compensate for loss of wages and other ancillary expenses and both sterilization and IUD insertions were to be performed after well informed consent.

Suggestions for disincentives were also made. The Third Five Year Family Planning Programme Advisory Committee examined this question in great detail and rejected any suggestion of reducing maternity benefits or any measure which would effect the care and development of the children Reduction of maternity benefit or a birth tax was considered punishing children for irresponsible sexual behaviour of their parents. Restriction of maternity benefits to those with two or three children was considered likely to cause serious erosion of care for children and mother, who needed the care most. Preferential treatment for those who had small families was not considered desirable. Any preferential treatment based on family size was expected to be availed of by the rich rather than the large number of poor. Preferential treatment could be considered only when the population in general achieve requisite level of social and economic development. It was the firm view of the members of the committee generally, that disincentives, would be counter-productive, the impact of monetory incentives would not be enduring, and the main focus should be on education.

Some felt that disincentives as a part of service regulation as in Defence Services could be considered. In the army, for example the married persons were not eligible for admission to the National Defence Academy and Indian Military Academy. A Commissioned officer was not generally expected to marry before the age of 25 years ; and if he marries before that age was not entitled to "married accommodation". These disincentives were not part of establishing a small family norm, but for enabling them to be unencumbered with family responsibilities during their rigorous training and development periods in the early years of service.

Gradually support for incentives and disincentives gained ground. The declared policy did not consider incentives as an alternative to education but as an intermediate step between slow process of behavioural change through education and quick response of the people through high incentives among poor couples. In 1960s 'the compensation money' advised by the Government of India was Rs. 11 (including Rs. 5 to the individual) for IUD ; Rs. 30 (including Rs. 10 to the individual) for vasectomy ; and Rs. 40 and Rs. 90 in camp (including Rs. 15 to individual) in case of tubectomy. Some States made higher provision for vasectomy and higher payment to individual, *e.g.*, Maharashtra paid to individual—double the amount suggested by the Government of India. Similar increase in payment to individuals in case of tubectomy and IUD were made in several States. A number of States introduced disincentives such as restricting some of the existing benefits : to the Government employees if they had three or more children, maternity benefits to Government female non-industrial employees (Andhra Pradesh, Maharashtra, Orissa, Mysore, Himachal Pradesh) ; medical treatment facilities in the Government hospitals ; Government scholarships which were being given to the children of the freedom fighters, teachers, soldiers, scheduled castes, loans, grants and subsidy, distribution of Sabha land under the Zamindari Abolition Act, loans for land and housing to low and middle income group by the Housing and Local Self Government (Uttar Pradesh). Haryana also initiated restriction of medical treatment and education available to families with three children, but also introduced a clause to give preference for scheduled castes, economically backward classes and scholarships to those with not more than three children.

On January 3, 1967, the Central Family Planning Council took serious view of such developments and recommended the appointment of a committee to study and make recommendations on proposals like No-Birth-Bonus, Maternity Benefits and Children's allowances as possible incentives to popularize a small family norm, and present their report by June 30, 1967. Ministry of Health and Family Planning appointed the Committee on January 28, 1967 with Govind Narain, Secretary, Ministry of Health and Family Planning as Chairman and Dipak Bhatia, Commissioner Family Planning as Member Secretary. The President Family Planning Association of India, representatives of the four labour unions and employers organisations were, among others, members of this committee. In July the committee was designated as "Small Family Norm Committee" earlier Resolution of the Government was partially modified. The committee was required to submit their report by 31 March, 1968. Homi J.H. Taleyarkhan and B.V. Pai, Manager M/s. Tata Oil Mills Company Limited to represent Employers were included in December 1967.

The prevalent view at that time among many of those responsible for moulding of public policy is reflected in the responses from a wide range of persons to the questionnaire circulated by the Small Family Norm Committee. The Committee received replies from 252 persons and organisations including government and voluntary organisations, organisations of employers and labour, members of Parliament and legislative assemblies, members of health and legal profession, Health Secretaries of State Health Departments, Administrative Medical Officers and Family Planning Officers. The picture that emerged was : Out of 252 respondents, 152 were in favour of discontinuing maternity benefits after the third child ; 129 were in favour of granting children allowance, of these 96 suggested giving such allowances in kind only like books, stationary, clothing, food, etc., majority of the respondents were against giving any direct incentive to avoid or postpone next birth ;

172 were against birth tax ; majority recommended restriction of existing facilities to government (non-industrial) employees with three children, *viz.*, allotment of accommodation, loans and subsidies, Travelling and Dearness allowances on transfer or otherwise, free studentship, scholarship ; majority considered that income tax structure needs revision ; "some of the respondents suggested : (*i*) sterilization after second/third child ; (*ii*) legalization/liberalization of abortions ; (*iii*) raising age of marriage of boys and girls ; (*iv*) wide range propaganda, publicity, education and motivation of the masses particularly in rural areas of the country ; (*v*) lower premium rates for sterilized persons ; bonus/increment incentive for those who restrict their family size by undergoing vasectomy/tubectomy operations".

The major recommendations of the Small Family Norm Committee were :

(*i*) in respect of individual incentives : to adhere to give compensation for meeting out of pocket expenses, "any additional amount by way of incentives need not be given because in the long run the real incentive should be the realization by the people that the adoption of family planning is for their own good" ;

(*ii*) in respect of maternity benefits : not to consider changing existing benefits for industrial workers 'now', but for non-industrial Government employees concessions may be reviewed for those with more than three children after ensuring provision of adequate facilities for birth control services and after giving due notice ;

(*iii*) in respect of children allowance : restriction to three living children except : (*a*) merit scholarships, etc. ; and (*b*) existing number of children (the restriction is for any additional child born after a particular date, *viz.*, a year after the date of announcement of restrictions) ;

(*iv*) in respect of No-birth bonus : For consideration of employers and Government that if a woman employee below a certain age group and age level gets sterilized, after second child, it will entitle her to one month's pay as bonus or if she gets sterilized after the third child, it will entitle her to half month's bonus ; some rebate in Life Insurance Corporation premia to those who have undergone sterilization after two or three children ; the Life Insurance Corporation of India and the Postal Life Insurance policies redeemable after 18 years of marriage with special benefits if family size is restricted to one, two or three children ;

(*v*) in respect of awards : recognition of promoting family planning efforts of State Governments, Local Bodies, Panchayats, Labour Unions and business organisations (group incentives) ; for education films, for books and the Press, particularly the language Press in India (dailies, weeklies, fortnightlies in each regional language) for promoting family planning.

The Committee emphasised that, "In our democratic society, individuals are free to take decisions regarding their family size. There is no place for the use of force, coercion or compulsion of any kind. The structure of the society, the social mores and cherished values have to be respected. The idea of small family does not have to come in conflict with religious and sentimental susceptibilities of the individual or the society and no new problems need be created in the process of its adoption as a practising ideal by the poople. The accent has to be on persuasion and education to secure the willing involvement of the people. In deciding the nature and quantum of disincentives it is essential to bear in mind that basic social welfare and health services are not denied to any one.[122]

General debate on incentives and disincentives continued. Those who subscribed to the great value of incentives in family planning programme were not able to prove their case. Their was sufficient evidence that incentives adversely effected the quality of acceptors (the volunteers for sterilization were older and high parity acceptor) and the quality of service. Paradoxically the programme support to incentives and disincentives increased. Arguments in their favour were drawn from isolated studies often of questionable design and quality. Just a few years after the Small Family Norm Committee submitted the report, the approach to individual incentives appeared to have changed—high incentives were advocated.

Mass vasectomy camps in the early 1970s highlighted payment of high individual incentives. A team of experienced researchers[123] showed that the largest number of cases in mass vasectomy camps in Kerala, Gujarat and Utter Pradesh were brought by revenue personnel (revenue or village officers in Kerala ; Talatis in Gujarat and Patwaris in Uttar Pradesh). "The higher incentives were perceived by overwhelming majority of respondents as 'means of help to bringing up a small family', followed by 'means of self-help', 'a means of corruption' and 'coercion'. . . .The main determinants of perception of higher incentives and in turn the acceptance of vasectomy appeared to be the economic status and the family size ; which means poorer the people higher the positive perception of incentives and greater the acceptance of vasectomy. Similarly, the lesser the family size (number of living children)—specially less the number of sons the more reluctance for acceptance of vasectomy and more negative perception of higher incentives. Condition for acceptance of vasectomy seemed more conducive where the age of the last living child of the cases has reached three to four years.

In 1976, the Government announced higher individual incentives. They were supplemented in cash and kind by local bodies and voluntary groups. Some disincentives were introduced by State Governments for non-industrial Government employees. The Government of India did not issue any advice to make sterilization programme compulsory. It also did not approve the compulsory legislation suggested by Maharashtra Government. It seems that the Government was almost ready to approve such a measure. In the *Hindustan Times* Sunday Magazine of June 16, 1985, Om Mehta is reported to have told Janardan Thakur that there was the bill brought forth by then Health Minister. "The matter came up for discussion in the Cabinet...There was a chorus of approval from all sides She (Mrs. Gandhi) was about to say "all right" when I (Om Mehta) intervened "Madam", I said, already we are suffering the serious consequences of sterilization. If this bill is passed people won't allow us to come out of our houses. The bill I maintained would give too much power to police. There would be no end to harassments and excuses...Finally, Mrs. Gandhi said "I think Omji has a point and I agree it is not the time to have a bill. We must motivate the people". This perhaps accounts for the clause relating to compulsory sterilization in 1976 Statement on National population policy made by Health Minister. The statement reads : "the question of compulsory sterilization has been subject of lively discussion over the last few months. It is clear that public opinion is now ready to accept much more stringent measures for family planning than before. However, the administrative and medical infra-structure in many parts of the country is still not adequate to cope with vast implication of Nation-wide compulsory sterilization. We do not, therefore, intend to bring in Central legislation for this purpose at least for the time being. Some States feel that facilities available with them are adequate to meet the requirements of compulsory sterilization. We are, therefore of the view that where a State legislature, in the exercise of its powers, decides that the time is ripe and it is necessary to pass legislation for compulsary sterilization, it may do so. Our advice to the States in such cases will be to bring in the limitation after three children and to make it applicable to all citizens resident in that State without distinction of caste, creed or community". The facts show that Mrs. Indira Gandhi was always against any compulsion or coercion. The question therefore sometime raised is whether "the permissive clause" in respect of compulsory sterilization in the National Policy Statement had the approval of Government of India or expressed the view of Ministry of Health and Family Planning. In a communication Dr. Karan Singh states that "the population policy statement was duly vetted and approved by the Cabinet.[124] The upsurge of support for high individual incentives and consideration of even near-permissive clause in respect of compulsory sterilization is surprising, especially in view of the observations made by the Small Family Norm. Committee and the views of Prime Minister Indira Gandhi. The Ministry of Health and Family Planning had a large group of social scientists in their own and other institutions. In fact many other parts of the National Population Policy Statement like age at marriage, education of women, reflect the approach of these social scientists. It appears that in respect of permissive clause the professionals were unable to put a convincing case against considering any measure even remotely associated with coercion or the advice given was lost in the din of achieving targets through aggressive measures, or the political and administrative climate was not such in which the voice of social scientists could be heard. There appeared to be a communication gaps between politicians, administrators and professionals. There is no scientific evidence to support the statement that "public opinion is now ready to accept more stringent measures for family planning than before". The subsequent events showed that such was hardly the public opinion. An objective look at the events reveal that: The official declared policy continued to be that the choice of birth control method was of the individual and was voluntary. The centres delivering the services continued to be called Family Welfare Planning Centres. There were still cases of coercion especially in Northern India. There appeared to be a climate of fear generated by real or alleged rumours. There seemed to be a wild chase for targets not only to achieve given targets but to exceed them. Some over-enthusiastic persons appeared to get berserk. Such a situation was highly politicized. The result was that the political party in power lost in the election. This forcefully demonstrates that in a democracy it is not enough to have official policy against using force, coercion or compulsion of any kind but such a policy should be viewed by the people as such and supported by measure to prevent its erosion by individuals or groups. This lesson was learnt at a very heavy cost.

The outstanding lesson of this period is that contrived measures, coercion and compulsion are disastrous and have no place in democratic societies.

On re-election of Congress (I) as a party with over-whelming majority, Prime Minister Indira Gandhi repeatedly referred to the official position regarding 'compulsion'. Addressing the Thirty fourth World Health Assembly in Geneva on May 6, 1981 she said : "I should like to clarify that we neither believe in nor have we practiced forcible sterilization as a matter of policy. We did emphasis what is called 'motivation', that is persuading people to participate in the programme ; operations were conducted by competent and authorised medical personnel. In this, due to mistaken over-zealousness or other mischief, there were some cases, but the margin was no larger than in other cases of medical or other error. What did incalculable harm was the baseless propaganda which some interested parties and individuals unleashed about our family planning schemes, and the political use that was made of it by gross exaggeration and even falsehood". She reiterated similar views in her address to the First National Conference of Indian Association of Parliamentarians for problems of population and development in New Delhi on May 25, 1981. She said : "I reiterate my Government's total commitment to voluntary family planning. We have been and are firmly against compulsion. There was hue and cry about individual cases where something had gone wrong. Later it was found that these were but insignificant fraction of the total number. After false propaganda to denigrate family planning, it is good that there has been perceptible improvement in performance during 1980-81".

Planning Minister S.B. Chavan, in 1983 stated "incentives that are offered can only be very selective and limited in scope ...as for policy of disincentives there is little room for such a policy in our democratic system based on conviction and compromise. Disincentives in the form of denial of food, clothing shelter and medical facilities are out of question, since these form a part of the basic human rights, more over it will cause hardship to poor families which are already deprived...Any drastic measure of disincentives could therefore be counter productive. However, some selective disincentives can be built into contractual benefits like service conditions of employees of the Government and organised sector. Here also there should be no question of withdrawing any benefits already available to the family.[125] This broadly reflects the general policy in early 1980s in respect of incentives and disincentives.

A notable feature now is the focus on group incentives—awards and preferential treatment. The amount given to individual has been increased, but it is still called as compensation not incentive. The payment of "cash compensation" continue to be raised periodically. The rates of Central assistance were revised : for a tubectomy Rs. 200 and vasectomy Rs. 180. This includes Rs. 100 for accepter and the remaining for drugs and dressing, diet, transport, and miscellinous including motivater fee in each case. An additional Rs. 20 is allowed to individual accepter of vasectomy and tubecromy with three and less children. The IUD insertion rates have also been revised to Rs. 12 per insertion, including Rs. 9 for accepter, Rs. 2.50 for drugs and dressing and Rs. 0.50 for contribution to ex-gratia fund in case of complications, etc. Several innovations are seen, *e.g.*, foreign tours for district officers and leaders where over 150 per cent of the targets are achieved ; tours in India for other officials to observe successful programmes, honouring presidents of Panchayats with successful programme with ceremonially tying a turban (*feta*, a traditional honour—Maharashtra). The State and Union Territory Governments have been requested to issue 'green cards' to individual acceptors of sterilization after two children 'as a mark of recognition and for priority attention' ; to provide five State lottery tickets to accepters of sterilization (Tamil Nadu was the first State to introduce this scheme in August 1983). The group awards include cash awards to the best performing States and Union Territories and monetary rewards in the form of community assets to organised and identifiable groups actively engaged in the implementation of the Family Welfare Programme. The Central Council of Health and Central Family Welfare Council in their joint conference in New Delhi in July 1983 recommended : consideration of "a scheme for giving continuing monetary benefits to accepters of terminal methods of family planning after two children" and preparation of scheme to recognise meritorious services of functionaries of Government, voluntary organisations and local bodies.

A great sophistication is seen in respect of incentives in recent years for contraceptive acceptance and birth prevention to accepters, motivaters and programme personnel ; to individuals employees of Central Government and other groups ; in cash and kind ; immediate, graduated and differed. On December 4, 1979 Ministry of Finance Government of India issued an office memorandum authorising incentives to Central Government employees for promoting small family norm. Bhatia has attempted to study demographic and monetary implications of incentives to the Central Government employees. His estimates show that both incentives and the cost of births averted are high. For example the incentive money to be paid to a First Grade male employee till retirement varies from Rs. 5,610 (for those who undergo sterilization at age of 49-50 years) to Rs. 16,505 (for those who undergo sterilization at age of 30 years). "The cost per birth averted for this category of male employees varies from Rs. 4,912 (for accepter at age 30) to Rs. 1,12,200 (for accepter at age 49-50) based on incentives till retirement and from Rs. 5,668 to Rs. 1,75,200, if pension benefit is also taken into account" "The incentives for Government employees are 14 to 236 times more than the incentives being paid to an accepter from general public".[126] The studies among Central Government employees also show that beneficiaries may include employees in unproductive group due to age or primary and secondary sterility, and about 82 per cent of First grade employees, 78 per cent of Second Grade employees ; 67 per cent of Third Grade employees and 58 per cent of Fourth Grade employees already practice family planning methods. Irrespective of these special incentives, a large proportion of Central Government employees would be using family planning methods. The expenditure on incentives according to one estimate is about 10 per cent of the financial allocation for family welfare planning. Such large investment on incentives appears to be based on familiarity of administrators with achieving results in other fields through measures like punishment and awards, subsidies and price support. Example of incentive in agriculture is often cited. The fact is that farmer adopts a new practice after going through a series of attitudinal changes through extension education, provision of fertilizers and seeds facilitating his experience to get a better yield and seeing results of a new practice. They are hardly comparable to incentives in cash or kind for adopting a small family norm.

Recently, Setia and Maru have reviewed the incentives and disincentives in India.[127] It is an interesting review. The conclusions (at least some) may be debatable. They observe that accepters of incentives contribute to an increased level of contraceptive acceptance and 'incentives do not seem to have any direct adverse effect on either the quality of accepters or a quality of services'. Such a conclusion may not stand careful scrutiny. There is ample evidence that incentives adversely influence quality of service, and may increase the level of acceptance immediately but will not have enduring effect. They concede that "incentives alone are not enough to increase acceptance, but they should still form an integral part of motivational activities". It seems advocates of high incentive view 'motivation' partly in terms of a bundle of crisp rupee notes and not in terms of perception of the people of such an offer and processes inherent in behavioural change.

In a statement on incentives, the need for review of the entire system of individual and community incentives has been emphasised. It is stated that : "Following are some of the incentives schemes which could be considered : A economic incentive to the small family to be built into all the socio-economic development programmes of the Central and State Governments which are beneficiary oriented. A preference is to be given for two or less child family norm in the selection of beneficiaries and also additional subsidy/grant and an interest rebate is to be granted on loan/payment. Schemes being considered for these economic linkages are the IRDP, NREP, RLEGP and other rural development programmes of assistance to individuals, loans under small scale and village industries, welfare schemes of all beneficiary—oriented development corporations, insurance schemes, banks and cooperative loans, allotment of land and housing and such other activities as have a strong bearing on the citizen's life. These benefits will be subject to a small family accepter being eligible otherwise under a particular scheme. The non-government sector including corporate sector and voluntary sector is to be persuaded to implement the same economic linkages under their activities. Accepter of sterilization with two or less children may be given "Honoured Citizen Cards" which will entitle them preferential treatment in all possible areas where facilities are available to the public. Accepters of sterilization after two or less children will be entitled to an Insurance Policy of high value but low premium to serve them in old age.

There are other schemes like a National Lottery Scheme for accepters of sterilization with two or less children offering attractive prizes, issuing of bonds of the face value of Rs. 25,000 maturing after 15 years to accepters of sterilization having two female children and Community Awards for Pariwar Kalyan Villages which exceed contraceptive prevalence of 70 per cent. Such schemes are to help in raising the age of marriage of women, their status and neutralise the male offspring preference.

State and National merit system and awards/recognition extend to workers, programme managers at various levels, individuals and corporate bodies in the private sector and voluntary organisations".[128]

Two major obsessions are discernible in family planning programme-targets and incentive and disincentives. While developing an incentive system certain basic considerations must be kept in view such as : the basic needs for food, clothing, shelter and employment are not denied to any member of the community irrespective of number of children ; facilities which promote social welfare, health and nutrition are availed by every one ; no preferential incentive should erode care of mothers and care of children and their development ; the relatively effluent in the community should not have the major share of preferential incentives ; and good work is recognised. It is well to keep in mind that the poor have more children and it is relatively effluent who stand to gain by the preferential treatment. There is enough evidence that incentives which are mainly for adopting terminal method adversely influence use of other methods especially for spacing, quality of accepters and services suffer and many distortions take place. In fact incentive system, as practised, has overall eroding impact on the family welfare programme. Incentives do have a place in any programs such as recognition of good work in various ways ; or relief of income tax for expenditure incurred on family planning by voluntary and other organisations. The strong support for incentives continue, among other reasons due to lack of evidence sufficiently convincing to programme managers. "How much part incentives play, in attracting (persons to use) family planning methods can be any body's guess, as no specific study has so far been conducted in our country on this aspect.[119] Unlike the areas like agricultural or industrial production, or many social policies, labour market, tax and other economic policies, incentives do not have long term influence on fertility behaviour whether it is to reduce or increase fertility. Pronatalist policies in Western Europe show no sign of success. There is an urgent need for a detailed study on the entire subject of incentives and disincentives to dispel prevailing confusion. There are reports the Government is re-examining the question of incentives and disincentives.

10

Training

Initially there was sometimes confusion in the preception of terms education, training, orientation and communication. Gradually, general concensus was reached. It may be of interest to define[130] these terms.

Education. "Education is a generic term that refers to all processes that bring about changes in levels of information, knowledge, understanding and performance, and in behaviour patterns of the individuals, to their fullest potential, to develop attitudes, values, skills, habits and roles appropriate for the societies in which they live. Although education in its broadest sense is a vital component of the whole process of socialization, objectives of particular educational programme may focus on specific aspects, *e.g.*, education of particular members of society, education in specific subjects, education towards specific goals, etc. It may be formal, informal, institutionalised, unstructured, etc. The educational process includes numerous components—the formulation of educational objectives, the development of curricula, communication, practice of skills, etc.".

Training. "The processes and aims of training are not at variance with the processes and aims of education. In training, the focus is more restricted and specific, the duration more limited and the setting usually institutionalised. One thinks of training in relation to acquisition of one or more skills or techniques required for the performance of specific tasks. Education may also include the development of skills and techniques in the context of a broader learning process".

Orientation. Orientation is a process of orienting, a process of enabling to understand how one stands in relation to his environment and adjustment to ascertained principles. Orientation is also not at variance with processes and aims of education and training. The duration could be shorter than for training. The setting could cover a wide range—institutional, seminars, small groups, etc. It may be a preliminary phase before imparting training.

Communication. "Communication refers to the process of the exchange of ideas and information among people (an interactive process). Components of the process include verbal or non-verbal messages, transmitted through one or more from message senders to receivers, who may provide feedback to the senders. Communication is not synonymous with the term mass media.* Those with some experience do not like to use the term "media" in isolation. They prefer the use the word communication processes or communication system. Each channel for disseminating information plays a role in effective communication. The goals of communication are parallel to those of education, that is to bring about changes in levels in information, knowledge, understanding and performance and behaviour patterns. Communication is a component of all educational and training processes".

Motivation. "Motivation is a term which refers to inner needs or drives which influence how an individual learns and behaves in relation to his aspirations, goals, or purpose in life. Motivation may be modified by internal change, or it may be modified by external stimuli. The motivation of individuals is inherent concern in the development of all programmes attempting to introduce social change, including those dealing

---

*Telecommunication is a recent and very useful development. It is a one-way process from communicator to receiver, with no participation by the latter.

with education, training and communication. Educators and trainers and communicators must assess motivation in order to implement programme objectives. The assessment of motivation, while essential in education, training, orientation, and communication programmes in family planning as in other areas, is nevertheless complex, *e.g.*, observed behaviour does not always correspond to motivation as it has been assessed".

The social scientists, and programme managers in India especially those working in Community Development programme and elsewhere were familiar with these terms since the inception of the programme. In the very first meeting of the Family Planning Research and Programmes Committee in 1953, considerable discussion took place on these subjects. Margaret Snyder had prepared a paper on 'Education for Family Planning, for consideration of the committee. She emphasized that "effective family planning education can be developed only on the basis of sound knowledge of community attitudes, beliefs and behaviour patterns relating to family size. This knowledge can best be acquired by using techniques of cultural anthropology and of opinion research".[131] Action was initiated to support such research. But at the same time it was felt that concurrently all available information on the subject and experience of knowledgeable persons should be pooled and the information, education, communication and training programmes should be developed based on such information. They could be modified in the light of further research.

Family Planning Training and Research Centre Bombay

In January 1954, the Family Planning Research and Programmes Committee recommended the appointment of Sushila Gore who was in charge of the Godfrey Clinic in Bombay. The Committee had visited the Godfrey clinic in July 1953 and was 'impressed with what Gore had accomplished in that clinic'. She was appointed as an officer on special duty on 25 June, 1955 to start a training centre. Delhi, Nagpur, Calcutta and Bombay were considered for the location of the training centre. While the proposals for establishing the training centre were being finalised, Gore with two social workers started training courses of short duration in different parts of the country. The candidates deputed to these courses were by State Governments and local authorities. As the work of family planning was to be integrated with that of maternity and child health (MCH) centres, the trainees mainly came from MCH centres. Some trainees from well established voluntary organisations also attended these short courses. Working conditions for Gore in Delhi were difficult. There was no office accommodation. She worked from her residence in the Western Court in New Delhi.

With the assistance of the Family Planning Association of India, Ministry of Health purchased the Parakh Hospital building at Sandhurst Road in Bombay at a cost of Rs. 3 lakhs in 1957. The Family Planning Training and Research Centre (FPTRC) was established in Bombay on the 25 March 1957 with Gore as its first officer-in-Charge. The training was both in the class room and the field. The former included besides teaching the techniques of contraception and allied subjects, instructions in the principles and techniques of social work, techniques of education of rural and urban communities and other behavioural sciences which have a bearing on a person and family relationships. Great emphasis was laid on imparting instructions in the techniques of motivating people for accepting small family norm. The trainees were helped in the field to organize mass and small group meetings and home visiting. The course was in nine parts, *viz.*, Family Planning General (including history, demographic, medical eugenic, economic and social aspects); Family Planning Technical; Administration and management of services; sex, marriage and family planning; social welfare; Dynamics of human behaviour, psycho-social development of the child from birth to adolescence, psycho-somatic ailments with special reference to sex, marriage and family inter-relationships; Public health and Family Planning; Principles and concepts of learning and teaching, social education, audio-visual aids, education in rural and urban communities; and Maternal and Child Health. The Family Planning Centre included birth control, pre-natal, post-natal, toddler's and well baby clinics, a children's preventorium, milk centre, marriage guidance and counselling, services for infertility and sterility and a 'mother's club'.

The FPTRC pioneered the methodology on team training (doctors, nurses, and health visitors and medico-social workers). The major part of the course was essential for the whole team but at certain stages of training further specialised training was given to specific group to equip them for their specialised job in their specific field. Although an advisory committee was constituted for the training centre, the main credit for development of the centre should go to Dr. Gore. With very limited staff, she developed the centre in record time. The centre was established in March 1957, the first course started in September 1957 and by October 1958, 149 persons were trained (mainly potential instructors from States of Andhra, Assam, Bihar, Bombay, Kerala, Madhya Pradesh, Madras, Mysore, Orissa, Punjab, Rajasthan, Uttar Pradesh, West Bengal, Delhi, Himachal Pradesh and Tripura.[182] There were changes in its role and activities over the years. The Centre is now located in the campus of International Institute of Population Sciences in Chembur, Bombay.

Touring Teams

In 1959 a training centre was set up in Delhi. State Governments started establishing their own training centres. The rapid pace of the development of the programme, and limited capacity of the training facilities led to setting up touring teams in the states in 1960.

Family Welfare Workers Training Centres

The number of persons qualifying each year as auxilliary nurse midwives (ANM) from ANM training centres was not sufficient to fill the posts in the family planning programme. A few selected voluntary institutions were given financial support to train women with basic qualification lower than required for ANM. They were designated as Family Welfare Workers. The courses for their training were job oriented and of shorter duration than for ANM. An expert committee laid down the carriculum, and examined the trainees. The performance of Family Welfare Workers in the field was reported to be very good.

EXPANSION OF TRAINING PROGRAMME

Training programme was inevitably influenced by the programme strategy and pace of development of the programme. Around 1958, the focus was on development of training in seven directions, *viz.*, a centre for training potential instructors ; a rural training, demonstration and experimental centre ; touring training teams ; development of selected clinics into regional training centres ; regional training centres for family welfare workers ; ad-hoc training courses of short duration where ever trained personnel and clinical material were available ; and incorporation of family planning in normal training programmes in teaching of doctors and medical auxilliaries. The titles regional centres over-time became a misnomer they in fact developed into State Training centres.

In March 1961, Jungalwala Committee recommended to give regular courses of instruction in family planning to the following categories of personnel : (*i*) all medical, para-medical and medical auxilliaries already employed by the State Governments, Local Bodies and Voluntary organisations ; (*ii*) private medical practitioners ; (*iii*) all personnel under training in medical colleges and medical training institutions for doctors, paramedical personnel and medical auxilliaries ; (*iv*) medical paramedical personnel and medical auxilliaries working in special establishments exclusively for the family planning programme such as staff of the family planning training and research centres, family planning clinics, members of touring training teams, and orientation training teams and also senior officers responsible for developing the programme in all States and at all levels ; (*v*) social scientists and those under training in social services ; (*vi*) extension workers, school teachers and voluntary social workers ; and traditional birth attendents (*Dais*). The Committee made observations on objectives, content and duration of training and interim arrangements for imparting such training, such as converting one regular course at All India

Institute of Hygiene and Public Health Calcutta and training centres in Bombay and Delhi for senior instructors and also observation tours for them to the following institutions: AIIH & PH Calcutta, FPT & RC Bombay, FPTC (later CFPI) New Delhi, CHEB New Delhi, Institute of Audio-visual Education Delhi, Health Centres Najafgarh, Poonamalle and Singur, Demographic Centres Bombay, Delhi, Calcutta and Trivandrum, medical and biological research institutes like CTU Bombay, Family Welfare Bureau Bombay, CDRI Lucknow, All India Institute of Medical Sciences, New Delhi, Post-Graduate Medical Institutes in Calcutta and Madras; and schools of Social Sciences, Bombay, Baroda, Delhi and Madras.

In October 1961, Tandon Committee was formed and recommended short term orientation courses for the following categories: the categories of personnel under the Central and State Governments other than those employed for the family planning programme and medical and health services be considered under the following heads: Senior Administrators; Community Development personnel; School teachers; Junior Officials in the administrative posts under the Central and State Governments especially in the Revenue Department; Staff of Training Centres run by different Ministries. The content and duration of courses for different categories would depend on the job expected of them, the length of their training course. The objective was to increase and improve their knowledge and understanding of family planning and population activities so that they appreciate their role and functions in their respective sphere in the nationwide family planning programme. The Committee also suggested courses for the training centres of IAS and IFS*. Special reference was made for action required by the Ministries of Education on teachers training, sex education in schools and Family Life Education in Colleges; Labour and Employment on orientation of trade unions and employers associations; Community Development and Cooperation for their different categories of workers including the members of Panchayti Raj bodies and Mahila Mandals and other Departments and Ministeries.[133]

*Indian Administrative Service. Indian Foreign Service.

Initial steps to establish linkages with Governmental and non-Governmental agencies were taken earlier in 1958 such as with the Central Social Welfare Board ; All India Women's Conference, Indian Council of Child Welfare ; Ministries of Information and Broadcasting, Labour and Employment, Home Affairs, Defence, Commerce and Industries, Education, Community Development and Cooperation ; Indian Medical Association, Indian Red Cross Society ; Medical Council of India ; Indian Nursing Council ; Bharat Sewak Samaj etc. The Family Planning Association of India was the most important partner in all these endeavours. A very close association with it was developed both at personal and official levels.

Indian Nursing Council

In November 1957, the Indian Nursing Council recommended inclusion of training in family planning in the basic courses for nurses, midwives and health visitors to all the State Nurses Registration Councils.

Medical Council of India

In October 1958, the Medical Council of India recommended that 'Medical students should undergo a short course of training in family planning during the period of their internship which they are required to spend in a health unit for participation in public health administration. Such health units should have at least one well developed family planning centre for carrying out this training progiamme, the centre being in-charge of a medical officer trained in the Central Government's family planning institute and with adequate number of social workers attached to it, to promote a sound system of home visiting and follow up, and the training should consist of about 6 lecture demonstrations at the family planning centre attached to a medical college or at a recognised health centre, provided that this training be undertaken during the post examination period. Jungalwala Committee considered such a recommendation restrictive and felt that the whole subject should not be left over for internship period only but should be initiated during the normal instructions in preventive and social medicine, midwifery and gynaecology ; surgery and paediatrics, and integrated syllabus could be prepared and overlapping avoided if a specific department in the medical college was made responsible for coordinating and initiating the subject and initially a lecturer appointed from a family planning training centre in the vicinity of the college. Gradually, instructions related to family planning began to emerge in different phases of teaching, *viz.*, anatomy, physiology, bio-chemistry and pharmacology ; later in para-clinical and clinical courses ; and still later during the period of compulsory housemanship. It was suggested that medical colleges should organise periodical seminars in which staff from all departments and the in-service trainees participate ; and some of the seminars were to be devoted to methods of teaching and evaluation of training. D. Anand carried out a research project on family planning through hospital care which further underlined the need and feasibility of family planning advice and services as an integral part of total patient care in a hospital. His report influenced the policy on family planning teaching in medical colleges. Greater understanding of the role of hospitals in family planning programme gradually emerged.[134]

Universities

Population issues were being included in some universities to a varying degrees for a long time. In order to achieve substantial improvement in all universities the Inter-University Board was approached. The Board was sympathetic and supportive, but actual development depended on the interest of university Vice-Chancellers. In 1960s the National Council of Education Research and Training (which itself was then in formative stage) found in a study that in eight States the syllabus did not refer to population problem in social studies, some reference to population problem was found in teachers training schools and colleges, human reproduction was included in some detail in teaching of biology in the universities and teachers training institutions, some teaching in marriage and family life appeared in home science teaching but mainly devoted to inter-personal relations and child rearing. The picture was a little different in respect of demography, which was taught in many universities at undergraduate level. A few lectures on India's population problem were given to graduates in economics, sociology or statistics. Demography was taught at post graduate level in a few universities like Aligarh, Banaras, Gorakhpur, Lucknow, Jaipur and Sagar. A compulsory paper in demography was included in Poona University for those taking master's degree in statistics. University of Kerala started a two-year diploma course in demography. Ujjain and Lucknow Universities offered as optional subject to the candidates for master's degree in sociology, biology and economics. Certificate courses and diploma courses in demography were offered in the Lucknow University.[135] These courses were in addition to those in specialised institutions like ISI Calcutta, DTRC Bombay, Demographic Centres in Trivandrum, Dharwar, Poona, Patna, Lucknow, Delhi and Madras and at institutions like AIIH & PH Calcutta, PRAI Lucknow, IRH & FP Gandhigram and CFPI New Delhi.

Delhi University was a pace-setter. C.D. Deshmukh, the Vice-Chanceller, Delhi University called a meeing of Heads of different faculties on May 5, 1965 to discuss promotion of studies in different departments and also undertaking studies of problems influencing the people in the area surrounding the university. A unique feature was that a group of devoted social workers led by Mrs. Durgabai Deshmukh and Mrs. Ganguli arranged to provide family welfare services and a field practice area. The need to provide information on basic nature of population issues and its importance in the country and advanced training where possible were developed by other universities. The multi-disciplinary nature of such training (behavioural sciences, medicine, public health, education, demography, management and administration and other disciplines) was appreciated. Implementation varied widely even in medical teaching institutions. This depended on local leadership. Some made outstanding efforts, *e.g.*, M.K. Krishna Menon made valuable contributions in the organisation of training centres in family planning for physicians and pre-medical personnel. At the Institute of Obsetetrics and Gynaecology Madras, he started for the first time a training centre for physicians in the mid-

1960s, besides pioneering social obstetrics and integration of MCH and family planning services.

Financial Assistance

The Government support for the training activities was extended from 1950s, the extent and scope increased with the development of the programme. In July 1957, 100 per cent financial support for training of doctors, health visitors, nurses medico-social workers and social workers and establishment of 36 regional centres was intimated to the Governments of Madras, Kerala, Uttar Pradesh, Madhya Pradesh, West Bengal and Punjab. This assistance was on relatively more liberal scale than extended earlier in September 1956. The assistance was further augmented in the light of experience in July 1958. This included support to medical colleges and other teaching institutions for health personnel in all States.

Further developments took place in early 1960. It was felt that there should be at least one training centre with adequate facilities in each state ; regional centres at the time were able to provide just basic training to put the personnel on the job as soon as possible. It was suggested that such a centre should preferably be located or associated with a teaching medical institution. The number of training centres to be set up was based on population (1961 census) ; one centre for 10 million, a total of 44 centres. The centres for the one year training for family welfare workers were gradually converted to training centres for auxilliary nurse midwives.

With initiating the extension approach of the programme in early 1960s, training needs had to be adjusted to meet programme needs. It was essential that the whole training system should be carefully reviewed and responsibilities of the central and state training centres delineated. The Central Family Planning Institute New Delhi took the initiative in developing the job description of programme personnel. The initial exercise had already been done at IRH & FP Gandhigram (by K.V. Rangnathan with help of Betty Mathews who stayed in Gandhigram for sometime and was mainly responsible for giving the job description its final shape); the Central Family Planning Institute (mainly Surjit Sandhu) and the All India Institute of Hygiene and Public Health Calcutta at Singur (by R. N. Basu and his team).

In 1966, the Central Family Planning Institute for the first time arranged a training workshop[136] attended by the representatives of the States and Union Territories, Central training institutions including NIHA & E and CHEB, regional ADG's FP, and CFP Field Units. The Secretary Ministry of Health and Family Planning (B. Mukerji) was almost a regular participant in this workshop. The recommendations of the workshop had a profound impact on training programme thereafter. Besides recommendations on further strengthening training of trainers and other personnel directly involved in the programme and others, the workshop recommended that Central Planning Institute should explore the possibilities of arranging symposia/seminars for legislators and other leaders of public opinion; and a training division adequate in size and capacity to undertake the responsibilities involved should be formed in the Family Planning Department. This led to formation of a Training Division in the Family Planning Department under the direction of a Deputy Commissioner and enabled further development of the Family Planning Training System and streamlining the existing resources, assessing training needs, and taking measures to meet those needs.

Thus emerged the training activities at four levels, *viz.* (*i*) Orientation of moulders of public policy the legislators, members of local bodies, employers of labour, trade union leaders and administrators; (*ii*) training of family planning trainers and persons directly involved in the programme; (*iii*) training of those who in their normal work can assist in the programme like those working in the fields of public health, community development, education, individual, group and mass communication; and (*iv*) training local leaders. Besides these four levels, it was recommended that the subject of population and family planning should also be included in regular courses of training in teaching institutions for medical and para-medical personnel, universities, schools of social work and later population education in and out of schools.[137]

The training resources eventually could be mainly grouped in about twelve categories : (*i*) Central Institutes ; the Central Family Planning Institute New Delhi (chiefly responsible for training of trainers from training centres in States including Central Family Planning Field Units ; (*ii*) Training Centres in States (responsible for training most of the categories of peripheral workers at block and village level ; (*iii*) Inservices training and refresher course ; (*iv*) training in demography at the DTRC Bombay besides several universities ; and other specialised centres ; (*v*) training in bio-medical aspects in universities and specialized training in reproductive biology initially in three centres : All India Institute of Medical Sciences, New Delhi, the Delhi University and the Central Family Planning Institute ; (*vi*) Medical practitioners courses held by the HQ of Indian Medical Association ; (*vii*) training of medical practitioners of other disciplines like Ayurveda, Unani, Homeopathy, etc., by their respective associations ; (*viii*) ANMs in over 300 training centres ; (*ix*) integrating teaching in medical colleges and in other teaching institutions like universities, encouraged by their respective organisations ; (*x*) training of other Government and non-Governmental personnel like Community Development, Food and Agriculture, Labour and industries railways, social welfare, Education voluntary institutions, etc., by their respective agencies ; (*xi*) Diploma Courses in health education at the All India Institute of Hygiene and Public Health Calcutta and the Institute of Rural Health and Family Planning Gandhigram ; (*xii*) training in various disciplines outside the country under a fellowship programme and observation tours.

The Central Training Institutes had a pivotal role in the training system. To the above mentioned training resources several others were added like the pilot demonstration district programmes, rural demonstration district programmes, rural demonstration areas attached to each medical college, and the National Institute of Health Administration and Education.

Organisational changes were made within the Central Institutions. The Central Family Planning Institute (later called National Family Planning Institute—NFPI) and National Institute of Health Administration and Education—NIHAE were combined to form National Institute of Health and Family Welfare NIHFW.

NATIONAL INSTITUTE OF FAMILY PLANNING (NIFP)

The institute had a modest beginning. Jayshri Katju, in 1959, started a training centre in a small room in residential type E Quarter of the All India Institute of Medical Sciences. In 1962 other small units each engaged in different facets of family planning programme were combined to form a single organisation and called the Central Family Planning Institute with Surjit Pannu (now Sandhu) as its Acting Director. In November 1964, the institute was registered under the Societies Registration Act.

The Ford Foundation (especially Moye W. Freymann and his chief Douglas Ensminger), gave substantial support to this Institute. Moye Freymann was an extraordinary consultant—young, innovative, pusher, practical with deep commitment, rich field experience in community health and social medicine and erudite. His perspective, developed through shere hard work, of the needs of the family planning programme in India was remarkable. His speed in formulating projects often appeared faster than the pace of generating resources. No foreign consultant in India influenced the development of family planning programme in 1960s more than Moye Freymann. In many activities his wife, Kathy Freymann, made rich contribution. She was frequently seen in her house with note-pads and pencil busy in statistical exercises or outside absorbed in discussion with Institute Faculty members like Surjit Sandhu.

Other international agencies extended help such as C. Chandrasekaran's services were made available for a month in 1966 by the United Nations ECAFE ; advice of Professor FAE Crew and Margaret Jackson's was made available by the United

Kingdom under Colombo Plan. Estella Brodman in 1968, Robert Blake, Thomas Poffenberger, Edward Pohlman and other visiting experts helped in the growth of the Institute to a varying degree;

The Institute had the unique distinction of adopting the motto approved by the President of India Dr. S. Radhakrishnan. The motto approved by the President of India reads : *Swrashtrasy Smradhiartham Farivaro Nyojitam.* "Let the family be planned for prosperity of the country".

The Ministry of Health declared it an autonomous body on 22nd March, 1965.

The objectives of the institute were :

(*i*) to develop more effective methods of applying relevant knowledge already available for strengthening the national family planning movement ;

(*ii*) to discover new knowledge relating to the educational, social, medical, biological, statistical, demographic, organisational and supply aspects of the national programme ;

(*iii*) to provide evaluation, information, training and other consultation services ; and

(*iv*) to serve as a coordinating body for the communication action-research programme and the demographic research programme.

For carrying out these objectives special Divisions were developed, *viz.*, administrative services, programme development and evaluation ; training ; demography and statistics ; social research ; information and audio-visual ; medical education and research ; biological research ; and population genetics and human development. A Division for management information alongwith other functions was suggested but did not materialise. Although there was a separate training division the responsibility of training was shared by all divisions. The titles of the divisions did not reflect the activities initiated or envisaged, for example the Information and audio-visual Division dealt with health education and information and education and communication system. It was also envisaged to develop in it a National documentation centre on population and family planning with information retrieval system. Amrit Mahal, a senior health educator from AIIH & PH Calcutta was transferred to the Institute to head the Information Education Communication Division. Assistance was sought of national and international experts to develop the Documentation Centre. An attempt was made to mobilize many different skills and scientific disciplines besides the medical and health field to meet the needs of the rapidly developing nation-wide programme. The focus was to develop an institution of excellence—a multi-disciplinary resource with special focus on training trainers in population sciences integrated with social and biological aspects and delivery of services; multi-disciplinary research, experimentation, demonstration and evaluation activities. To achieve the desired excellence, attention was given not only to selecting the best available talent within the available resources and staff development, and associating other National Institutions with its activities but also to have an advisory committee for each division with experts in the countries with wide experience and thus pooling the best talent in the concerned fields. A notable feature was use of field practice areas with emphasis on community participation, especially at Najafgarh, developed in the early years by D. Anand, Surjeet Sandhu and the health team. Later it was further developed by Padma Kashyap a young, and perceptive medical officer with attractive personality. She subsequently joined the All India Institute of Medical Sciences.

In the efforts to reorganise the institute and to develop divisions on the basis of learning and research for various special functions, procedural problems arose from time to time, such as staff recruitment, revision of pay scales of the staff to attract young persons and other issues specially at junior levels. The attempts to get real autonomy (which could resolve these problems) did not succeed. The senior government officials were always ready to help (and actually provided strong support), but were bound with rules and regulations and reluctance to loose administrative control.

The experience shows that research and training institutions should have real autonomy. The Government can lay down policy, provide funds subject to audit and carry out general monitoring with a view to ensure that the funds are utilised properly. Training, research, demonstration, experimentation and evaluation can best progress if institute functions with maximum flexibility. Research and training blossom in a free environment. They can then effectively feed back to administrators the findings for further development of the larger programme.

The Institute made significant contributions to the programme, besides training, in the field of evaluation, research in biomedicine, communication and socio-psychological aspects, and programme operation, notably "Action Research Projects.

The Institute conducted several evaluation studies including the evaluation of family planning activities by different States of the country. The studies carried out were mainly directed to find answers to practical problems faced in the programme, *e.g.*, the Institute demonstrated that a period of about 3 months or 15 ejaculations are necessary to get rid of the residual sperms from the tract of vasectomized individuals Several biomedical studies conducted in the Institute identified the causes of the complaints with existing methods of family planning. The Institute demonstrated how 'Nirodh' could be commercially distributed. The studies on socio-psychological aspects of the family planning programme, including vasectomy camps led to the norms laid down for related workers about communication and medical approaches. The Institute trained many key personnel in the programme for family planning. The approval of IUD insertion by paramedical staff was obtained on the basis of studies conducted by the Institute. The introduction of TCu 200 IUD in the programme was also based on studies conducted by the Institute. Similarly, studies on oral contraceptives, studies on drop-outs, studies on medical termination of pregnancy, aud studies on condoms helped in the advancement of the programme.

THE NATIONAL INSTITUTE OF HEALTH ADMINISTRATION AND EDUCATION [NIHAE]

An ad hoc Committee of the Planning Commission in early 1962 proposed, *viz.*, establishment of a Central Family Planning Institute ; a National Institute of Health Administration and Education : and intensive rural and urban health and family planning projects. The proposals were agreed in May 1962 by the Planning Commission and Central Ministries concerned. The Central Family Planning Institute was already in the process of development. In October 1962, the Central Council of Health at the meeting in Mahabaleshwar considered the proposals of the ad-hoc commitee and recommended that : "Pilot Demonstration District programmes should be undertaken on an experimental basis in each State". The Council recognizing ; "the crucial importance of administrative and educational problems in implementing health and family planning programmes" and "the great need for facilities to carry out high-level training and research in health administration and education" also welcomed "the proposed establishment of a National Institute of Health Administration and Education".

In early 1963, the Ministry of Health invited a team of consultants. The team included Dr. Hugh R. Leavell, Professor of Public Health Practice, Harvard School of Public Health ; Dr. Edward G. McGavran, Dean School of Public Health, University of North Carolina and Dr. Willian Mayes, Chief Office of Research Grants, Bureau of Community Health US Public Health Services. The team concentrated its attention on the plans for NIHAE and intensive Rural Health and Family Planning Programme. The team took into consideration three dimensions of health programmes, *viz.*, technical (the specific biological and physical knowledge related to a specific programme), administrative or organisational (ways in which human, physical and financial resources could be meaningfully related to each other and supported and maintained to achieve programme goals) and educational (methods and techniques whereby personnel within the programme achieve satisfactory consensus on their goals and patterns of work and whereby people can be helped to learn new health concepts and undertake the process of moving as a group towards adoption of new practices). In respect of the first dimension it was felt that the knowledge was largely available in the country and the urgent need was to consider dealing with administration and health education dimensions. The team further observed that "it is with these broad considerations in view, plus the particular urgency of developing a strong organisational base for the national family planning movement", that National Institute of Health Administration and Education has been proposed.

"The basic planning document included the following as objectives and activities of NIHAE : *Training* : the Institute will provide post-graduate courses in the principles and practice of public health administration, for physicians and other highly qualified health workers. It will also provide post-graduate training courses in health education, for medical and non-medical personnel. In addition, a regular programme of advanced training for leaders in public health administration will be developed. Other educational activities will include short courses, conferences, seminars and study groups for various types of health personnel, in connection with particular problems in the field of health and family planning administration ; *Research* administration and educational problems in implementation of health and family planning programme will be the primary research interest of the Institute ; *Services* : the Institute would be used as a resource to which problems could be referred or which could help to carry out special training needs.

The team of consultants suggested a tentative organisational set up including five Divisions, *viz.*, Administration ; Research Methods ; Health Programmes ; Health Education and Service Units. The health programmes included sections on family planning, maternal and child health, nutrition, nursing, environmental sanitation, medical care, communicable disease control (including microbiology), industrial health and accident control. It was envisaged that the Division of Health Education will be concerned with professional training, general educational methods, audio-visual media and school health. It would also develop courses for specialists in health education and courses in techniques of community and staff education for students other than specialist. A strong social science base was considered essential. Types of education and training included D.P.H. programme, Diploma course in health education, Ph.D. programme and Staff college function.[138] With such a conceptual frame the NIHAE was established in 1962, and started functioning in hired buildings in Greater Kailash-I, New Delhi. (Initially at planning stage it worked in three rooms in Patiala House, with Dr. M.S. Chadha as its first Director who had just retired as DGHS).

Over the years the NIHAE developed under the successive distinguished directors and faculty members and made valuable contributions in various directions, especially in developing professional managers. But in some areas the hopes of those (at least some of those who were associated for its establishment) were not fulfilled, *e.g.* : when the family planning programme with extension approach was launched extension personnel could be trained in existing centres, but for supervisory and guidance levels there was urgent need for Diploma courses in Health Education. Initially, AIIH & PH, Calcutta provided such a course ; later IRH & FP, Gandhigram also initiated such a course. These two institutions could provide 60 health educators in a year, against the requirement of over 10,000 health educators in the country. CHEB also initiated action to arrange such courses. Other institutions were also identified where such courses could be held. The NIHAE was expected in February 1963 to start a diploma course in health education, as it was a priority need for family planning programme ; but this did not materialise. The NIHAE was also expected to function as a staff college to update training of existing staff in the field of public health administration and also to undertake the training of a new type of public health administrator, innovative and creative with a "peoples participation" perspective.

Substantial contribution was made by NIHAE. But it did not appear to blossom fully and appeared to face financial constraints.

The NIHAE had a special role in the development and supervision of Intensive District Health and Family Planning Projects.* These projects were expected to provide leads for programme operation. They ended before they could be fully developed.

NATIONAL INSTITUTE OF HEALTH AND FAMILY WELFARE

Many predicaments of NIFP and NIHAE were similar. Both were functioning in hired buildings one in Green Park and another in Greater Kailash-I in New Delhi. Both faced financial constraints. Both were not really autonomous. When the NIFP acquired land for its own buildings and was planning to have sufficient space for its future expansion, the proposals started being made to combine NIFP, NIHAE and CHEB, into one institute. There were differences of opinion in integration of the three institutions mainly based on the experience that when a discipline reaches maturity it blossoms in an independent environment. It was suggested that some activities could be combined and institutions function closely linked but independently as in a university setting. After considerable discussion over a long period (delay being mainly due to lack of resources for the building project), it was finally decided to integrate NIFP and NIHAE. The name was changed to National Institute of Health and Family Welfare (NIHFW).

The NIHFW has now departments of Communication; Community Health; Administration, Education and Training, Medical Care and Hospitals Administration, Population Genetics and Human Development, Reproductive Biomedicine, Social Sciences, Statistics and Demography,

* The Intensive District Health and Family Planning Projects are discussed in a separate chapter.

National Documentation Centre and Administration. The Institute has a very experienced staff.

The annual reports of the institute are an impressive reading. The degree of excellence of the Institute will rest a great deal on the leadership ; the staff, their job satisfaction, and opportunities for their advancement ; real autonomy ; flexibility in and freedom of operation not only for the Institute as whole but also each of its departments creating the environment for each of them to blossom fully.

The population and family welfare problems are not transitory. Many aspects are not fully appreciated and when appreciated remain at conceptual level. There are great possibilities for expansion and development of the combined institute. The skills exist in the country. The competence to utilize the skills also exist. A great deal has been accomplished. But a great deal remains to be done. Mobilization of the existing knowledge and continuously enriching it requires full appreciation of the dimensions of the problem, its complexity, its interdisciplinary and, highly technical nature of the problem as a whole and each of its components and environment free from extranuous pressures and financial support and real autonomy. The institutional role conflicts which may arise have to be overcome. The administrative proceedures required to serve this type of institute should be quite different from those of Governmental or para-Governmental organisations. Such an organisation would require maximum flexibility and climate of research and different proceedures for selection and filling of posts and audit methods. There may be a situation when there is no post sanctioned, but a young promising scientists comes up with a innovative idea. It should be possible, as mentioned earlier to recruit and build the project around such a person.

Attention has to be paid for a long term manpower projection and developing programmes for professional development of each member of staff in any institute of excellence. Terms and conditions of service at all levels should obviously be such that staff continue to work in the institute and not drift to other institutions in India and abroad either for higher remuneration or better opportunity for work, specially in case of first and second level scientists. The institute will then attract top quality young persons. High level technical advisory committees can advise in specific problems. Research scientists from India and abroad should be encouraged to come and work on specific problems for varying periods ; some may spend their sabbatical leave in the institute. The faculty members likewise could have study leave and spend it in institutions abroad.

DEMOGRAPHIC TRAINING AND RESEARCH CENTRES

The training and research in population studies have been developed as an integrated programme. A committee on Demographic Studies with V.K.R.V. Rao as convener was established early in 1954. On the 12th March 1954, the committee suggested formation of a Council of Population Studies composed of selected non-official institutions engaged or proposing to engage in population research, representative of Ministries and other offices of the central government in population research and selected individuals who would be experts in one or other aspect of population problem. The functions of the council broadly conceived were : to promote research on selected aspects of population problem by individuals and institutions in different parts of the country and support the same by adequate financial assistance and technical guidance where needed ; to hold seminars, conferences and discussions groups on various aspects of the population problem ; to promote and finance the setting up research and training sections in demographic studies in selected universities and research institutions in the country ; and to promote the training of research workers in demographic studies by award of scholarships, fellowships, etc., to selected individuals for study either in India or abroad and also if necessary, by special training programmes. In a meeting held on the 23rd May 1954, Rao further outlined preliminary pilot research and long term studies in a special paper. For pilot research he suggested : analysis of data that may not have been published ; field studies aimed at direct collection of data. The committee recommended that units should be set up with a view to studying the 1951 data, the statistics of some of the larger maternity hospitals in the country ; field studies should cover different types of areas, *e.g.*, tribal, areas with assured rainfall or irrigation facilities, those with uncertain rainfall and frequent famines, rice, wheat and millet areas, town, city and country. Obtaining of correct basic data on birth rates, death rates and specific fertility rates were to be primary object of field studies envisaged. The services of the following institutions and organisations were proposed to be utilised : the National Sample Survey, the Central Statistical Organisation, the Registrar General's Office, Universities, Research Institutions (Gokhale School of Politics and Economics Poona, School of Economics and Tata School of Social Sciences Bombay, The Delhi School of Economics, J.K. Institute of Sociology and Human Relations and other similar institutions), Rural Extension Units set up by Ministry of Agriculture, Health Survey Units being set up by Central Health Ministry, and Public Health Departments of States. A few intensive studies were also recommended. The Committee underlined the fact that an effective and rational scheme of family planning requires a careful study of various factors that were responsible for high birth rates in the country. In a country like India, with a large area and people diverse in their social and cultural habits, the of a single birth rate was somewhat of an abstraction. It was, talk therefore, suggested that it would be useful in the first instance to carry out a series of pilot studies in different parts of the country with different social groups. After some preliminary idea was obtained it would be possible to plan a programme of long term research.

While the above suggestions were being considered Leona Baumgartner and Frank Notestein visited India and submitted a report to Health Minister Rajkumari Amrit Kaur in December 1955. Notestein, in this report, suggested that in view of limited number of personnel trained and experienced to staff research centres and meet the needs of National and local Governments for trained analysts and the needs of the universities for specialised teachers in demography, a demographic training centre to conduct training and research at advanced level should be established. The research at this centre, he suggested should be in two fields, *viz.*, analysis of trends in population growth and distribution in relation to socio-economic change and evaluation of their meaning for health and welfare of the population ; and analysis dealing specifically in the field of family planning. It should be directed towards finding the most efficient means of modifying interest, attitudes and behaviour in variety of settings and towards evaluating the consequences of such changes in terms of health and welfare. The research on medical and biological aspects of the problem were to be conducted in a medical centre, but close liaison between the demographic and medical and biological research was considered essential. Immediate need, in view of Notestein was establishment of one such centre which should : "have appropriate academic affiliation but given considerable autonomy under direction of a governing body, have possibility of close liaison with medical and biological work ; be directed by a fully experienced demographer and have a staff on which skills in public health, sociology, social psychology, economics, and statistical methods are represented ; and take part in the design of a limited number of field trials in family planning and be given assistance in the collection of information necessary for their evaluation".[139] The need for training demographers was underlined at the United Nations Asia and Far East Seminar on Population at Bandungs in 1955. This time the Economic and Social Council of United Nations had recommended by unanimous vote establishment of regional centres for demographic training and research.* The plans included one centre in South East Asia. The Government of India decided in July 1956 to establish such a centre in Bombay. On the 15th November 1956 the Demographic Training and Research Centre was established in collaboration with the United Nations and Sir Dorabji. Tata Trust with John Mathai as Chairman Governing Body and K.C.K.E. Raja the Coordinating Officer of the centre as Secretary of the Governing Body. On the basis of previous

---

*It may be added that the idea of starting regional demographic centres first emerged at the First World Population Conference held in Rome in 1954, sponsored by the International Union for the Scientific Study of Population helped by the Population Council, New York,

negotiations with the United Nations it was agreed that the Centre would be a regional institution to serve the needs of other countries in Asia in the ECAFE (now called ESCAP) region. The countries covered by the Centre included Afghanistan, Pakistan, India, Nepal, Burma, Thailand, Malaya, Laos, Cambodia, Vietnam, the Phillipines, Taiwan, Japan, Korea, Indonesia, Ceylon (now Sri Lanka), Sarawak, North Borneo, Brunei, Singapore and Hongkong. The United Nations undertook to provide long term advisers and short term consultants on different aspects of demography and related fields of training as well as equipment and technical literature and other reference material for building a library and fellowships for students from the countries of Asia other than India. The Government of India undertook to provide the building, scholarships to trainees from India and in association with Sir Dorabji Tata Trust to establish and maintain the Centre. The provisional allocations for 1955-61 were : Government of India Rs. 13.12 lakhs, United Nations Contribution Rs. 10.20 lakhs and share of Dorabji Tata Trust Rs. 1.25 lakhs. Collaborative relationship was established with Departments of Economics and Sociology, Bombay University ; the Department of Economics and Statistics Government of Bombay ; the Tata Institute of Social Sciences Chembur Bombay ; Indian Cancer Research Centre (Human Variation and Physiology of Human Reproduction Divisions) Bombay ; and the Gokhale Institute of Politics and Economics Poona. K.C.K.E. Raja, played the major role at the initial stage in the development of the centre. He relinquished the post to join as member-secretary of the committee to review the health programmes in India. He was succeeded by C. Chandrasekaran, who was designated as Director. The research and training programmes gradually expanded. The centre was recognised for training leading to Ph.D degree in demography by the Bombay University. Chandrasekaran left the centre in August 1965 to join ECAFE (now ESCAP) as Regional Demographic Adviser. The post of the Director was later held by S.P. Jain (965-67), S.N. Agarwala (1967-73), and JR Rele (1973-1978). Rele was succeeded by K. Srinivasan. V.K.R.V. Rao served as Chairman of the Governing Body for some years. In July 1970 the name of the centre was changed to International Institute of Population Studies.

The words 'Population studies' were later changed to Population Sciences. Major organisational change took place in 1966. The Centre (later Institute) was registered as a Society under the Indian Registration Act on August 26, 1966, with a General Council (Minister of Health and Family Planning* as President), and Executive Council (a nominee of the President of the General Council as Chairman), and Director of the Institute as Secretary of both the General and Executive Council and Academic Council with the Director of the Institute as Chairman, four outside experts, all professors, two readers and one lecturer of the Institute and senior most professor of the Institute as Secretary. Sir Dorabji Tata Trust withdrew their financial support from 1970. The support from other agencies like the United Nations, continued. The USAID provided assistance during 1966-69 to 1971. Notable contribution to development of the centre was made by the United Nations and other experts. Eminent demographers like Frank Notestein, W. Parker Mauldin, Donald Bogue, M.A. El-Badry and others worked in the centre. Parker Mauldin took leave from his position in the Population Council and spent one academic year on the faculty of the Centre, from September 1957 to 1958 to help in organizing teaching and research programmes. During 1956-1981, 429 Indian students and 260 foreign students were trained at the Centre/Institute and a large number of research programmes were undertaken.[140] The Institute has been declared as a "Deemed University".

Since starting of the Demographic and Research Centre in Bombay other similar centres have been established, *viz.*, at Santiago in Chile, Cairo in Egypt, Accra in Ghana, Yaounde in Cameroon, and Bucharest in Rumania. The DTRC Bombay (IPPS) holds the unique position as the first to be started.

DEMOGRAPHIC RESEARCH CENTRES

It was obvious from the very beginning that the one centre

*It may be noted that the Minister of Health and Family Planning replaced non-official chairman of the governing body.

in Bombay, though a valuable demographic studies and training resource, will not be able to meet the needs of the family planning programme. The size of the country and its diversity required a number of centres and wide support of universities and other institution. Despite the limitations of trained personnel, it was felt that at least a few institutions should be identified where demographic research centres could be started. Training in formal demography was still in its formative period. The experts in population studies were drawn from a variety of disciplines such as statistics, economics, sociology, anthropology, mathematics, biology and public health. A number of Indian scholars had already made valuable contributions to population studies like P. C. Mahalonobis, V.K.R.V. Rao, Gyan Chand, B.N. Ganguli, Radhakamal Mukerjee, C. Chandrasekaran, B.S. Guha. Some departments of Statistics were well staffed like in Trivandrum Kerala. Three demographic centres were, therefore, established to begin with, *viz.*, at the Delhi School of Economics, Delhi University (later shifted to Institute of Economic Growth) on 29-10-57; the Indian Statistical Institute Calcutta on 28-12-1957; and the Department of Statistics Government of Kerala, Trivandrum on 22-9-1958. Further centres were proposed to be established as trained personnel were available.

An Advisory Committee on Demographic Research was formed with V.K.R.V. Rao as Chairman, P.C. Mahalonobis Hony. Statistical Adviser to the Government of India, P.J. Thomas, member of Rajya Sabha, Asok Mitra the Registrar General and ex-officio Census Commissioner as members and Director Family Planning as member-secretary. The functions of the Committee were to advise on research and studies on inter-relationship between economic, social and population changes on the reproductive pattern, attitudes and motivation affecting the size of the family; advise on programmes of training and research keeping in view that such training and research will assist the Government to take economic and social action and thereby facilitate the sound national programme of reconstruction; coordinate demographic research schemes receiving financial assistance from Ministry of Health; review progress made in the centres and examine and recommend proposals which may be received by the Ministry of Health for financial assistance for conducting demographic research. (The secretariate for the committee was provided by the Central Family Planning Institute immediately after its establishment with D.V.R. Murty head of its Division of Demography and Statistics as its important member). Within this framework the Committee devoted its attention to demographic manpower planning and development of a pool of trained manpower ; developing a network of demographic research centres which would in time produce demographic data of adequate reliability, so that their collective efforts would give an all-India picture ; demographic research ; and studies on dynamics of human fertility behaviour. In demographic research special encouragement was given to identification of high and low fertility areas, communities and groups for the study of factors responsible for fertility differentials, ensure comparability of studies undertaken by different centres, at least minimal uniformity in respects of concepts, design, tabulation and analysis of data ; detailed family planning knowledge, attitude and practice surveys with fertility components, periodically in a number of districts ; intensive depth studies to ascertain differential receptivity to family planning programmes as between different areas, communities and groups ; resurvey of villages and areas in which demographic surveys was carried out sometime back ; demographic studies in areas which witnessed high rates of economic development ; improvement in methods of measurements of fertility variables ; studies of economic, social and demographic factors associated with migration phenomena ; demographic studies of tribal areas ; mortality and morbidity surveys ; and studies to improve registration of vital statistics.

Fellowships

Population Council gave valuable assistance in training of personnel abroad.

During 1955-1974, sixty persons were given fellowships in demography for training abroad.[141]

Training in Demography in Other Centres

Gradually, it was possible to increase the number of demographic research centres. There are seventeen centres, all financed by the Ministry of Health and Family Welfare. There are ten centres in universities (Trupati ; Waltair ; Trivandrum ; Guwahati ; Patna ; Baroda ; Udaipur, Chandigarh ; Srinagar and Bhubaneswar) ; one in Bureau/Departments of Economics and Statistics of States (Madhya Pradesh, Bhopal) ; and six in other institutions (Indian Statistical Institute Calcutta, Institute of Rural Health and Family Planning Gandhigram, Gokhale Institute of Politics and Economics Pune, Institute of Economic Research, Dharwar ; Institute of Economic Growth Delhi, and Institute of Social Economics Change, Bangalore). There are two more population research centres at Bangalore and Lucknow firstly set up under World Bank assistance and then taken over by the State Governments. Besides there are other important centres engaged in population studies such as those in universities ; Statistics, Demography and Evaluation Divisions in the Family Planning Departments at the Centre and States, Bureau of Health Intelligence in the Director General Health Services, Department of Statistics and Demography National Institute of Health and Family Welfare, New Delhi.

The stewardship of the Demographic Advisory Committee changed in 1966 when Rao became a member of Planning Commission (later Minister of Education and Youth Services 1969-71). P.C. Mahalonobis became its new Chairman. The Demographic Advisory Committee became the Demographic and Communication Action-Research Committee.

Some years after the Advisory Committee was abolished. The experience showed that there was a need for an institutional arrangement to give professional advice to the Family Welfare Department. A population research advisory committee was formed and reconstituted in March 1985.

Indian Statistical Institute Calcutta

The Indian Statistical Institute Calcutta, founded in 1932 and nurtured by Professor Mahalonobis has a unique position in the history of development of research and training in statistics and fertility studies in India. The Population Data Committee 1945, noting that the Indian Statistical Institute had gathered from time to time a considerable amount of data on fertility, recommeded to entrust to the ISI to conduct type studies in fertility. Leads in developing methodologies to obtain satisfactory age, life tables and population projections were provided by ISI. From 1950-1972, the ISI was entrusted to conduct the National Sample Surveys. The Government took over this activity when the Department of Statistics was established. Even after formulation of Department of Statistics ISI continued to provide technical support and trained personnel. In 1959, the Indian Statistical Institute Act was passed by the Parliament declaring it an Institute of National importance and besides other things empowered it to give degrees and diplomas in statistics.

A number of centres for teaching statistics and research developed in universities and research institutions. An outstanding among them is Gokhale Institute of Politics and Economics, Poona developed in early years by Professor Gadgil.

Demographic Studies and Training Centres Plans

A number of aims and factors were considered while planning demographic studies and training centres. The needs for personnel with professional knowledge of demography in the family planning programme at the various levels were expected to increase. The normal management information system was required to be supplemented by information through population studies, collaborative fertility surveys and diagnostic studies. These activities also required demographers. There were other activities which required demographers such as in universities and other teaching institutions, in-service training for persons needing skills in techniques of demographic analysis; orientation of persons to take professional interest in demography, although demography may not be their main avocation ; training of public health personnel, economists, statisticians, sociologists, psychologists anthropologists, who in their professional work make use of population data and analysis ; training and orientation of administrators, social scientists and others to familiarise them with available demographic data and importance of their improvement and development, the need of building appropriate infrastructure and training a large number of workers honorary and paid at different levels—community development blocks, Tehsils, District, State and Central levels. The infrastructure for normal health and family planning programme management information was practically absent or weak. The Reorganised Family Planning Programme of 1960s had made provision (as minimum requirement) of a statistical clerk at Block level, Statistical Assistant at District level, a Statistician at the State level, Statistical Officers at the Regional Level; and staff for Statistics, demographic and evaluation section at the Central level. This network was expected to increase. Training assumed an important place in manpower planning.

Population Studies were promoted in universities mainly to provide a regular flow of personnel trained in demography. It was hoped that overtime all universities in India will have population studies and training centres and needs of each State will be met by universities within the State and the Demographic Training and Research Centre at Bombay will continue to serve the nodal centre for National and Regional training in demography.

The development of population studies centres was for meeting special needs. At one stage it was felt that they should be developed as population laboratories and so distributed in the country as to provide the complete fertility trends in different regions of the country on a continuing basis and also carry out diagnostic studies as required. This basis of developing the population studies centres was slightly modified. Initially those centres were developed where requisite interests and skills were available and the main expectations of the output from each of them was in the areas of their special interest and expertise, *e.g.*, the Institute of Economic Growth Delhi had special interest and expertise in urbanisation.

Population Studies Centres were free to conduct research as they deemed fit. But they were expected to initiate population studies and give emphasis to those studies as programme managers may require and also advise and assist the central and local programme managers, to undertake collaborative studies and diagnostic studies to provide the information which could help in developing effective population activities. The population studies centres were also expected to provide field training to young researchers.

In the early years the development of Nation-wide activities in demographic training and research in a systematic manner to fulfil the manpower requirements, to conduct collaborative fertility surveys and demographic research was guided by the Demographic Advisory Committee at the National Level (Later Demographic and Communication—Action Research Committee) with the Secretariate at the National Family Planning Institute New Delhi. The Secretariate function to the National Family Planning Institute was given, as the Demographic and Evaluation Division of the Institute had the professional staff to process the proposals received for consideration of the Demographic Advisory Committee, and also to make periodical estimates of manpower requirements to identify priority areas of research and serve as nodal centre for collaborative research such as fertility surveys. The attempts to establish an autonomous organisation on population Studies were made in 1954 by Dr. V.K.R.V. Rao in 1954. They were revived by him some years later, but were again not successful. The Population Council with Home Minister Govind Ballabh Pant as Chairman (with committees on Census and Vital Statistics, Demographic Studies, and Social and Economic Studies) formed in 1960 was short lived. The coordination and development of population studies and training under a high level professional autonomous organisation with adequate resources, is necessary now more than ever before.

Studies and Training in Human Population Genetics

The studies in human population genetics were carried out on very modest scale mainly by independent workers in research institutions. The Human Variation Unit and other workers did bring out the nature of genetic variation in some social groups through systematic studies. It may be recalled that Notestein in his proposal for establishing DTRC had suggested close liaison with medical and biological work. On the formation of DTRC liaison with Human Variation Unit was established. Progress in the human genetic research in India was just beginning. In 1960s when Central Family Planning Institute (now National Institute of Health and Family Welfare) was established, the Population Genetics and Human Development Division formed its important part. The objectives of this Division were : to compile and interpret available information on the genetics constitution and inherited characteristics of human populations, the changes and trends which might occur in these characteristics under different conditions and effects of such changes on human adaptation and development ; to identify meaningful research problems in this field in India, especially as might be related to the possible genetic effects on differential fertility and family planning programmes ; to help to stimulate, coordinate and assist in the development of studies on these problems in various institutions and also carry out directly such studies ; to help in strengthening teaching in this field in various institutions, and provide consultative services ; and to maintain close contact, for the above purpose, with other research institutions concerned with human population genetics studies. It was envisaged that over time a relatively fuller picture on the genetic constitution and inherited characteristics of human populations groups of India would be made available, a centre would be developed at the Institute where all genetic abnormalities could be reported like Indian Tumour Registry, the cytogenitic laboratories in selected centres will be established throughout the country, genetical counselling services would form a part of family planning programme and gradually human population genetics, medical genetics and cytogenetics would become a part of general health services as universally as maternal and child health. The Division had two great advantages, despite its being a small Division of the Institute—it was headed by a very experienced and capable cytogeneticist Somnath Roy and for a short period had the benefit of advice of Professor F.A.E. Crew a doyen amongst world geneticist who worked as WHO consultant at the institute.

Training Local Leaders

Appreciation of the need for peoples participation in population and development, emphasised the need for their training and orientation. The mechanism evolved was formation of village health committee and training of the member of this committee.

The earliest formation of such a committee, was in the experimental health unit established at Singur (in 1939) by the All India Institute of Hygiene and Public Health Calcutta, to foster community organisation and initiative in the solution of health problems and self-help. Each village Health Committee covered a population of about 1000. The Committee consisted of five members from the community, duly elected by the villagers. The sanitary inspector served as secretary. Each of the five members volunteered for one of the five specific health activities, *viz.*, maternal and child health, environmental sanitation, vital statistics, control of communicable diseases, and control of malaria. Each was trained to perform his specific function, supervised and guided by the health professionals at the Singur Rural Health Centre. The work of village Health Committees was co-ordinated by the Union Health Advisory Committee and Parent-Teacher Association at the Union level. The Rural Medical Officer of Health was Secretary of the Co-ordinating Committee.[142] Many years after, R.N. Basu in Singur and others in different places in India developed strategies for community participation in family planning programme and developed education/orientation/training programmes for the members of the community. The Singur model was modified to suit different local situations. The number of activities had changed. Further knowledge on methods of selection of members has been gained. The structures and functions of the Committee may change. But one aspect should remain unchanged, *i.e.* : specifying training objectives and tasks and training of each member of the village committee for a specific task well, and for reasonable duration, so that they can perform the tasks (for which they volunteer) efficiently. Collecting the a large group and giving them one or two days' orientation is wasteful.

Health and family planning committees were formed is some places. Their training however, did not generally take the form as originally envisaged.

At later stages, orientation camps were introduced. Guidelines for such camps were prepared, tested and circulated to all concerned. The weaknesses in some camps were observed to be mainly due to insufficient training, personal guidance and supervision of workers conducting the camp. Where trained workers were available, it was found that people themselves were able to plan and arrange camps very well and such orientation camps were very successful. A general trend was that programme personnel arranged the camps with very little involvement of people. The number of orientation camps of varied quality considerably increased over-time. The actual time available for free discussion and development of skills to form voluntary groups in villages appear to have been reduced and the emphasis on achieving "targets" further seemed to have reduced the desired impact. The periodical re-assessment of orientation camps, and of the duration and the methodology used therefore, seems necessary.

Another dimension is of training of community leaders in the broader field of population and development which will require greater attention than at present. Self help and self-management require management and administrative skills, knowledge of rudiments of planning ; techniques of community organisation ; skills in organising community groups ; information on resources available from programme already launched by the Government which have relevance to their problems, co-operative efforts which are feasible, even ways to negotiate with bureaucracy. This means the people, especially their leaders, need training.

The major element of the strategy should be training of People by People. A reappraisal of plans and methods to train members of the community is essential to avoid weaknesses such as those noted in the orientation camps and to strengthen training by the use of new technology. In respect of the latter, National and International experience and assistance will be valuable.

In the country, the Self-Employed Women's Association (Video SEWA) is a notable example. SEWA "is a trade union of some 24,000 poor, self-employed women in Ahmedabad. The organisation provides its members with skills, training, cooperative mechanism to aid in production and marketing, child care and health benefits SEWA also advocates women's rights before the authorities and operates a cooperative bank. By combining struggle and development, SEWA enables its members to protect their interests and to gain their rightful place in the economy". Ela Bhatt is General Secretary of SEWA.

The Video Cooperative of SEWA has demonstrated that modern technology can not only be applied at local level in villages and slums but is also more effective than centralised communication training. It can be adapted to suit the local language, dialect. culture. environment and development problems, and cross the illiteracy barrier. The Video SEWA was formed by the participants of a three-week workshop, in which the participants prepared their own video programmes. The interesting feature is that "one third of participants were illiterate and another third had less than high school education". One of them Leelaben Datania, an illiterate vegetable seller for generations, was able to produce instructive video tapes. Video SEWA tapes are used as one of the training tools during training sessions of SEWA members. They include several programmes including health. The Coordinator of Video SEWA, Jhoti Jumani "has helped to train women in Thailand and Guyana"

At International level the help of Village Video Network New York has been fruitful. The members of the Village Video network, founded in 1981, include family planning workers in the Caribbeans, literacy teachers in Mali and scientists and farmers in China. The Village Video Network "provides technical assistance, facilitates exchange and works in partnership with local governmental and non-governmental organisations to plan, fund equip and train local development video teams".[143]

11

Communication System

In 1950s, action was initiated in three major directions, *viz.* :

(*i*) investigations on knowledge of community attitudes, beliefs and behaviour patterns relating to family size and encouragement of adoption of the techniques of cultural anthropology and social science research ;

(*ii*) development of information, and education and communication material on family planning ; and

(*iii*) testing of material so developed by their actual use for their effectiveness measured by suitable ad-hoc research techniques.

The United Nations—Government of India study in Mysore State and Ramanagaram study related to rhythm method had provided useful information. But it related to Mysore. An attempt was made to collect information from rest of the country to varying extent.

The education programme was mainly based on the experience in the fields of health, community development, the paper prepared by Margaret Snyder on 'Education for Family Planning', and recommendations of the Family Planning Research and Programme Committee in July 1953.

Margaret Snyder had suggested anthropological studies within limited geographical areas and extensive opinion research covering an area of two or three districts with a population of 5 or 6 million.

In 1954, on the recommendations of the Family Planning Research and Programme Committee, an expert Committee on Socio-economic and Cultural/demographic studies was formed with V.K.R.V. Rao, as convener and P.C. Mahalonobis (Statistician) Gadgil (Economist) B.S. Guha (anthropologist), K.C.K.E. Raja (Health expert), L.D. Sangvi (expert in genetics), and M.V. Govindaswami (psychiatrest). Later, the Demographic Advisory Committee and Communication Action Research Commitees were formed ; still later, both were combined into one committee. The research initiated by the advisory committees provided some leads to the development of the programme and greater understanding of the population issues.

Focus on Media

In 1950s major focus was on mass communication. The content of the message generally was : the family planning will contribute to health and happiness of the family. Hoardings on railway station, buses and other places and other mass media were used. The debate on investment in mass and individual/group communication began at later stage. This was highlighted in the proposals on Health Education for the Third Five Year Plan by the Central Health Education Bureau New Delhi and the discussions at the Family Planning Education Seminar in March, 1960.

Personal Contact

The 1960 seminar emphasised that not more than 25 per cent of the total expenditure on family planning education should be allocated to mass communication. In support of this suggestion observations of an international expert (Derryberry) and the Vice President of a large New York Advertising Agency were cited. Derryberry had stated that, "the most extensive use possible was made of all known information media, including news articles, bill boards, radio, exhibition, pamphlets, motion pictures, etc., in an effort to induce people to buy bonds, not only for financing the war but also for curbing inflation. When the final tubulation was made, it was found that over 80 per cent of individual purchases were made on personal solicitation, which shows the need for intimate and personal contact in order to induce action in a large proportion of the population". The Vice-President of the advertising agency in his article on "How to interest People in Things they do not want to know" stated : "Our mass media or so-called major media of communication are relatively minor media, when it comes to moving serious ideas into the heads of the people. They have, I believe, only a secondary role in helping you with your problems, and it is important that you do not divert too much of your limited resources, chasing after these media. They are not the first or second or even third media you should think of, in efforts really to reach people and to teach them serious things for their own good.[144] V. Ramakrishna, the first Director of the Central Health Education Bureau, besides impressing on family planning programme managers that the posters, pamphlets, hoardings, exhibition radio broad casts, etc., were channels of information and had their value in the family planning programme, they could not bring about changes in attitudes and family planning practice. He underlined the importance of individual and group contacts and team work. In support of the latter, he circulated views on the dynamics of planning in health education of his mentor Dorthy B. Nyswander. Nyswander at the Health Education workshop at Asilomar in 1955 had said : "we bring structure to life through 'team work'... —'all must share in planning' : We must communicate". She underlined two empirically derived steps. The first in that our contribution to planning have their roots, deeply imbedded, in a philosophy of democracy. It is a philosophy which implies that leadership is not a prerogative of status or power personages, but the leadership is a shared responsibility of all members of a particular group......The second assumption is that each life situation with problems whose solution involve planning, has its specific degree of freedom within which planning must be done. Democracy in practice is an orderly process : a process in which responsibility and authority are given to agencies and persons. But in each agency in each differing situation within an agency, there are degrees of freedom of action specific to the situation".[145] Observations of both experienced young researchers and not so young further contributed to giving more emphasis to face to face and group communication.[146] Communications research in family planning was in a formative period. K.G. Krishnamurthy, a young and vibrant sociologist, amongst some others, was critical of research designs aad conceptual tools of several studies in the country and attempted to impress that their findings had serious limitations for policy formulation.[147]

Potential of Mass Media

Mass communication enthusiasts were anxious to demonstrate the potentialities of mass media which had remained unexplored. Lajpat Rai Nayyar, the Director of Audio Visual Publicity in the Ministry of Information and Broadcasting, with assistance of his consultant and team, launched a two month multimedia publicity Campaign in Chandernagore, Chinsurah and Serampore in Hoogly District West Bengal and demonstrated effects of the publicity campaign.[148] The in-puts in mass communication increased in 1960s. But the declared major emphasis was given to individual and group communication.

Mass communication is readily seen and heard. Support to it came from many quarters both in India and abroad. Donald J. Bogue was prominent among the promoters of mass communication. Bogue, first appeared on the Indian scene as United Nations expert at the Demographic Training and Research Centre Bombay in September 1958—July 1960, subsequently paid several visits to India. One of the successful ways to promote a specific approach in different countries has been to introduce the subject for discussion at international, regional and national conference/seminars/workshops and circulate a prestigious document. The same method was used in case of mass communication. "The bold new strategy on Mass Communication" was highlighted at Regional Conference in Singapore sponsored by the United Nations Economics Commission for Asia and Far East in 1967, and similar concepts at a conference in Bangkok arranged by the university of North Carolina and USAID in 1968, and at the Eleventh World Conference of Society for International Development in New Delhi 1969. A paper entitled 'Towards a Master Plan for Family Planning Communication' presented by Donald J. Bogue (Professor of Sociology and Director, Community and Family Study Centre University of Chicago) and S. Bert Johnson (Chief, Field Support Division Office of Population, Bureau of Technical Assistance, USAID) at the World Conference of the Society for International Development in November, 1969, became an important impetus for developing communication strategies in India. Bogue and Johnson in this paper, in respect of the content of messages, hypothesized that : "before any couple will adopt family planning six psychological conditions must have been established : (*i*) *Information.* Knowledge of methods and how to use them must be possessed. (*ii*) *Motivation.* A sense of need for benefits confered by family planning must be created. (*iii*) *Credibility.* The information and motivation must be trusted or believed. (*iv*) *Legitimization.* The practice of family planning must be felt to be socially acceptable, at least in the eyes of some respected social reference group. (*v*) *Positive attitude.* The overall reaction to at least one available and reliable method and its use should be one of approval. (*vi*) *Self referal.* A sense of urgency that action needs to be taken on the problem of family size, of apprehension that delay might be mistake should be felt". They further added that "we fail to see any reason why mass communication cannot be used in massive way to promote all six of these conditions".[149] Their hypothesis is a valuable framework for an effective communication strategy. Persons responsible for communication programmes in India at the time appear to have given policy support to it. But at the level of implementation, we generally find a different picture. Mass media started to be viewed as mover rather than facilitator and health education and extension education was given a back seat. In practice, the inter-personal communication" was vertually drowned in "the mass-media sea".

Red Triangle

The Chief of Media, D.K. Tyagi was given a place in the Secretariate (Wing of the Family Planning Department (not under Commissioner Family Planning). Ford Foundation consultant Frank Wilder joined him. Both developed, what they called 'India's New Departure in Mass Communication'.[150] This 'New Departure' had one very visible programme—an unstructured symbol, the inverted Red Triangle and a stylised picture of four smiling faces (a man, a woman, a male child a female child), with a solgan 'two or three that is enough' (*Do Ya Teen Bache Bus*). A man and woman and two children within a triangle had been used earlier in Meerut District Study of the Central Family Planning Institute. Tyagi, with his tremendous drive, saturated the whole country on a massive scale, from villages to towns, with paintings of the Red Triangle and the stylised picture of four faces with the slogan. The inverted Red Triangle caught the imagination of people both in India and outside (several publications both in and outside India use Red Triangle). It became identified with family planning.

Tyagi was quite a unique person, with very strong commitment to "the Red Triangle". When an un-employed elephant keeper met him, he formed a small group, raised money from membership of this group, designed a badge with elephant and Red Triangle to be worn by members. With financial support of this private group, the elephant decked with Red Triangle moved from place to place distributing flyers and condoms. Tyagi died young. His death wish was to shower paper Red Triangles on his body and his funeral march should be accompanied by his favourite song on family planning written by a popular Indian song writer and recorded on tape by an equally popular singer. Both his wishes were carried out, amidst moist eyes of both his ardent supporters and also those who did not wholly agree with him.

The strategy of intensive and extensive use of a simple

symbol (inverted Red Triangle), easily reproducable and recognisable was an outstanding success in creating awareness of family planning throughout the country including places where other media could not reach. There is, however, no firm evidence that such a strategy alone contributed to bringing about change in attitudes, or removed doubts, combated rumours and dissonance that emerge in programmes, or in changing traditional norms. There are reasons to believe that in some cases the Red Triangle motivated people to seek advice on family planning, for example the Health Education Bureau, Lucknow, in a study in 1978 found that some persons after seeing the wall-painting visited the family planning clinic ; of these two volunteered for sterilization and the remaining received supplies of conventional contraceptives.

Expanded Information Programme

The Meerut District Project had given insights into the power and limitations of, and methods to, achieve optimum results from mass media within a communication programme. Knowledgeable media specialists laid emphasis on communication systems rather than just on media. Proposals for an 'Expanded Information Programme in Family Planning' was prepared in November 1963. They were related to accomplish two tasks, *viz.*, organisation of a programme by which teaching aids, of all types, can be produced for use in the training centres. A part of this job, envisaged was that the workers themselves could be taught to make and properly use these materials, and to make information about family planning available to the people in group meetings and personal contact. Content of messages obviously required considerable attention. This required guidance and active involvement of people and group of experts in a number of disciplines including health, population, social sciences. These activities were proposed to be centered at the Central Family Planning Institute. Appreciable progress had been made at the Institute in developing these activities, in the following years.

Family Planning Department Media Office

Soon after the establishment of the Family Planning

Department, these activities were transferred to the Chief of Media in the Department and activities of the Institute in this field were considerably pruned. This was presumably based on the view that the Institute was giving greater importance to individual, interpersonal and group communication than to mass communication and desired results could be achieved most expeditiously instead by expanded role of Media office. Many other activities in the field of communication of the Central Family Planning Institute were curtailed. For example the financial resources for production of *Family Planning News*, nurtured and ably edited by Brajesh Bhatia, were stopped. *The Family Planning News* was published on behalf of the Ministry by the institute "to keep field workers informed of the plan, activities and progress in family planning programme in different parts of the country, to educate public opinion in matters of family planning to disseminate correct information which will contribute towards better understanding of the family planning movement and other associated issues, and "feed back from the field". The favourable response from readers had led the Institute to prepare plans for increasing its distribution and publish supplementary reports. At this stage, publication of *Family Planning News* ceased. The Family Planning Department started the publication *Centre Calling*, It has its merits, but no where near the role of *Family Planning News*. *Swasth Hind* of Central Health Education Bureau partly provided the information needed, but to a limited extent. The major void was filled by the publications of Family Planning Association of India especially *The Journal of Family Welfare and Planned Parenthood Bulletin*. Some even now consider that revival of *Family Planning News* will enrich the communication programme.

The vital functions of developing communication systems and other associated activities such as press liaison, internal news letters and reports, technical bulletins, audio-visual material production, briefings for conferences and speeches and professional inter-agency communication became major responsibilities of the Media Office. The Family Planning Department also assumed responsibility for printing, graphics facilities, photography, writing, mass mailing and other activities. There was a major shift from inter-personnel communication to mass media. The declared policy support to health education and extension education continued, but not in practice.

Mass media specialists were appointed as the heads of information, education and communication cells in the State Family Planning Bureaus. They were not generally equipped with the knowledge to develop effective communication system. There was a great deal of emphasis on "vibrating multi-media strategy". But such a strategy requires a sound behavioural science base. Surprisingly the communication-action-research advisory committee was also discontinued. Awareness increased but behavioural change lagged behind. In 1987 V.K. Kakkar, former Chief Media Family Welfare Department discussed communication strategy and programme in India. Some of his observations may be debatable and other valuable. They may provide same insight on past activities as seen by a mass media specialist.

Focus of Communication Programme in 1980s

In 1980s communication programme appears to take a more balanced view of mass communication and extension education but this change seems to be still in its formative stage. From the National Workshop on Communication in Health and Family Welfare in August 1981, it seems that over emphasis on Mass Communication continues. The involvement and advice of social scientists, extension specialists and non-government communication experts were not saught by many State Media Heads. There are some encouraging reports Media committees at District level, are reported to meet regularly and decide on programmes based on socio-cultural factors, local needs and resources. Linkages between mass communication and extension education are increasing. The health education and communication programmes are reported to work together.[151] Suggestions have been made to merge health education and media cells at the State and District levels and also revive communication-action-research centres in the country. There are some indications that infra-structure for information, education and communication, will be restructured and strengthened. The policy makers "are increasingly turning towards social scientists and workers and providing them all possible financial and other support to come forward with practical, feasible and effective communication strategies". The 10th Joint Conference of the Central Council of Health and Family Welfare recommended that "appropriate operational research in all aspects of the family welfare programme...and continuous and close contacts be promoted among researchers, programme planners and implementers".

The implications of the expression 'communication" really is that there is interaction between two groups, interchange and sharing of thaughts, opinion and discussion between them. Such interaction is conducive to changing attitudes and practices, especially what are called the hard core. The expression "communication" in the above context is now delineated as personal communication or inter-personal communication, Another facet of communication system is mass communication, which is also called public education. The mass communication is a one-way process, in which the communicator transmits a message or messages through a media or package of media, the receiver of the messages has no part in the process except receiving information and getting aware of the issue contained in the messages.

The family planning programme managers appear to have been trying to find the answer to the question : What should be the proper mix of inter-personal communication and mass communication ? Swings in the favour of the one or the other are noted over the years. In 1950s the main inputs were on mass communication. In the 1960s primacy was given to inter-personal communication. In late 1969 and 1970s media ruled supreme. Around 1980s the importance of inter-personal communication re-emerged. This seems to be due to not fully appreciating that both have their values and place in the communication system and not fully making use of research.

Mass communication, is a powerful 'facilitator' in communication process. The roles of each should be recognised and the anomalies that occur removed, and results of research finding used fully. The findings of a collaborative study on Evaluation of Media Reach and effectiveness in family planning programme 1983 have drawn attention to strengths and weaknesses in communication programme and the need for action along a broad spectrum including planning, management, training, implementation and evaluation. The study revealed that inter-personal communication was used to create general awareness, a task of mass media, Home visits and group meetings did not cover the whole community and 'the contacts were of the touch and go type'. Folk media had a very high acceptability, but the community exposure to them was limited, between 8 per cent and 15 per cent. Family planning reach of the radio was very high. The messages heard on the radio were discussed with others both in rural areas and urban deprived areas, more in the former. The major content of the message was on need and importance of family planning (76 per cent) and problem of over population (57 per cent). More males than females were reached by the radio. The diversification of messages are obviously needed especially to remove doubts, to counteract rumours, to disseminate successful stories related by persons with public credibility and to take care of what Wilbur Schramm calls 'the dissonance over having abondoned old norms'. Television reach in rural areas was found to be meagre. But among those who watched television reach of family planning programme was high and, unlike radio female reach was higher than male. The messages on immunisation and age at marriage conveyed on television recently are impressive.

The Satellite Instructional Television Experiment (SITE) in 1975-76 showed that "awareness, knowledge and adoption of new agricultural practices was higher in experimental villages and television viewers than non-experimental villages and non-viewers in four villages in Bihar besides gain in knowledge of improved agricultural and other practices, the television programme incalculated modern values in its viewers. There was a significant gain in knowledge of new extension workers and farmers through farm telecast training.[162] Television was found to be 'an important source of information for rural females' and 'substantial proportion of viewers of both sexes belonged to the low socio-economic category. At the sametime, higher socio-economic status was found negatively related to television viewing'. With recent extension of television coverage in the country and developments in video-films these media can be brought nearer to the people. Diagnostic studies and research are always required even for simple activities such as the content of the messages for different groups, the manner and the channels for conveying the message, the timing and frequency of message, the response of the people to the messages.

Research and training in communication are essential for development of effective health and family planning communication system. While in the begining it may be necessary for a National Institute to prepare prototype material and other aids, based on studies in the field, to be adapted by the States to suit their immediate requirements. The training research and development in communication should become responsibilities of the institutions developed in the States. The National Institute should be a catalytic agent, the National clearing house of information, stimulating innovative activities, supporting enrichment of knowlege, full harnessing of tools now available and developing new skills. The communication strategy (with adaptations and reinforcements) of 1960s needs revival.

This underlines the value of the communication research and a National Expert Committee to guide it.

Messages can be designed with assistance of social scientists, based on local situations. Local people in their own environment can participate in the video-films, such films shown in their own community. Success stories with local cast can be shown in neighbouring community. Visual aids and where ever possible audio visual aids should be an essential part of inter-personal communication. There are numerous ways of using such a media with great effect.

Other Dimensions and Issues

The complexity of factors involved in social change require consideration of various other factors, exchange of information and research. It has been observed that one of the hinderances for development programmes becoming people's programme is that the people view it as Government responsibility. Uma Narula has studied the development communication problem in rural and urban-slum communities. She observes that 'there is a lack of co-ordination between three agents of development, *viz.*, planners, change agents and the masses. This lack of coordination has resulted in such consequences as (1) discontent and perceived helplessness ; (2) learned dependency and neo-fatalism ; ethics of proportional efforts ; and (3) the counter-productive effect." The syndrome of 'learned dependency' described by Narula is 'not only as the absence of development motivation but a cluster of beliefs and attitudes and folkways which are undesirable alternatives to it'. Traditionally dependent on local social heirarchy and on fate they (people) have transferred that dependency to Government as a very appropriate response to multiple messages which Government gave ; that they were ready to take responsibility for everything ranging from economics, to birth control' Fatalism was replaced by Neo-fatalism' in which people were not content but had learned to depend upon Government to make things better'. 'It seems that the feed back from the masses have also serious weaknesses. "The masses are not at all sure that they have been heard, and if heard understood ; and if understood taken seriously, and if taken seriously become the cause of Government action. The most frequent responses to their feedback are disclaimers from the change agents (who say they have passed the message through proper channels and do not know what is happening to it now)." It is also observed that "with high level of awareness and information, people are ready to accept and participate in development, but their participation is ignored by the development functionaries". Uma

Narula has suggested Development—Dialogue—Action Strategy to counteract the low development motivation among the people. 'The assumption is that such a strategy can focus on self-participation, self-reliance and self-management of the socio-economic facilities provided by the Government. The strategy suggests the active involvement of both the development functionaries and the community as a whole (not just the group leaders) in a mutual search for a solution. A methodology for such a strategy has also been suggested.[163] Testing the methodology suggested in an action research project could be very fruitful.

Communication research in the country has played important roles in the field of agriculture and family planning. The contribution of such research has been significant. There are, however, critics as in any programme. The criticism of some aspects may be justified, of some others highly exaggerated and of many others without any real basis. The inadequacies of many studies in the early phases of the programme, referred in the first review of Indian studies by K.G. Krishnamurthy are generally accepted. The comments of Lakshman Rao and Lim generally appear valid that "our attitude to information exchange seems to be a selfish, one sided affair in which we extract that we can from the system without considering the necessity of putting back into the system what information we can contribute".[164] Likewise some observations of B.R. Patil in his very provocative statement on 'Community and Communication' are thought-provoking such as : "communication scholars have chosen research areas and topics which are 'in things', fashionable, and catchy which ensured some pages in magazines, tables in conferences, trips to foreign countries or just some lines added to our curriculum vitae.[165] This may be a generalization, but such an approach is discernible not only among communication scholars but also in other fields.

The observations sometime made, that sufficient attention was not paid to communication programmes and studies have been useless, are gross exaggeration. The available knowledge at that time was harnessed and major attention was given to training programmes in and outside India. In the meantime, research activities were encouraged in institutions where experienced persons were available. As trained manpower increased it was possible to establish communication research centres in different parts of the country ; and both the number and quality of research improved. Nation-wide surveys are time consuming and if not well planned and well conducted lead to wrong conclusions. The emphasis was, therefore, laid on small diagnostic studies. Some of them provided valuable leads. In the 1960s in the reorganised programme, resource inputs into communication infrastructure increased and seem to have remained at that level, though not fully used because of the change to media bias.

Early in 1960s, a 15 year perspective plan including communication programme and research was prepared. It was re-emphasised in this plan that the aim should be to "educate people at all levels and create among them a consensus to understand the problem of population growth and effect its solution, through *community action*". The 15 year perspective plan among other issues discussed : details of programme needs, training (both in mass and community education), infrastructure, supervision and guidance, preparation of training staff, provision of equipment, supplies and facilities, mass education and extension education and their mix, diagnostic studies to resolve specific problems, appraisal concurrent and periodical, and communication research. Some of the basic assumptions in the proposed programme were : efficient use of high calibre professional talent that is in limited supply, through a central servicing and coordinating mechanism ; assistance in by-passing local bureaucratic hurdles ; measures to facilitate cross fertilization of ideas and exchange of experience ; efficient use of the administrative flexibility and highly co-operative atmosphere ; recognition of the need for research centres manned with highly skilled researchers ; strengthening agencies and institutions that will have to carry on research and development of a pool of personnel with training and experience for conducting and promoting research ; creation of environment conducive to conducting and promotion of research and establishment of institutional ties at the coordinating and outlaying centres.

The conducive environment for research is essential for recruiting and retaining a high level and competent staff. The conducive environment implies a climate to develop new ideas, free exchange of ideas, freedom from dampening effects of the hierarchy of cadres. The appropriate conditions of service, pay, allowances, fellowship grants and other facilities should be such as to attract the best talent in the country.

Applied research to solve problems faced in the programme and those directed towards social and economic development needs priority, at the same time there is need for inputs in basic research (about 20 per cent). The action-research strategy is directed at evolving the most effective communication system. It must be also realised that much of what is already known has not been applied by skilled educators under conditions of maximum flexibility and that this itself can be very significant learning research experience. Needs for immediate results are great but at the sametime the foundations can be laid for reaping future gains from longer-term research ; that acceptance of a change by individuals is a product of sequence of events and influence operating through time.

Information Services

In the field of population, a greatly needed and valuable development has been POPLINE. It is a computerized literature service, offers bibliographic citations and abstracts covering all aspects of family planning and population. POPLINE is produced by the Population Information Program of the John Hopkins University Baltimore, Maryland, the Library/Information Program of the Centre for Population and Family Health Columbia University, New York, and Population Index of Princeton University, in cooperation with the US National Library of Medicine, and with financial support from the US Agency for International Development.

In Asia and Pacific, this service is now available from United Nation Economic and Social Commission for Asia and

Pacific Bangkok Thailand. Such services are being further extended through centres in different countries. In India National Institute of Health and Family Welfare New Delhi has developed a documentation centre.

Other facilities for providing information are available such as *Population and Development Review* and *Studies in Family Planning* published by the Population Council New York ; *Population Reports* by Population Information programme the John Hopkins University Baltimore ; *International Family Planning Perspective* by The Alan Guttmacher Institute New York. In India, News letters issued by Population Studies Centres ; *Demography India* published by Indian Association for Study of Population. *The Journal of Family Welfare* by the Family Planning Association of India Bombay and *Health and Population Perspective and Issues* by the National Institute of Health and Family Welfare New Delhi are notable sources of information. Among the Indian publications, the recent publication *Population Research Abstract* by the Applied Population Research Trust ("the brain-child" of C. Chandrasekaran Banglore the first issue 1990 June) is a valuable source of information. The pace of development in communication technology has accelerated in recent years. The span of communication has enlarged. Not very long back discussion on communication was mainly on interpersonnel communication and mass communication. At present to these sub-groups a number of others have joined, such as tele-communication (telephones, telex, facsimile) ; organizational communication (within the organisation and outside like electronic mail and teleconferencing), computer-mediated communication (such as total automated system in institutes ; Local Area Network, Inter-city communication through Wide Area Network, storage and movement (short and long distances of computerised information) ; Development communication.

Modern Technology

Use of modern technology is now appearing to a varying extent in the developming countries such as satellite transmission of television, data base management system, computers with versatile capabilities, personal computer with desk-top publishing, portable videotapes, the Cable, VCRs and so on. Remarkable developments have taken place in increasing the capacity of storage of information, its conductivity and reach. Its power in various areas is often underlined such as impact on changing social organization and even toppling governments. "The communication horizon for the 1900s is a dizzying mixture of marvels and menaces, of exponential growth in power and reach, yet also of concentration, both institutionally and geographically".[166] India entered the space age in 1967, when the Indian Space Research Organisation was established. In August 1975, Satellite Instructional Television Experiment (SITE) was launched. Since notable developments have taken place. The INSAT I-B launched in 1983 provided increase in communication facilities. The modernisation and expansion of communication are being stepped-up to meet the needs of various sectors of social and economic development such as education, health, family planning, agricultural and rural development, industry, transport. A noteable development has been in the linking of foremost research centres and universities in India through Biotechnology Information System Network (BTISNET). The Government of India established nodal agencies under various departments. One of them is CMC Limited, as public sector enterprise. Information technology is applied to core sectors like agriculture, rural development, health, education and industries. Besides BTISNET, there are communications and networking such as INDONET, India's first national commercial computer network commissioned by CMC INDONET in 1986 ; NICNET, an extensive network of computers and interactive terminals in Delhi, regional centres, State capitals and district headquarters set up by National Information centre ; CALIBNET, a network of 35 science and technology libraries in Calcutta. The application of information technology is extending, *e.g.*, Indian Institute of Science is installing an intercampus Local Area Network.[167]

Some Simple Facts to Remember

In this bewildering world of communication some simple factors in family planning communication strategy (in fact in all communication strategies at grass roots) should not be overlooked like : we are concerned with people. "Computer linkages would be stultifying, if they were not anchored in a process of face-to-face contact".[158] among people there are groups with different needs, different resources, different social and economic conditions and perceptions, speaking different languages and dialects, the messages should suit each group ; within each group there are priority sub-groups for special attention like adolescents, newly-wed*, low parity women and their husbands ; exploration and promotion of existing informal traditional communication network,** popular theatre ; paying attention to details like timing of message on television or radio for different priority sub-groups, *e.g.*, the efforts will be infructuous if the messages are relayed at a time they are normally otherwise busy ; utilization of research and experience and appreciation of the fact that changes do not take place in the whole population at the sametime, the change follows descernible pathways.

During the last few decades, the expression "information revolution" is frequently heard. Is it a reality or a myth ? In India, it appears to be both. The brief mention above of some developments in communication systems in India shows that a high level of communication technology is available in India and communication net-work has reach to remotest parts of the country. At the sametime, it appears that the available technologies are awaiting full utilization. In the vast rural areas of the country, the modern communication technology does not seem to have made full impact. The ubiquitous

*"In China, a manual and sex guide for the newly wed is made available to young married couples and gives advice and guidance on sexual behaviour, family life and the prevention of sex-related diseases. Young girls and boys in some Chinese schools are invited to sign a pledge to postpone marriage until age 25". The family planning information to newly-wed is given in other countries also such as Indonesea, Mexico, the Philippines, and number of localities in the USA.[159]

**Ashish Bose had drawn attention to the information received by millions of people about the precise day and time of bathing in *Kumbh melas*.

media is the radio. The radio-network is not always of local interest. The development communication suited to the needs and interests of the rural 'population has still not been completely developed. Centrally designed, stereotype programmes for the rural areas are not unusual.

The reasons for not fully utilizing the modern technology may be : lack of resources ; high cost of technology ; limited number of trained personnel ; unwillingness of those trained to work in or near villages; weaknesses in communication policy and/or structure or both ; lingering urban and elite orientation, etc. There appears to be greater interest in information relating to politics, foreign affairs, sports than on development communication.

Mann V. Sichalwe, Director Zambia Institute of Mass Communication, commented on some of these aspects. His comments are applicable (to varying extent) to most developing countries, including India. He said : "Since dominant media in most of our countries is largely meant for the elite, the media practitioners have to make sure they serve needs and aspirations of this 20 per cent......It is, therefore, understandable why the journalist and the management continue to publish or broadcast less material on the rural areas where 80 per cent of the population live. They are only serving the interests of their audience, who are not 80 per cent of population......Rural broadcasts are not listened to by many, because they cannot afford the receivers. The educated elite do not enjoy listening to or reading rural material. It bores them and is seen as just the unfortunate side of the society which we cannot do much about at the moment. Rural affairs only make news when a Minister visits the area, makes a speech about it or something dramatic happens, or when a foreign donor makes a grant and establishes a project". On the rural reporter Sichalwe observed, "The rural reporter knows that he is covering an area which the audience does not care much about. It is not interested. It also means rough travelling in areas where roads may not be tarred, with no hotels or modern bars. In some areas, drinking water is even dangerous. The rural reporter also knows that the people whom he interviews in the rural areas hardly have a chance to read, see or hear their interview. They are not the audience for whom the story or programme is being produced. Back at the offices in the city, the rural reporter meets other reporters who speak very highly about the interesting political stories they are working on. They are admired by city public and the reporter is respected. But working on rural development is not so exciting and is rougher than working in the cities. Working among the 20 per cent of the population gives the reporter more national limelight and exposure than working with the majority".[160]

It will be obvious that some priority areas for serious consideration are : examination in detail communication policy and structure ; re-education of media personnel for development communication ; removal of barriers to effective development communication especially flexibility and freedom of action of communication staff and organisation including upgrading working conditions to attract and retain competent persons ; decentralization of production to suit the local needs and interests.

It has been well established that as the programme production gets nearer to the consumer, its acceptibility and effectiveness increases. Innovative low-cost participatory programmes have been developed with production unit close to the village, even with employment of illiterate persons. Maria Perugacki a farm broadcaster in Otavallo Equador is a very good example. "She's a Quecha Indian. She can't read or write but understands and speaks Spanish. She receives information (*from Farm Radio Network*) (like how to keep weevils out of grain with wood-ash) recorded in Sapanish on a cassette. She listens to the casette and stores up the information in her mind. Every single morning, this illiterate woman farm broadcaster speaks on the radio to 100,000 Quechua Indians living on the slopes of the Andes. She is passing along information that comes from farmers, with similar problems, perhaps on the other side of the world".[161]

The experience of Farm Radio Network can be used with advantage for health, nutrition and family planning programme. The family planning communication programme integrated with development and environmental communication programme will be rewarding.

The processes of behavioural changes in a population should always be kept in mind. The sequence of change may not necessarily always be the same. But it should be expected that "there are segments of the population that are already practicing family planning, others that are ready for it, still others are beginning to get interested. An entire society does not adopt a social change at the same time ordinarily the change moves from convinced group to ready group to a potentially interested group. As acceptance grows members from ane group move upto the next group, so that ultimately the barriers of disinterest and hostility begin to fade, and some of those people join the potentially interested. It is more helpful to think mass media as facilitators than movers. They are most useful in multiplying and directing the flow of information that would go on any way, and to speed up the change that would probably in time even without them. They are not something apart from other communication and, therefore, we must take special pains to keep necessary related word of mouth communication flowing. Because they feed the appetite for change, we must take special pains to make available the material and services that are necessary for change. Because they foreshorten all the time scales of change, we must take special care in planning their use. But essentially they are not tools to knock down walls of opposition ; rather they are tools to build roads into and out of walled cities".[162]

12

Population Education

The preparation for one of the most important career-parenthood—in almost all societies does not seem to receive sufficient attention. The family and the school are considered responsible for it. Parents can play their expected role effectively, if they in their childhood and adolescence receive orientation in these fields. The basic attitudes towards important areas of life such as sex, parenthood and family life are formed long before they become parents. The cultural, moral and legal traditions regulate the conduct of members of society. They change over time, some become irrelevant and others are added. The social and scientific and technological changes weaken or strengthen the traditional controls. The conflicts between the old and new streams of thought focus attention on education in new fields like sex and family life.

Dr. A.P. Pillay pioneered the spread of sex education in India. He was editor-in-chief of the quarterly MARRIAGE HYGIENE, 'the only scientific journal (in 1934) in the world at that time devoted to advancing our knowledge of conjugal hygiene'.[163] The term sex education or conjugal hygiene was viewed in broad perspective. The journal was devoted to secure for conjugal hygiene in preventive medicine by setting forth its significance and interactions on personal, domestic, and social life and its importance for national welfare ; to publish scientific contributions treating marriage as social and biological institution especially the factors and forces influencing its welfare...and to promote, co-ordinate and unite the interests of contraceptive clinics and marriage hygiene consultation centres in various parts of the globe". The all inclusive scope is reflected in the subjects included in the Indian Population and Family Hygiene Conference Bombay 1938, planned by A.P. Pillay and his associates. The subjects included sex education, economic, sociological, anthropological, nutrition, maternal child welfare, health, birth control, health and statistical aspect of population, etc.

There was certain amount of vagueness, in the beginning, about the terms like sex education and family life education. Operational definition later led to some precision. The sex education was associated with sex hygiene especially prevention of sexually transmitted diseases and disorders interfering with sexual and reproductive functions. Its scope was subsequently extended to overcome false beliefs and other psychological factors which interfere in full enjoyment of sexual relationship in marriage and control of sexual and reproductive behaviour. The goals of family life education recognised were the fulfilment of those conditions which are necessary for welfare, harmony, happiness of the family from social, economic and cultural point of view. The conjugal relationship, family size, parental responsibility, preparation for marriage, house keeping, family needs, family living, maternal, parental and other family problems figured in it. The family planning programme managers at that time considered the population awareness, sex education and family life education as a single package mutually supporting and not necessarily exclusive.

In 1953, when the scope of family planning was officially defined, it included besides 'assistance enabling (the family) to regulate and space appropriately the bringing forth of children", also "advice and guidance to those who propose to unite their lives in marriage. Sex education both of parents and children in order to provide the background necessary for successful adjustment to many difficulties that sexual urge with all its demands may bring into being".

The above approach determined the initial action taken by the Governmental institutions. In 1957, Sushila Gore at the Family Planning Training and Research Centre Bombay besides population dynamics and family planning programme included dynamics of human behaviour, psycho-social development of the child, psycho-somatic problems of adolescence with special reference to sex, marriage, and family relationship.

In 1958 a School Health Education Division was established in the Central Health Education Bureau (CHEB). Promotion of Education in family life including sex education was one of the function. The overall aim of this division was to help in bringing about desirable change in health knowledge, attitudes and practice of the school population. This was proposed to be done through carrying out the following functions : (*i*) to interpret the importance of health programme in the schools and teachers training institutions and carry out general programme of planning ; (*ii*) to assist States in developing students Health Education Units in the State Health Education Bureau ; (*iii*) to promote and guide studies and research related to health education work in schools ; (*iv*) to plan and conduct training for school health personnel in positions in Central and State Governments and other agencies and institutions ; (*v*) to provide services to State educational institutions connected with the Central Ministry of Education, Central Health Schemes and other important to the development of school health programme ; and (*vi*) to prepare suitable material for students : teaching aides and guide books for teachers and collect material for reference.

In respect of population and family planning the CHEB worked in close collaboration with the family planning organisation in the Health Ministry and Central Family Planning Institute. Miss Kamla Sud in the CHEB prepared with meticulous care a syllabus on health education for age groups 6-11, 11-14 and 14-17 years and for teachers training colleges. One of the subjects in the sub-areas in each syllabus was family life education including sex education.

Mrs. Prakash in the CFPI started a pilot project in family life education. Sushila Gore in FPTRC Bombay carried out a survey of the age at menarche and problems associated with puberty among girls. About the sametime David Mace visited India and discussed the subject of family life education with officials and non-officials. At the All India Conference on Family early in 1957, he gave an account of marriage guidance programme in the West (marriage counselling and concilliation : specific preparation for marriage for couples on threshold of marriage : and general education for marriage in the home, schools and the community). The discussions with him gave reassurance that the all inclusive approach in the Indian programme was on sound basis. It seems that there were two prevalent attitudes regarding marriage guidance. "One : with so many enormous social and economic problems to be urgently faced, marriage guidance was irrelevant" ; and two : just beneath surface there were serious marital tensions which would soon break-through and (it was a matter of urgency to develop necessary services to cope with them)". The family planning programmes managers subscribed to the latter view and encouraged young investigators like Prema Bali in the All India Institute of Medical Sciences to pursue research on sex and family life to build the scientific basis for planning and develop programme on sex and family life education in India.

In 1960, a committee was appointed by the Ministry of Health and Family Planning to survey the existing situation of school health education programme in the country and make recommendations. In 1961, another committee with Secretary Health and Family Planning Mr. B.R. Tandon as Chairman recommended that Ministry of Education should prepare a note for starting a pilot project for (*i*) teachers training centres ; (*ii*) sex education in schools (which included population awareness and family planning programme in the country) and family life education in colleges.

In 1966, Ministry of Health and Family Planning had

requested Ministry of Education for involving universities and college teachers in the family planning programme. The Ministry of Education referred the request to the University Grants Commission (UGC). The UGC committee in 1967 made the following recommendations : "Well prepared charts indicating comparative population explosion which may appeal to the intellectual community may be sent to universities and colleges for exhibition ; well written monographs making a critical study of the population problem and its consequences may be sent to post secondary institutions. It was very desirable that this work should be done by skilled persons in an instructional way and not merely in a professional way ; selected persons with expert knowledge on population problems may go round the universities and give extension lectures which may be instructive and educative. Financial help may be provided to the universities for arranging such lectures ; academic conferences in the country may discuss topics related to population growth. In these conferences attractive exhibitions on family planning and welfare may be put up and experts in population problem invited to address such conference : there should be active collaboration between the Departments of Social Sciences in the universities and medical colleges to provide an idea of community service to students coming out of medical colleges. Medical graduates should not only know how to provide family planning services, but also an approach to the community in this regard ; social research fellowships, scholarships may be provided for research in this field either within the country or abroad ; the Ministry of Health may consider creating a few visiting fellowship for teachers for advance study and research in population problems at DTRC Bombay ; extension work and field service should be linked up with the research/doctorate programme in universities and financial assistance provided to research scholars for field and extension work ; financial assistance may be provided to university teachers with expert knowledge in the field for undertaking research work ; financial assistance may also be provided to experts in the field to organise seminars. It would be desirable to plan such seminars an year in advance so that some field service on the topics to be discussed could also be organised in the intervening period ; a joint committee of the Ministry of Health and Universities may be set up which may guide in the production of literature and also suggest topics for research in the field in universities ; and a bibliography of the material available for studies and research may be compiled". This was in addition to training in population sciences in universities and institutions.

The pace of development of these activities was slow. About mid-1960s a survey by the National Council of Educational Research and Training (NCERT) showed that of the 17 States in 16 States "population" was not mentioned in the syllabus ; some reference seemed to have been made in the teachers training schools and colleges. In some areas like Bombay the syllabus included human reproduction. The response to syllabus circulated by Kamla Sud of CHEB, teachers seemed to have reservations on discussing sex education. The Planning Forums, initiated and supported by the Planning Commission, varied in their opinion on including 'population' as one of the subjects for discussion. In places where there were demographic training and research centres like Delhi, Bombay and Madras the subject received relatively greater attention. Some members of staff from these centres were requested to hold lecture-discussions. The Regional Centre for Educational Planning sponsored by the UNESCO appeared to take interest in including 'population' in the carriculum. Ved Prakash, the Deputy Director of this centre at the World Population Conference in Belgrade in August-September 1965 stated, "if education is not to indulge in fence-trading on major issues of our times...there is no major reason why in some countries population control and family planning could not serve as major focus in adult education programme. Likewise curricular offering in secondary schools, colleges and teachers preparatory institutions offer much scope for improving the individual's understanding of the problem and making him aware of his personal and social obligations in meeting it".

While the programme on population awareness, family life and sex education was being developed in India, Sloan R.

Wayland, Consultant from Columbia University, visited the country. In May 1965, he submitted a paper entitled "Contribution of the Formal Education System to Family Planning Objectives in India". Wayland influenced the change in the definition of the term 'Population Education' and its scope. The major focus was laid on dynamics of population growth, and its influence on achievement of health, education and other National goals. The new approach steered clear of sex and family life education and focus was on size of the family and rate of growth of population in India. Among other suggestions of Wayland, two had long range impact *viz.* (*i*) formation of a special task force by the Ministry of Education in consultation with Ministry of Health to make rapid analysis of the basic ways whereby the formal education system could contribute to family planning programme, to suggest specific goals and procedures for the implementation of their conclusion and to maintain contact with the progress of implementation of such proposals ; and (*ii*) to hold a National Conference on Population Education involving persons from the Centre and States, specialists in demography, family planning, health education, economics, social scientists and representatives of the Planning Commission.

Before the NCERT took the major initiative in holding the National Conference, the Family Planning Association of India submitted a Memorandum to Maharashtra Government on population education and also provided a forum for first public discussion at their Sixth All India Conference held in Chandigarh in December, 1968, at a special seminar on Education for the Younger Generation. At the All India Conference, Avabai Wadia President FPAI, Edward W. Pohlman (CFPI and Carolina Population Centre) K. Seshgiri Rao (The Path Finder Fund), Prem Bali (AIIMS), Sarah Rao (FPTRC Bombay) Malika Ghosh and Baago among others made observations. Pohlman and Rao presented their interesting report on research on children, and parents view on "birth planning". The first such report in the country. The subject which led to major discussion was their views on population education. The approach advocated by them was: "School systems in rural areas of developing countries should develop ways to teach population education, but this is clearly and soundly divorced from sex education, family life education and contraception education". The argument in support of this approach was based on the assumption that parents, community, educational and governmental leaders would accept population education in such a restrictive sense and that any efforts to teach an all inclusive population education might be blocked : and that it was much easier to find or train group of teachers if 'sexless' education was emphasised. Pohlman underlined this argument by the statement : "music is wonderful, but the man entering a life boat to escape a sinking ship may miss the boat if he insists on taking his grand piano along". Prema Bali, Sarah Israel and Malika Ghosh strongly opposed such a view, Sarah Israel's observation based a ten years experience in secondary schools for girls showed that 92.3% of girls found training in reproductive physiology and family living helpful and 100 per cent teachers found training rewarding. Prema Bali's studies reinforced the feeling that family life education was essential. Similar view was expressed by Malika Ghosh who had worked for a long time with the Association for Moral and Social Hygiene. The approach of the Family Planning Association of India mainly developed by Avabai Wadia was all-inclusive. Avabai Wadia subsequently described the different components of population education. The scope described by her and presented in a schematic form is an notable contribution to population education programme. It covered five areas :

(*i*) Population, its determinants and consequences—births, deaths, migration, rate of growth, etc. ;

(*ii*) Human ecology and Environmental Aspects—Man and his environment, pollution, high rate of consumption, resource depletion, etc. ;

(*iii*) Social Economic and Developmental Aspects—Productivity, GNP, health, education, housing, employment, etc. ;

(*iv*) Family Life and Individual Aspects—Family and social

institutions, family life education, sex education, status of women, etc. ;

(*v*) Basic values and quality of life—Goals of society, technology, consumer society, use and development of resources, etc.

It is not surprising that the advice of Family Planning Association of India on population education continues to be sought. It is reported that "during 1986 FPAI Headquarters and 40 Branch units covered 2,03,594 school and college students ; 81,444 out of school youth. In addition, over 65,000 teachers, teacher trainers were oriented in population education concepts and 300 youth educators in family life and responsible parenthood.

In 1969, Ministry of Education in collaboration with Ministry of Health and Family Planning organised the National Seminar. A number of officials and non-officials organisations helped in preparing background material, especially Central Health Education Bureau, the Central Family Planning Institute and the USAID. The responsibility for providing the academic services rested with the Department of Social Services and Humanities of the NCERT. The main person behind the preparation and organising the seminar was T.S. Mehta. V.K.R.V. Rao the Union Education Minister at that time set the tone of the discussion of the Seminar. He emphasised that : population should not be treated merely as a quantitative phenomena or just an essay in numbers. It is the quality of population that is most relevant both as factor of growth and end product of growth and numbers have to be treated in terms of the effect they have on quality of citizens, on deterioration or improvement. Population education is a part of human resource development. Quality of population among other things would seem to be determined not only by numbers, but also by health maintenance and nutritional betterment". The recommendations of the Seminar vertually was the first step in integrating population education in the education system. The objectives of the population education defined at the seminar were more or less the same as in Wayland's paper of 1965.

The Seminar recommended that "a separate Population Education Cell should be established in the NCERT in order to develop suitable curriculum in population education at the school stage. The cell should work in close collaboration with the Central Health Education Bureau, the Central Family Planning Institute and other agencies interested in the programme both official and voluntary.

In May 1970 the Population Education cell was established in the NCERT. The cell initially included T.S. Mehta, R.C. Saxena, Ramesh Chandra and Supta Das. Later the cell was designated as Population Education Unit including besides Mehta and Ramesh Chandra, S.P. Chawla. Health and nutrition as suggested by the Education Minister Rao became a component of population education and A.K. Sen, an experienced health educator also joined the population education unit. Within a couple of years the Population Education Cell /Unit developed a comprehensive population education programme at the school and teachers education levels. The salient features of the programme were : (*i*) to conduct various studies of the curricula involving analysis of syllabi of the various states ; (*ii*) to identify core concepts and develop a well articulated curriculum in population education ; (*iii*) to clarify the concept of population education, develop stagewise objectives in behavioural terms ; (*iv*) to develop detailed curriculum guides ; (*v*) to develop various types of instructional materials-textual, supplementary reading and audio-visual ; (*vi*) to take up 'try' out of material on sample basis ; (*vii*) to prepare programmes for teachers both in-service and pre-service ; (*viii*) to take up programmes and develop strategy for the implementation of the programmes at state levels (working with states) ; (*ix*) to conduct and promote research in the various aspects of the programme ; (*x*) to develop a good library of reference material both Indian and foreign, and to perform clearing house function for agencies working within the country and also keep contact with organisations in other countries working on population education. The NCERT Population Education Cell organised a number of workshops and issued a number publication such as *Points for Population Education in*

School Curricula and the Population Education a Draft Syllabus. These publications were followed by others such as *Indian Population Situation* by S.P. Jain (subsequently revised under the title *Indian Population and Development*), *Population Education Selected Reading, Teaching Units on Population Education, Nutrition and Population Education* by A.K. Sen, *Bibliography on Population Education.*

Activities in population education with a wider scope continued by the FPAI, CHEB and to some extent by CFPI. In 1971, the CHEB started a WHO supported project on health education including family life education. In the same year a workshop (Government of India and WHO) on health and population education and workshop on instructional material on population education for teachers and representatives of selected health and education organisations in Delhi were organised. In 1970 CHEB had developed a Population Education Guide for Secondary School teachers and also issued a document entitled population education lessons giving some sample textual material. A diploma course in health education was also started under Delhi University on the initiative of CHEB.

In October, 1971 the NCERT organised a National Conference on population education to discuss the problems of implementation of the programme. Avabai Wadia again emphasised at this conference that population education should be all inclusive.

Avabai Wadia's view was widely shared in the country as is reflected in the recommendations of the National Seminar on Population Education at Sri Venkateswara University in Triputi. One of the recommendations at the Triputi National Seminar was "sex education and health education should be the component parts of population education in creating responsible attitude towards planned and healthy parenthood and that various issues have necessarily to be imparted to the youngsters in this regard".

At the 1971 National Conference, the official approach

seems to have remained unchanged except for a minor changes. One of the such change was: "Out-of-school youth is a group either very close to matrimony or already married. Hence the concept of responsible parenthood may be emphasised more in the programme developed for this group. Reproduction and other elements of family life and sex education may find a place in the programme developed for them". Other recommendations related to population at school stage, teachers education and machinery for implementation at the National and State level. Formation of quasi-government organisations with representatives of Ministries of Health and Education was also suggested.

The task of NCERT in developing population education (even with restricted scope) was by no means easy. Education is a transferred subject to States. Education policy itself was faced with general criticism. Basic questions were raised, such as those underlined by Ralh Tyler as far back as 1949; *viz.*, "what educational purposes should the school seek to attain? What educational experiences can be provided which might help pupils to attain these purposes? How can these educational experiences be effectively organised? How can we determine whether these purposes are being achieved?" The general view was that the education provided in schools do not serve the purpose they seek to attain. In this climate a consensus had been reached that population education is important component of educational experience, feasible approaches had to be developed and resources had to be found.

There was hardly any previous experience on teaching population education in the country. A number of approaches were discussed such as 'permeation strategy, unified package, and teaching units. Kamla Sud, of the Central Health Education Bureau, was experimenting with the permeation strategy introducing the subject at the special points in the existing curriculum. The supporter of unified package argued that in permeation approach it might not be possible to communicate the population situation and issues in a unified form and such an approach would involve repetition and overlapping. The unified package, however, virtually meant introducing a separate subject and adding another subject in an already overburdened syllabi and difficulties of finding teachers with a multi-disciplinary background. The idea of self-contained teaching units/modules, which could be introduced at various levels emerged. It was obvious that a lot of experimental work and preparation were needed, specially building of trained man power, preparation of well pre-tested educational aids, building of organisation in the States and finding financial resources. Considering the overall constraints, Mehta and his colleagues at the Centre and persons dealing with the subject in the States did an admirable job. The teaching units were developed with much care and it was possible to develop population education in the country without making a major change in the school education system. Other strategies were also useful in different situation, for example, unified course could be offered during out of school and adult education and as an extra-curricular activity.

Training of teachers continued to be difficult. The family planning managers felt that training of teachers could be designed in two phases one a short unified course to cover in a specified time all teachers in the country and followed by teaching in greater detail over relatively prolonged period. The teaching/learning activities could be devised with care to achieve three objectives, *viz.*, to enable the trainee to define common demographic terms and measures ; to list the causes of the rapid rate of growth of population ; and to answer questions on the population problem in India and its implications at micro and macro level and the need for two child family (girls or boys, or girl and boy) ; timing (with emphasis on age at marriage), spacing of births and care of mothers and children with special emphasis on infant mortality ; and education especially of women and status and their employment ; and National Family Welfare Programme.

The financial constraints were gradually over come and Ministry of Health and Family Welfare provided financial support on increasing scale. In the Sixth Plan a sum of

Rs. 1.5 crores was transferred to Ministry of Education for population education. By the end of March 1983, 27 States and Union Territories were implementing the programme ; 16 States had developed population education syllabus for Primary and Middle level school stages and 14 for Secondary school stage ; 12 states introduced population education in their Elementary Teachers Training Curriculum; 16 States had developed instructional material for teachers. Population education was introduced in various other fields 28 Universities introduced the subject in the B. Ed. Course ; the subject was incorporated in the activities of various development Departments such as Agriculture, Rural Reconstruction, Co-operation, Labour and Employment, Sports (Nehru Yuvak Kendras to begin with in Uttar Pradesh and Madhya Pradesh).

As the population education programme was being developed in India, the interest in this field was being taken in other developing countries. The third Regional Conference of Education Ministers in Asia in Singapore in 1971 showed interest in the subject. A regional workshop was held in Bangkok in 1970. Mehta was a consultant in this workshop. Meetings or workshops were held in Columbia (1970), Malaysia (1971), Thailand (1971), Iran (1971). By 1971 about 20 countries had active programme of population education. The Singapore meeting led to another regional workshop in 1974 under the auspices of UNESCO with financial support from UNFPA on preparation of a source book on population education. The source book, a very useful document, was issued by the UNESCO Regional Office for Education in Asia Bangkok in 1975. All these programmes, except for a few exceptions such as Philippines excluded sex education and family life education.

The question sometime raised is : why there has been so much hesitancy in including sex and family life education in population education in India ? It does not appear to be due to (or entirely due to) opposition of youth, parents, community, or Government leaders. It was also not based on any comparative studies on the so called sexless education. It does not seem to be also based on any cultural taboos, as in India traditionally sex is not associated with 'sin'. The main reason appears to be that major focus (or the entire emphasis) of the promotors of the new concept of population education was on rapid rate of growth of population in developing countries. Other supporting reasons appear to be that of the educationists responsible for school education in India did not feel comfortable in discussing subjects like human reproduction, human genetics, human sexuality, not necessarily in all cases because they had any conscientious objections, but perhaps mainly because their unfamiliarity and lack of knowledge of these subject. They seem to feel that let these subjects alone for dealing by other people. Another factor may also be that supporters of broad all-inclusive concept of population education were not as influential as supporters of the restrictive concept of population education.

Even at present, the scope and purpose of all inclusive 'population education' is not fully realised on a countrywide scale. Such a situation is obviously mainly due to lack of education and training among teachers themselves, and official support.

The momentous technological and social changes in the world are having profound influence on behaviour, including in the area related to human sexuality among the younger generation. These changes are perceptible in urban India, especially in large cities. How far they have influenced the rural India or how soon they will come under such influence or what are precisely their present problems both in rural and urban areas can only be a matter of conjecture. The few studies already available do not reflect the situation in the entire country. The sex education, in the country, wherever promoted generally appears to be restricted to information on what is popularly termed 'facts of life'. The education in human sexuality has much larger scope. "The purpose of individual or collective sex education is to help people to lead healthy sexual lives, and the concept of sexual health (in the view of an international group of experts) includes three basic elements :

—the capacity to enjoy and control sexual and reproductive behaviour in accordance with social and personal ethics.

—freedom from fear, shame, guilt, false belief and other psychological factors inhibiting sexual response and impairing sexual relationship.

—freedom from organic disorders, disease and deficiencies that interfere with sexual and reproductive functions. Sex education is a component of family and community health, related to such issues as family and marital relations, the improvement of maternal and child care, family life education for school age children and young people, the treatment of sexually transmitted diseases, the promotion of mental health and even desegregation of the sexes in education, employment and social life".

The Expert Group suggested the following short and long term activities :

Short Term Activities

A survey to provide a reliable picture of present programmes, activities and services. The convening of series of meetings to facilitate the sharing of experiences by health practitioners who have established successful programmes, to study socio-cultural factors in regions where programmes are to be launched, to pool research findings and agree on the health implications of wide range of sexual phenomena and to allow discussions of policy among representatives of the national and international health organisations. The provision of immediately needed resources, such as an information exchange centre, a comprehensive bibliography, a directory of agencies, and some assistance for new programmes, especially in the developing countries.

Long Term Activities

The training—through fellowships, seminars and study meetings—of specialists to provide leadership at national and regional levels, selected on a wide geographical basis from among health practitioners with extensive knowledge of one or more aspects of sexology. Programme development through meetings on a national level of deans and administrators from school for the health sciences ; assistances to school in curriculum development and teachers training courses ; and continuing support and evaluation of new teaching programmes. The provision of library facilities, audio-visual aids and a central clearing-house for information with regional branches and advisory services ; and maintenance of an up-to-date directory of agencies and organisations. The initiations and support of research-cross-cultural and within individual cultures in human sexuality ; co-ordination of existing medically oriented research ; and continuous evaluation of training programmes".[164]

These recommendations were made in 1972. Their relevance has not ceased. The Family Planning Association of India has pioneered activities in this field. Their activities like 'Teenagers Ask and Doctor Answers' and on human sexuality and family life education have been widely welcomed. Their experience will be valuable in future planning.

There is an urgent need to give serious consideration to the suggestions made by the Expert Group in 1972, as the much needed activities covering the whole country do not appear to have been launched. They can be adapted to suit the national situation. The training should not only focus major attention on school teachers, medical men and women in the health system, but also health visitors, Auxilliary Mid-wife and Social workers. The health visitors and Auxilliary Midwife already give advice on birth control, timing, spacing and number of children, care during pregnancy, labour, post-partum periods, maternal and child care. "They should also aid parents to deal constructively with sexual behaviour and questions of their children, and assist teachers concerned with sex education in schools". Health educators, extension educators and other members of health team should be able to strengthen activities in this field. The first step which may be taken is to designate an organisation responsible for professional development of the programme, such as Family Planning Association of India. The first step the designated institute may take is to survey in close collaboration with NCERT, NIHFW, CHEB and other selected institutions and experts. The Schematic Plan for Population Education presented by Avabai B. Wadia, at the FPAI's Seventh All India Conference on Population Education for younger Generation at Manipal in 1971 can form the basis for the survey and one of the major background document for discussion on further development of population education in the country. This exercise can be followed by a National Workshop for preparing a plan of action and action-research projects in selected areas. This may assist National Council of Education Research and Training and the agencies concerned in the health sector to have another look at the population education programme and develop a well co-ordinated all inclusive population education programme in the Country.

13

Peoples' Participation

It was apparent, from the very beginning, that the success of family planning programme rests on it becoming a people's movement. This implied that for bringing about change in people's behaviour, efforts have to be made by the people themselves. It was recognised that the action by people are determined by their own perception of their situation and experience. The problem of arousing the desire to make necessary adjustments in family life, in so intimate and personal matter as family planning was not simple. The adults learn best when the felt needs are identified by them and not determined by others ; when they feel that the new practice will contribute to fulfilling their urgent needs like improvement in their environment and social and economic conditions, when they are confident that the new practice conforms to their traditional values, when they are sure that the new practice has the approval of the social group to which they belong, when they fully understand and accept goals, and when they see visual proof that the new practice will lead to the achievement of their desired goals.

Much was talked in the 1950s about illiteracy in India, as an almost unsurmountable barrier to the modernisation process. Massive inputs in education were (are) considered one of the highest priorities. But near universal education in the country takes time. One reassuring experience of field workers was that villagers might be uneducated or semi-educated but they have intrensic intelligence to solve their own problems often of higher order than the educated urban population. They were cautious, in some cases suspicious of the advice given by those outside their social group. Some organised machinery was considered necessary to arouse people's interest and make the movement as their own, arouse in them the feeling that a small family is desirable, the desire to seek knowledge and the drive to take action. Some of the questions faced by the programme managers were : Who could be the change agents among the people ? Who could provide professional and other support ? What form of organisational steps or structure could give the desired results ? What could be the ways and channels that could be tried to make family planning programme people's movement ? Several ways to operationalise the above goal were considered such as developing health education and extension education activities through Government agencies ; mobilising support through the people's institutions like Panchayati Raj and Cooperatives ; using infrastructure that was being developed by the Central Social Welfare Board and State Social Welfare Boards ; harnessing the network of voluntary organisations especially the Family Planning Association of India.

Government Channels

The Government channels and personnel were reported to be generally identified by the people with executive function. The memories of colonial past still seemed to linger, which had created a general apathy, often distrust and even element of fear of bureaucracy. Any attempts wholly through Government channels could be viewed as an external imposition with unknown and unpredictable results. At the same time the development of health education organisation within the Government set up was essential. But it required support from people and peoples' organisation.

Panchayati Raj Institutions

Democratic decentralisation was being brought about

through Panchayati Raj Institutions. The Panchayati Raj and Cooperative organisations were supported and assisted by the various Government Department and agencies. Earlier in the First Plan the community development and rural extension programme were initiated. The community development was considered to be the method and rural extension as the agency 'through which Five Year Plan seeked to initiate a process of transformation of the social and economic life of villagers".

The programmes in the rural areas including health and family planning had to operate through Panchayati Raj Institutions. The mechanism to involve them intimately through village health family planning committee was suggested. The suggestion generally was not implemented. The formation of village health committee was revived in 1960s. The health and family planning committee was expected to be composed of peoples representatives who would be responsible for planning implementation and evaluation of their program. The officials' would play supportive role. The details were worked out in health centres such as Najafgarh. The health committee was to form a part of Panchayat Raj Institution (formal leaders). It was noticed that formal leaders of Panchayati Raj institutions did not always represent the feelings of all members of the committee. The community in the villages was not homogenious. There were classes and factions. The opinions of the underprivileged. who required, the assistance most, were not necessarily reflected by the formal leadership. Some ways appeared necessary to involve all the groups in the community in the programme.

Social Welfare Boards and Voluntary Agencies

Among the voluntary organisations with experience in social service and special experience for family planning work the obvious choice was the Family Planning Association of India. The activities of FPAI where limited to urban areas at that time. The organisational structure of the Association also did not lend itself to natural flow of the activities through State, District, Block and Villages. The Association had branches in cities with direct affiliation with Headquarters.

The Central Social Welfare Board and State Welfare

Boards (composed predominantly of non-officials with experience of promoting voluntary activities), under the dynamic leadership of Durgabai, were developing infra-structure to mobilise private voluntary agencies in the field of social welfare like welfare of women and children, social education, community organisation and develop new programmes. In early 1960s, the Central Social Welfare Board had about 7000 centres, each centre having 3 to 4 workers like the Gram Sewak and Sevikas, teacher or a *dai* (traditional birth attendant) living in the village and had a jeep to go round the whole area of 25 to 100 villages. Each centre had a 'balwadi' (child care centre). In addition to maternity and child welfare services, the welfare board centres provided adult Women Social education, adult literacy classes, craft training, recreational and cultural activities. They also had developed production units providing employment. Durgabai submitted a detailed note for coordination of the work of the Central Family Planning Board (CFPB) with that of the Central Social Welfare Board. One of her suggestions was that the Central Family Planning Board could take advantage of the Samaj Kalyan Centres (Social Welfare Centres) and post one family welfare social worker at each of these centres. She had urged the CFPB that the family planning programme should be considered not as a programme but as a movement, a people's programme".

The proposals of Durgabai which had great potential for providing family planning with involvement of people especially woman at grassroots did not get full support. Differences arose on the various aspects of their involvement. It was finally agreed that family planning should form part of their activities especially through the Mahila Mandals, Balwadis and the Samaj Kalyan Centres.

Gradually a plan emerged to form a cadre of voluntary outstanding public leaders with record of social service especially in rural areas at Divisional, District, Tehsil and Block levels and natural group local leaders at village level, to sensitize the people to accept innovative ideas which could lead people to plan, implement and periodically review and modify their plans in respect of family planning and mobilise resources of voluntary organisation and social welfare boards. They would not receive any pay, but could receive an honorarium for the expenses incurred. It was felt that if they were paid they would be considered just another category of Government functionaries. It was envisaged that the whole chain of these honorary workers would have freedom of action, and reporting system of progress of their work would be from one level of honorary worker to the next higher level of honorary worker. For getting support through National voluntary organisations already established it was decided that there would be an honorary leader in each of voluntary organisation who would stimulate and extend activities in their own organisation. Their would be mutual support between the organisation thus formed and Government organisation at all levels, and coordination at National level by a coordinating honorary leader.

Honorary Family Planning Education Leaders

A cautious approach was adopted and initially a few Divisional and Institutional Leaders were identified and requested to undertake the work. Durgabai Chairperson of the Central Social Welfare Board was personally aware of the work of leading social workers in the country. She helped in identification of the first group of leaders. There was no difficulty to identify National Voluntary organisations. Thus in 1959 Premlata Gupta, Shakuntala Paranjpya ; Avabai Wadia, S S. Kulkarni, Soundram Ramchandran, Shakuntala Kurtkote, Hem Sanwal and the President All India Women Conference in Rajasthan started working as Honorary Family Planning Education Leaders. In the following year they were joined by Shyam Kamari Khan and Begum Ali Zahir in Uttar Pradesh, Bhakti Sen and Aroti Dutt in West Bengal, L.N. Jha in Bihar, Minnakshi Amma and Leela Damodaran Menon in Kerala, Vishakha Dixit, Sushila Dixit, Krishna Agarwal, Suraj Kala Sahai, Kamlabai Jadhav in Madhya Pradesh, Indira Puri in Tamil Nadu. Gradually the list of Honorary Family Planning Education leaders became virtually a 'Who is Who' of social workers in the country.

The Honorary Family Planning Education Leaders were free to carry out their work, within the general scope of their activities. The scope covered the fields of information, education and communication ; of identifying persons and organisations who could be drawn to carry out the work and to mobilise them into active self-help groups ; to stimulate people's organisations to undertake the work themselves, preparing the ground for intensive work by the people, their activities supported by the Government and other agencies at all levels especially village, block, Tehsil, District. They were also to serve as a valuable channel to feedback progress of the programme carried out by both Government and voluntary agencies and help in resolving problems as they arose.

The Family Planning Education leaders had the wide experience of social work. But family planning was a new field. Except a few like Family Planning Association Institutional leader, for most the task was by no means easy. Still in a very short time they established rapport with all official and non-officials, peoples organisation, individuals and organisations in the family planning and other allied welfare fields. They sponsored Family Planning Association Branches and other voluntary groups to start family planning activities, arranged orientation camps, group discussions. and mass meetings. They received valuable support from organisations like branches of Family Planning Association, Red Cross, Social Welfare Board, Bharat Sewak Samaj and local welfare organisations. They received help from Labour and Development Commissioners and other Government officials especially health and family planning in their work in rural areas and among underprivileged in the urban areas. The response of the people in some places was overwhelming.

District Honorary Family Planning Education Leaders

The response of the pioneering work of Divisional Leaders led to the appointment of the leaders at District level. The individual appointments were made on the recommendations of the Chairperson Central Social Welfare Board and the State

Governments. The regional leaders were also requested to make suggestions. Unexpectedly one distortion in the extension of honorary education leader programme was that the appointment of new regional leaders was discontinued, and in the districts under regional leaders district leaders were not appointed.

Pariwar Kalyan Sahayaks and Sahayakas

At the village level there were already Gram Sewaks, Gram Sewakas, Mukhya Sevika (social education organisers) and other village level workers. Steps had been taken to include family planning activities especially education and weave family planning activities in the general health and welfare activities. The Community Development Organisation considered Gram Sewakas too young in age to discuss contraception. It was agreed that they would take active part in education programme with certain reservations relating to methods. The main question that arose was : whether with already a number of workers at village level was there a need for separate workers for family planning ? A close look at the existing workers showed that they were not necessarily natural group leaders and their existing responsibilities were already so many that they could not pay sufficient attention to family planning. It was suggested that the latter situation could be solved by increasing their number to reduce the workload. At the village level it seemed necessary to identify natural group leaders to form the base of the honorary leadership programme-Pariwar Kalyan Sahayaks and Sahayaka at village level and honorary family planning education leaders at Block, Tehsil, District, State levels with a coordinator at the National Level. The local leaders at village level were to be those who had the confidence, affection and respect of the group to which he or she belonged in the villages. They could be village elders, could be a Panchayat member, school teacher, social worker or even an illiterate or semi-illiterate person whose advice was sought when problems arose and decisions had to be taken by the community. It was expected that if such natural local leaders were members of the health and family planning committee of the formal organisation like the Panchayat it would facilitate family planning programme becoming the people's programme.

There were two problems—How to select natural local leaders ? and How to train them to work effectively ? Initially the selection was made on general impressions and their performance at the family planning orientation camps. This was hardly a satisfactory procedure. Methods for selection of local leaders were developed at Gandhigram, encouraged and supported by Soundram Ramchandran. The identification of informal leaders was based on two methods, *viz.*, selective group method and systematic sampling method. In the systematic sampling method a map was prepared of the area listing every household. Enquiries were made in two series. In one, a male in every fifth household was visited and in the alternate series a female in every fifth household was visited. The programme was explained to them and they were asked to suggest one or more persons whom they considered competent to carry out the programme. In the selective group method first formal leaders were requested to identify the social groups and their intergroup relationship. The investigations through their observations also identified the major groups and groups-wielding influence in the community. A map of the colony and a socio-gram (graphic representation of inter-group relationship) were prepared. The formal leaders were interviewed and requested for a list of informal leaders who in their opinion would be suitable for family planning work. The informal leaders suggested by them were interviewed and requested to give a list of leaders they consider suitable for the task, the inherent degree of influence and source of their leadership. Each individual in the list was given a score for influence and interest. Finally the list of informal leaders was prepared ensuring that all groups were represented, each one of them would be acceptable to the community and each one was interested in the programme. For their education and trainning short term orientation camps were developed to be followed by continuous professional guidance. It was hoped that with such orientation they could be important channels of communication ; could form local groups and stimulate and assist the people's organisation in planning, implementing and evaluating family planning programme and make it an integral part of health, education and welfare activities of the community. Three terms were considered for the designation of the informal local leaders, *viz.*, *Neta* (Leader), *Sewak* (servant) as in Community Development programme and *Sahayak* (helper). To emphasise that the community view them as one of them, a companion and helper they were designated as Pariwar Kalayan Sahayak and Sahayaka. (Family Welfare Helpers). They could be from any group—literate, semi-literate, illiterate, teacher even a formal leader. They were to be a part time worker, without seriously interrupting their normal occupation. It was envisaged that they would be within the framework of Panchayat Raj Institution and would also find a place in village committees especially village health committee. All Pariwar Kalyan Sahayakas and Sahayaks might not necessarily find a place to work in such a committee. But would spend some time for the promotion of family planning. They were not to be paid any honorarium, as that would make them (or would be viewed by the community) as another wing of the Government organisation.

The Health Education Seminar

The leadership programme developed slowly. By early 1960 there were fourteen voluntary Honorary Family Planning Education Leaders. The area covered by them was large. A stage was reached to bring them together for exchanging experience and also orient them with educational approaches and health education principles and methods and their application to the family planning programme for making it a people's programme. The Central Health Education Bureau was in its formative stage. Its Director, V. Ramakrishna, had profound insight in health education. A seminar was planned and conducted in March 1960 by the Central Health Education Bureau and the Family Planning Section of the Directorate General Health Services, in fact by Ramakrishna and his staff with marginal assistance by the Family Planning section. The seminar was unique in many ways. This was the first such experience for most of the Health Education Bureau staff. Generally the guide and concepts recommended in the report of the International Seminar on Education in Health and Nutrition sponsored by F.A.O. and WHO were used in planning it ; the seminar provided opportunity of identifying gaps between theory (recommendations) and practice (this seminar). It also provided an opportunity for a dialogue between family planning education leaders and State Family Planning Officers, State Health Education Officers, representatives from various training and research institutions, health education experts and social scientists. It became a forum for discussion on development of health education organisation at local, Block, Tehsil, District, State and National level. This was first meeting where the family planning education leaders discussed their problems and made recommendations on their duties and responsibilities in the light of their experience and the need for coordination. Although the major part of the report of the Seminar devoted to discussions aimed at further development of health education organisation in the country, it provided orientation of family planning education leaders and a broad view of health and family planning education organisation and their inter-relationship and bringing them closer to each other.

Honorary Family Planning Coordinating Leader

The work of honorary family planning education leaders was being initially coordinated by an officer in the Family Planning Section. As the leadership programme was conceived to be done entirely by non-officials with such Government assistance as might be required, the advice of Malika Ghosh, the Honorary Family Planning Education Leader for Delhi was sought. She had exceptional experience in social work and family planning while she was in Bangalore, and had close contact with the Family Planning Association of India and several prominent social workers and organisations in Delhi and other States. She had taken prominent part in 1960 Seminar as leader of the group on family planning education leaders especially on what major contribution they could make in promoting family planning programme. She was requested to work wholetime as the Coordinator of this programme. She agreed and was appointed Honorary Family Planning Coordinating leader in April 1961 on a honorarium of Rs. 1/- per month to satisfy Government rules for such appointment. There were 25 honorary education leaders in the country at the time. She travelled extensively giving help and guidance to and coordinating the activities of voluntary organisations and individuals.

Around mid-1962 there were 31 regional leaders and 62 District leaders. She called an ad-hoc committee meeting of selected leaders to review the work and to suggest measures for further development of the programme. They included Hem Sanwal, Sham Kumari Khan, Premlata Gupta, Mary Clubwala Jadav, Leela Damodaran Menon, Vishakha Dixit, Krishna Agarwal, and Shakuntala Kurtkoti. There were a few special invitees. Prominent among them were Phulrenu Guha, an outstanding social worker and organiser of social work ; S. Sundaram from Ministry of Community Development & Cooperation ; and Dorothy Nyswander a mentor of many health educators round the world. By this time the scheme of natural local leaders at village level (Pariwar Kalyan Sahayak and Sahayaka) was also nearing fruitation. The ad-hoc committee recommended that the stage was reached to appoint honorary leaders at Block, District Division and State level. It was felt that it was not possible for a Divisional or Regional leader to perform her function without District leaders. Suggestions were made on joint planning, enlisting support of leaders of all categories at all levels, work at various levels, relationship between honorary leaders with the Government Departments and other voluntary agencies ; measures for strengthening of knowledge of the leaders : exchange of experience and operational problems at periodical intervals.

Change in Emphasis of Their Role

The programme was geared to organise a strong cadre of voluntary workers to support the Government machinery at all levels and mainly to involve people with the programme and bring about a situation when people themselves plan and implement the programme to establish a norm of small size family. The task of family planning leaders and natural local leaders was centred on education and motivation, bringing others into the programme, forming local groups arousing people to solve their problems, help the people in this process by becoming an effective liaison between the Government and other agencies and the community, supporting them with orientation and training facilities.

The original concept, however, changed with "the target approach". District honorary education leaders were required to hold 6-10 orientation camps per year and in such camps attempt to arrange for at least 50 vasectomy operations or 100 IUD insertions. The focus shifted to targets for sterilization and IUD insertions. With this change in concept, the performance of Honorary F.P. education leader was measured in terms of "targets". They were unable to pass the new test. The family planning education leader programme was terminated. The natural local leader at village level programme (Pariwar Kalyan Sahayak and Sahayaka) continued to be given general support. But it also withered before it blossomed. The orientation camps conceived originally were for orientation of workers for upgrading their knowledge of family planning programme and group dynamics and to acquire skills to form peoples' own groups in the community for promoting family planning. Special emphasis was given on educational skills and organising the community. The new approach appeared to be focussed on achieving sterilization and IUD targets. The erosion of the basic concept thus began to the great disappointment of those who nurtured natural leadership programme and were associated with developing the programme.

Continuing Activities of the Former "Leaders of Family Planning"

After the termination of honorary family planning education leaders programme, no substantial change occurred in the activities of institutional leaders. They continued to extend their activities with perhaps enhanced professional knowledge and experience. Many regional and district leaders continued to be active workers in social and family planning field in the voluntary sector some holding responsible positions. The investment on them is still paying dividend. It is not difficult to visualise the scene which may have emerged if their was more understanding of the programme, and less impatience to see results in terms of sterilization operations and IUD insertions and if the cadre of voluntary workers with in-built training was allowed to be developed as a strong pyramid with natural local leaders at the base in villages and slums and honorary leaders at Block Tehsil, Districts, Divisions and States and a coordinator at the Centre all non-officials, with commitment and experience in social work, health and family planning mobilising people's support, building peoples action groups and voluntary organisations at all levels.

Questions often asked are : why a programme commended in early years was terminated before it was fully developed ? Was this due to weaknesses in concepts and goals ? Was it due to inadequate planning and management ? Was it due to inability of professionals to get administrators sufficiently interested ? Why declared policy since the First Five Year Plan to give high priority to peoples participation was not fully implemented ? There has been great emphasis on peoples participation in development in the Government Plans. Why then a programme with potential of generating peoples participation collapsed ? We may examine some aspects of people/participation in development, to find answers to such questions.

Peoples Participation in Development

The people's participation does not imply people as an extensions of programmes devised by higher levels. It means assisting people to discover their own needs, creating situations in which people make decisions, set goals, formulate policies and plans, implement and evaluate them, modify them in the light of their experience and changing needs, contribute their labour and resources and equally share the fruits of their efforts. Often quoted statement is : "Popular participation entails the creation of opportunities that enable all members of community and the larger society to actively contribute to and influence the development process and to share equitably in the fruits of development". The popular participation can be : spontaneous participation (voluntary based up, without external support) induced participation (sponsored, mandated and officially endorsed) and coerced participation (compulsory, manipulated and contrived.[165]

The contrived, manipulated, compulsory people's participation can have transitory desired effect, but is counter productive. Indian programmes are voluntary and participative and come in the category of 'induced participation'. The induced participation, however, has the potential of becoming or generating spontaneous participation (which is ideal) through diffusion of communication. News spread from an area where induced participation shows benefits to the families and the community to neighbouring areas and people there are aroused to take action, and spontaneous participation emerges.

The major constraint to people's participation is that it implies sharing of power (political and economic) between administration (development functionaries) and the people, between the affluent and the deprived, between men and women between different groups and communities.

The progress in the Community Development may be a good illustration. It had high political support in the early years mainly due to political commitment of Nehru to democratic decentralisation. As the programmes progressed, tensions arose. The old influential classes generally continued to retain power. They continued to get major benefits. In places where the community development programme was successful and people began solving their problems themselves, the local political leaders appeared to be apprehensive of loosing power as people then were not dependent on their patronage and largesse. Some observers feel that increasing power of the community development officials was also seen by the local political leaders as erosion of their authority and even the Block Development Officer moving extensively in a jeep was irritating to them. The support to community development declined. The election to Panchayat Raj Institutions were delayed for long periods.

There are several essential requirements before the people

can contribute to development such as an organisational structure ; freedom in local decision making ; financial and other material and technical support ; continuous dialogue (not one way communication) between development functionaries and the people ; availability of information, including technical, for planning and implementation ; urge for selfhelp ; desire for change and development ; and commitment to sharing equitably the benefits of development.

Self-help and self efficient management require management and administrative skills, knowledge of rudiments of planning ; techniques of community organisation, knowledge of available resources for programmes launched by the Government which have relevance to their problems, co-operative efforts which are fessible, even skills to negotiate with bureaucracy. This means the people. especially their leaders, need training. The training is also needed for planners at higher levels and government development functionaries especially at implementation level to promote effective people's participation.

An illustration of training local leaders is provided by "People's school in the Philippines. The International Institute of Rural Recoustructional (IIRR) set up the People's school in seven municipalities in Cavite Province of the Philippine, to train community residents as diffuser of appropriate technology in rural reconstruction. The commencement of the course was preceeded by discussions at conferences on feasibility of such training with "Village Captains" of 38 villages. The villagers agreed to pay for transportation and food. IIRR provided lodging, free tuition and free training material. The trainees were selected by the Village Council. The selection of courses and raising of funds were also done by the Village Council. The courses were followed by continued education, support, supervision, motivation and evaluation. The subjects covered in the courses included : agriculture, health, nutrition, family planning, sanitation, literacy, self government and folk singing. The experience showed that success of the programme was due to careful planning, involvement of local leaders, selection of courses by villagers, use of integrated approach and emphasis on self-help. The problems faced were : lack of funds and poor selection of trainees.[166]

Another aspect which may be reiterated is what has been termed as "Learned dependence" or in simple words the attitude of dependence on the Government which contributes to absence of development motivation. Uma Narula, in a seminar, mentioned two hypotheses in respect of "Learned dependency", *viz.* :

(*a*) It is a result of poor communication between development functionaries and the masses. Both blame each other. The masses perceive the Government as the perpetual provider of modernity, uninterested in their suggestions or initiation in their development programmes and they (people) themselves are ineffective in accomplishing development objectives. The development functionaries complain that the people limit their participation in development process to passive acceptance of what government does for them and complain about what it did not do, have no useful suggestions and did not maintain or repair what the government gives them. Such attitudes lead to frustration among both and increase 'learned dependence'. On the assumption that this hypothesis is correct Uma Narula suggested a 'Development-Dialogue Action Strategy' Project, which could 'replace erroneous with correct perception of each other'. The interesting feature of this strategy Project is that it is aimed at a dialogue between the community as a whole not just the group leaders in the community and programme functionaries.

(*b*) The second hypothesis is that the "learned dependency is a manifestation of a pattern of meanings which make active participation paradoxical". Development is seen by the masses as something for which government has assumed a parental control. Self is seen as one of the masses, a complex concept which reflects the lack of what Pareek called 'extension motive', and the presence of what is designated by Uma Narula as 'ethic of proportional effort'. The concept of 'ethic of proportional effort implies that masses are not willing to put more effort for development in kind, labour or cash, if the development benefits accrued are not in the same proportion).

There are two consequences of such a move :

(*i*) the haves of the society may have more development resources but they are not willing to contribute those resources for the simple reason that both they and the have-nots will be equally benefitted. The havenots also reciprocate the same attitude. "Such an attitude of the masses is, obviously, not conducive to active participation of the masses".

(*ii*) "masses are not willing to put more in development effort since they feel the government should put more government effort, as it is the government responsibility to deliver development both adequately and efficiently, why should they (masses) participate actively".[167]

The people's participation is not as simple as some may be inclined to believe. There are several grey areas which require further investigation. Such a statement may be generalisations, but draw attention to important factors which should be kept in view in approaches adopted in the alternative strategies. There is, however, sufficient knowledge of approaches and experience which can be followed. They can be improved as additional knowledge gets available through further field experience and research.

It is evident from some of the projects such as Malur, Jamkhed and Gandhigram that the success was due to identifying local needs and helping to mobilise the community to plan, implement the programme to meet their needs including health and family planning and development activities and delivering of services through carefully selected local village workers who after training irrespective of their literacy status became valuable assets to the community. The mobilisation of women and youth clubs provided valuable support to the local leadership.

There is a very strong case for developing a cadre of voluntary workers. A modest beginning can be made to start such a cadre in selected villages. A charismatic person from among the local informal leaders have to be identified by local leaders who can gather around him a few other local leaders. This group must be committed to mutual sharing of some of their time and labour for common good and happiness of the community. They can survey the community needs in their neighbourhood, assess resources, start whatever activity they can undertake fulfil the needs without conflicting with the work of others but supplementing their work. There is so much to do that the question of overlapping activities does not arise, *e.g.*, in the health sector they can undertake improvement, of environment, day care of children of working women, community kitchens to which the whole neighbourhood can contribute, or perform simple tasks like taking children when sick to health centre or for immunization or just talk to an old person, infirm or disabled. The members of this cadre should start health practices first themselves, then in their families, then extend to the neighbourhood and the community. In every community such local leaders will be found. Often they do not know how to go about it. They need training and support. The development of such a cadre may be a gradual process. Beginning with a few person giving spare time. Assessment at various stages may be necessary to make modifications. It has potentialities to grow. Some whole time workers may emerge. They can undertake training of new enterants. With dedication and hard work the cadre can spread widely. This cadre can be a powerful force for awakening the community for self-help, for improving their quality of life and Pariwar Kalyan can became a real people's movement. Such strategies have already shown results in Sri Lanka. Ariyaratne, the leader of the Sarvodaya Shramadana Movement in Sri Lanka, identified ten basic human needs :

(*i*) a clean and beautiful environment around us. Environment here means the physical, social, emotional and mental environment ;

(*ii*) an adequate and safe supply of water ;

(*iii*) minimum requirement of clothing......two for daily home wear, two for school or the work-place, one for night wear and the other for occasional wear ;

(*iv*) a balanced diet essential for energy growth and protection......establishing conditions to supplement the dietary needs especially of pre-school and school going children, expectant mothers, lactating mothers, invalids, and the old ;

(*v*) well planned, simple and pleasing small houses, with adequate light and ventilation, utilizing locally available timber and other building material ;

(*vi*) Health care, physical, mental and social......priority ...given to implement Health Promotional Programme provision of education and services which includes the training of Community Health Sevaks and Sevikas and conducting various preventive, curative, rehabilitational and protective health measures for expectant and lactating mothers, pre-school children, the handicapped, the malnourished and the aged ;

(*vii*) Suitable means of communication, in keeping with our progress and in relation to our economic conditions ;

(*viii*) Until such time as we are able to produce energy through solar rays, wind and water etc.......to meet fuel requirement through planting of more such trees that later can be used as a source of fuel ;

(*ix*) Life long education for upholding the highest ideals and values of our culture and satisfying our modern day requirements ...through formal, as well as non-formal educational methods ; and

(x) giving all development activities a spiritual and a cultural base.

Ariyaratne has demonstrated these basic needs can be satisfied through Sarvodaya development programme in which people with assistance of community workers become self-reliant. For example, activities carried out by just three of his community workers in about one year included motivation of 2710 families to drink boiled water, taking 1149 children, 500 mothers and 629 others to clinics/hospital ; detection of 1578 children with nutritional deficiencies of these 1108 cases nutritional defects were corrected, several thousand immunizations arranged, several hundred latrines built.[168]

Sarvodaya programme strategy adopted in Sri Lanka is replicable. The support for people's participation is re-emerging.

On March 11, 1987, Minister of Health and Family Welfare, in reply to Shri Subas Mohanty M.P. informed Rajya Sabha, that a Standing Committee on Voluntary Action (SCOVA) has been established to promote formulation and implementation of integrated projects on health and family welfare with community participation in the rural and urban slums and voluntary organisations are being encouraged for greater participation in the family welfare programme. During 19·5-86, 403 voluntary organisation projects were given financial support. The FPAI has been provided a rolling fund of Rs. 5 lakhs for providing consulting services and financial assistance to small voluntary organisations. These are very welome developments in promoting peoples participation, especially giving consultancy status to FPAI, an institution with long experience of successful projects with peoples participation. Major thrust is still needed on larger scale for making the programme Nation wide as peoples own movement through peoples own institution (Panchayats in rural areas) gradually taking full responsibility for planning, implementing and evaluating the programme with the necessary support from the Government functionaries and the professionals. This will need serious consideration of some of aspects discussed above.

14

Intensive Health and Family Planning Districts Project

India had long experience of health programmes, but not sufficient knowledge to motivate people to adopt a small family norm through practice of family planning methods. The experience on Nation-wide family planning programme outside India was "precious little". The emphasis was, therefore, laid mainly in three directions, *viz.* :

(*a*) to analyse critically the existing programmes and field experience and build the programme on that basis. "The Reorganised programme, with extension approach", emerged from this exercise ;

(*b*) to gain from experience in the field after putting "the Reorganised programme" on the ground through action-research and diagnostic studies and modify the programme from such experience ; and

(*c*) to give highest priority to quality of services and high level of competence in programme personnel and research through training and fellowship programmes in India and abroad and building training institution in India and to make the country self sufficient for the future needs.

The implementation of "the Reorganised programme" was facing the difficulty of finding sufficient number of qualified persons to fill the sanctioned posts. The All India Institute of Hygiene and Public Health Calcutta was the major resource for training public health administrators. Personnel were also drawn from other medical and nursing teaching institutions in the country. The progress in health and family planning programme, however was slow.

It may be recalled that in January-February 1963 a report on intensive health and family planning project was submitted by Dr. Hugh R. Leavell, Professor of Public Health Practice, Harvard School of Public Health ; Dr. William F. Mayes, Chief Office of Research Grants, Bureau of Community Health, US Public Health Service and Dr. Edward G. Mc Gavran, Dean School of Public Health University of North Carolina. The major recommendations in their report were: establishment of the National Institute of Health Administration and Education (NIHAE) and intensive health and family planning Districts Project. The NIHAE was required to assist in the identification of districts considered suitable for the project and later focus their attention on coordination of activities in these districts. One part of their report discussed objectives, organisational principles, importance of intensive rural health programme to family planning programme and importance of family planning programme to health in India, evaluation function, terms of agreement with participating States and role of State health planning and evaluation units. As the projects were to be operated by States, a meeting of Administrative Medical Officers, of Andhra Pradesh, Gujarat, Kerala, Madras, Maharashtra, Mysore, Punjab, Uttar Pradesh and West Bengal, was convened by Ministry of Health in New Delhi to discuss the project. The administrative Medical Officers attending the meeting expressed their enthusiastic support to intensive health and family planning Districts Project.[169]

The 1961 Census had shown that about one-third population of the country was contained in 51 districts in various states. It was felt that if sanctioned staff and some financial in-puts were provided in these districts, results would be 'rewarding'. Ministry of Health proposed to start the programme initially in 17 districts. States were required to provide a few basic requirements before additional support could be given. These requirements included : "unified control of all medical care and other health activities in the District under a medical officer trained and well experienced in public health. In case there was a District hospital of over 200 beds a separate administrative arrangement might be necessary. But in such a situation a very close liaison between them would be maintained. The Chief District Health Headquarters could "coordinate the activities of all agencies and institutions in the District who are interested in health work". Other imperatives were : highest peoples participation from the very beginning ; decentralisation of financial authority for specific budget expenditure and uncommitted discretionary fund, to enable the Chief District Medical Officer to sanction expenditure expeditiously; freedom to the Chief District Medical Officer "to review, modify and test out various alternative methods of reporting and record keeping for purpose of increasing administrative efficiency and effectiveness and minimising the paper work of technical personnel" ; consultation with District personnel ; monitoring and in-service training ; making salary scales and living conditions attractive enough to get and retain good quality staff ; the transfer of the personnel only if desired by the Chief District Medical Officer, not to be transferred before at least three years (if due for promotion ensurance of salary increase and seniority in his cadre in the present position, the principle being to retain administrative leadership without adversely effecting pay, promotion, seniority and pension for reasonable period ; maximum use of junior personnel especially para-medical staff ; the state planning and evaluation unit to work in close collaboration with National Institute of Health Administration and Education and provide support in planning and evaluation of intensified District programme ; appointment of a high level state advisory committee and an executive committee ; giving consideration to factors conducive to rapid development of the programme like contiguity of health training and research centre and intensive District agricultural programme, presence of well developed hospital in the District, absence of hinderances to programme development, favourable socio-economic factors, the additional costs borne by the Government of India and activities should be such as could be readily reproduced in other parts of the country, and readiness to incorporate expeditiously lessons learnt in the intensified District programme into regular operation of other Districts within the States.

By 1967-68 the intensive Districts Project was in operation in Guntur (A.P.), Kamrup (Assam), Darbhanga and Muzaffarpur (Bihar), Mehsana (Gujarat), Hissar (Haryana), Kozhikhode (Kerala), Raipur (Madhya Pradesh), Coimbatore (Tamil Nadu), Poona (Maharashtra), Dharwar (Karnataka), Cuttack (Orissa), Jullundur (Punjab), Udaipur (Rajasthan), Gorakhpur and Kanpur (Uttar Pradesh) and Nadia (West Bengal). The objectives of the programme laid down for these 17 district projects were : to create an awareness for the need of small family amongst every married couple and group acceptance of small family norm by all the communities in the population ; to impart knowledge about specific family planning methods to all eligible couples ; to assure adequate supply of contraceptives to all eligible couples within easy reach ; to arrange for clinical and surgical services to achieve the set target ; to organise good follow-up services so that sustained interest among eligible couples to have a small family is maintained ; to offer continuing care and concern for married woman throughout her reproductive period and for her offspring during the childhood, by integrating the family planning services with maternal and child health services ; to have an effective evaluation procedure including simple record keeping that can be easily interpreted and evaluated ; and find out which additional inputs will yield the best results with least cost and which can be duplicated. These objectives were in conformity with the recommendations made in 1962-63 Report of the Director Family Planning.

Considerable efforts were made to determine additional inputs required, through wide discussions and study of local situation. The additional inputs in each district included : 2

Medical Officers, 2 Operation Theatre Nurses, 2 Operation Theatre attendants, 3 Extension Educators, 3 Projectionists and 3 Drivers ; 3 Multi-purpose vans equipped with generator, audio-visual equipment and surgical instruments and equipment for doing sterilization operations and IUD insertions, two exhibition sets, one transistor set for every sub-centre, at least one wall paining in each village, tubular tent equipment for keeping cases after tubectomy operation, additional sets of surgical instruments to each Primary Health Centre for vasectomy operations and IUD insertions, a vehicle for District Family Planning Officer, and a vehicle for each Primary Health Centre. Other facilities included : special training of nurses and senior health visitors for IUD insertions, one trained *Dai* for every 1000 population, extending depot holder and the commercial distribution scheme for *Nirodh* in the District, Oral contraceptive project in districts where there were facilities, involvement of other development departments like Community Development, Social Welfare, Education in family planning programme, and construction of Primary Health Centre buildings and staff quarters on priority basis.

The main declared purpose of the intensive Health and Family Planning Districts project was to strengthen the family planning programme. But as the programme progressed it was noticed that major efforts were devoted to build health infrastructure and family planning figured as somewhere fifth on the list of objectives. This is understandable, as family planning programme depended on health infrastructure and ultimately was to be integrated fully as a part of the health system.

As minor adjustments were being considered, it appears that the project was losing administrative support. Several causes have been mentioned for such a development like induction of a large number of consultants, with varied experience, often with no clear cut assignment, which in itself proved as an irritant ; financial constraints ; time-bound and target approach overtaking strategies proposed to have been used in the intensive districts. It was commented by some observers that the Health Minister at that time was interested in the Ford Foundation support for family planning to strengthen public health services and institutions. It was also rumoured that the relationship between Finance and Health Ministers at that time were not cordial, which accounted for financial constraints.

A well conceived project met almost the same fate as the Reorganised Family Planning programme with extension approach, before it fully developed. The principles and guidelines given in the report of consultants on intensive health and family planning districts project are relevant even now, perhaps they are more important at present than before. The intensive districts health and family planning project seems to get support in 1970s and 1980s. The strategy of the Intensive Districts Health and Family Planning Project, with some modifications are reflected in the World Bank India Population Prcjects, and Area Projects with partial assistance from the World Bank, the United Kingdom, United Nations Fund for Population Activities, DANIDA and USAID.

15

India Population Project

Around mid-1970s, the World Bank Population Project India was launched in six districts of Uttar Pradesh and five districts of Karnataka. Partial assistance to the Project, besides World Bank was provided by Swedish International Development Agency. The studies in Uttar Pradesh commenced in May 1973 and Karnataka in April, 19 6. The experimentations in the two States was not always smooth sailing. At one stage the drive to achieve targets seriously effected the studies, especially in Uttar Pradesh.

UTTAR PRADESH

The objectives stated were : to complete the health infrastructure, training facilities and equipment as laid down in the Government of India pattern ; to provide additional in-puts in some areas to supplement the Government of India pattern ; to assess the results of alternative strategy to Government of India Programme especially linking the family planning services with maternal and child welfare (supplementary nutrition programme concentrated on recently delivered mothers and malnourished infants and children) ; to increase the use of mobile teams for motivation and services ; to give special attention to training and supervision ; to create the Population Centre to design a Management Information and Evaluation System (MIES) to evaluate the performance on continuous basis, to recommend changes in the project area and to ensure that the recommendations emerging from the studies carried out in the Project area are expeditiously implemented.

For achieving the above objectives four units were established, *viz.*, Project Coordinator's Unit, Project Implementation Unit ; Project Construction Unit ; and the Population Centre. It will be seen that emphasis was laid on improving facilities, staff and human resources development, accommodation, working conditions, equipment, mobility, monitoring, evaluation and feed back of information and results of the integration of family planning and child welfare studies. Such improvements were expected to provide satisfaction to the clients who would not only continue using the services, to create conditions for raising the morale and efficiency of the staff and speedily plough back the gains from the project in non-project areas. The progress in implementation in various aspects varied. For example, from May 1973 to March 1976 out of 122 major and 54 sub-centres buildings to be constructed, 63 major and 429 sub-centre buildings were completed.

Marked differences were noted in achievements of the Project and non-project Districts.

The percentage of women provided ante-natal services in Project Districts increased from the level of 3.9 per cent (1974-75) to 23.9 per cent (1977-78). Where as during the same periods the percentage increase in non-project districts was 5.9 to 10.9. The deliveries conducted by the trained staff in Project Districts increased from 0.8 per cent (1974-75) to 23.9 per cent (1978-79). The increase in non-project districts was from 0.7 per cent to 1.9 per cent. Maternal (1977-78) and child (1979-80) beneficiaries were 60 per cent and 400 per cent higher respectively in project districts as compared to non-project districts. The number of children immunised was also higher in the Project Districts than non-project districts.

In acceptors of IUD and conventional contraceptive practice, there were no significant difference between Project and Non-

Project districts. But there was appreciable increase in acceptance of sterilization. The acceptance of vasectomy in the Project Districts was 120 per cent higher than Non-Project district during 1979-80. Similarly more tubectomies were performed in the project districts about 200 per cent higher in the Project Districts compared to Non-Project Districts in 1978-79. The notable acceptance of sterilization may also be due to Nation-wide greater emphasis laid on sterilization. The comparisons of data collected in baseline survey carried out in 1974 and repeat survey in 1979 80 in three districts among other changes showed the percentage change in couples protected by different methods from 2.8 to 3.9 in Partapgarh, from 3.5 to 6.4 in Sultanpur, and from 7.3 to 11.0 per cent in Muzzafarnagar. The impact on birth rate was not large enough to show significant decline. The crude death rate and infant mortality rates also did not show significant change.[170]

KARNATAKA

The stated main objectives of studies in Karnataka were : to identify the strategies that would lead to better family welfare coverage including maternal and child health services, in terms of quantity as well as quality of acceptors, so that the strategies identified could be recommended for replication in other rural areas ; to study the processes involved in the implementation of various strategies for developing better insight into programme implementation, so that corrective measures could be suggested for efficient and effective implementation of the programme; and to develop indices for evaluation of family welfare programme in rural areas, so that the programmes could be effectively monitored and the goals set are achieved. For systematic evaluation, like in Uttar Pradesh, Management Information and Evaluation System (MIES) was developed (initially called Family Planning and Health Information System).

Five strategies and later a combination of strategies, were tested, *viz.*

Strategy I : Involvement of voluntary organisations in the

implementation of family welfare programme at the Primary Health Centre level. Two hypotheses tested were :

(*i*) the family planning and MCH performance would be better when the implementation of the programme in the rural areas is entrusted *exclusively* to a voluntary agency than when implemented exclusively by the Government ; and

(*ii*) the family planning and MCH performance would be better if it is implemented in co-operation with a voluntary agency than that of being implemented exclusively by the government.

For testing the forme Family Planning Association of India was allocated the Primary Health Centre Malur (Kolar District); for the latter Rural India Health Project a local voluntary agency was entrusted with responsibility of involving local people and creating demand for the services in Primary Health Centre Singasandra (Bangalore District). The Government continued to provide family planning services in this PHC.

Strategy II : Application of management principles at the Primary Health Centre level to test the hypothesis that "Introduction of modern management concepts and techniques at the Primary Health Centre level for improving the existing management practices and skills by decentralizing the authority, role classification and better co-ordination would bring about better family planning and maternal and child health performance than that of the existing system of management prevailing at the Primary Health Centre Level". The strategy was experimented in Primary Health Centres Honnali (Shimoga District) and Holakere (Chitradurga District). The Administrative Staff College of India Hyderabad was given the responsibility for implementation of this strategy.

Strategy III : Improvement of technical competence of medical officers and para-medical personnel at the Primary Health Centre level. The hypothesis for testing under this strategy was that "the training of medical officers in modern methods of medical termination of pregnancies and training of Health visitors for prescribing oral pills and inserting IUDs would bring about better family planning and MCH performance than that of the existing system of provision of services by the medical officer only". This strategy was experimented in Primary Health Centres Bagepalli (Kolar District) and Bidadi (Bangalore, District).

Strategy IV : Entrusting the responsibility of achieving the family welfare targets to non-health departments at the Primary Health Centre level. This was based on the assumption that the Panchayat Chairman, the village level worker and the village accountant have greater social interaction with eligible couples in the community than health personnel and sharing responsibility with all other departments would relieve the burden of health personnel who would be able to pay their full attention to provision of 'good' family planning and maternal child health services. The strategy was experimented in Primary Health Centres Nonavinakere (Tumkur District) and Thalak (Chitradurga District).

Strategy V : The role of incentives in family welfare programme at the Primary Health Centre level. The hypotheses were :

(*i*) provision of services in kind such as better food, drugs and follow-up care instead of cash incentives, would bring about better family planning and maternal and child health performance ; and

(*ii*) allocation of the entire "sterilization money" to doctors who would be responsible for providing food, drugs, follow up care and who could save if possible some money would bring about better family planning and maternal and child health performance than that of the existing system. These hypotheses were tested at Primary Health Centres Talaguppa (Shimoga Distt.) and Holavanahalli (Tumkur District).

At a later stage a combination of strategies were tested : *viz.*

(*i*) a combination of management, involvement of village level functionaries and up-grading the competence of medical and para-medical personnel ;

(*ii*) a combination of management and involvement of village level functionaries. The combined strategies had their limitations and did not include components which had given encouraging results in several action research programmes and even in one of the Karnataka projects—the Malur Project.

The strategy relating to a coordinated programme involving both the Government and voluntary organisation was short lived. It seems that the voluntary organisation lacked the requisite experience of family planning programme operation and depended mainly on clinical approach. Perhaps the roles of the Government and voluntary organisation were not clearly defined. It was soon obvious that the voluntary organisation working in the area could not play the role of a catalytic agent between the community and service giving agency (the government). The experimentation of this strategy was therefore, discontinued. There is however ample evidence in other parts of the country that voluntary organisations provide valuable contribution in supporting role to Government health and family planning programme. The weakness in this project was in selecting the voluntary organisation or inadequate planning and preparation of agencies concerned, or both.

The experimentation with introduction of management concept at the Primary Health Centre level did not show significant improvement in family planning performance. It did appear to have some impact on maternal and child health services. The failure seems to be due to the agency, responsible for introducing management concepts in the Project, was not able to establish adequate rapport with the administration and personnel responsible for the programme. The management professionals may have adopted aggressive postures or shown impatience in the pace of adoption of new concepts of management by the local health administrators which led to their alienation. It seems that the modern management concepts were not given a fair trial. There is enough evidence in other areas in the country that the performance can be improved considerably by adoption of management skills. In fact there is need to create a cadre of health managers with full grasp of management concepts. The National Institute of Health and Family Welfare could serve the function of staff college for the purpose.

Significant results including distortions in health delivery system were observed in the Primary Health Centre in which measures to improve the technical competence of the medical and para-medical staff were introduced. The personnel in the Primary Health Centre concerned laid greater emphasis on family planning which adversely effected the maternal and child health care. Such unbalanced delivery of family planning and maternal and child health services in integrated family planning and maternal and child health approach can be traced to training of workers and attitude of administration. In has been demonstrated in many other places that if the integrated programme is properly carried out it is not only feasible but improves overall performance.

'The involvement of the village level functionaries under leadership of the Panchayat Chairman did not yield significant results concerning family planning and maternal and child health'. Personal factors may have been responsible for such a result.

The introduction of the payment of incentives in kind showed 'some improvements in both family planning and maternal and child health, which was significant in the case of latter'. The strategy however was faced by a number of problems-organisational, administrative, credibility of workers (in-kind items sometimes were reported to have generated suspicion as to their value).

The experience of combined strategies showed that "the introduction of 'in-kind incentives would bring about immediate negative reaction, the strategy of management component helps in systemising maternal and child health performance though not helpful in bringing about positive increases in the level of family planning acceptance and the strategy of effecting improvements in the technical competence of the lady medical officer in conducting medical termination of pregnancies and health visitors in prescribing oral pills and inserting IUDs enhance the level of family planning methods although not fully helpful in bringing about a positive increase in maternal and child health performance'.

Several other outcomes can be identified in this project such as development of Management Information and Evaluation System, identification of a number of problems and conflicts that arise during implementation of the programme in the field, experience in designing similar experiments and rich experience to personnel involved in conducting the experiments.[171] The experiments in Malur stand out, in this project, as an out standing example of a successful programme.

THE MALUR PROJECT

The voluntary organisation requested to implement family welfare programme in the India Population Project was the Family Planning Association of India (FPAI). There could not have been a better choice. The President of FPAI, Avabai Wadia, in a number of forums had underlined the important role of voluntary orgnanisations in innovative approaches for family planning programme implementation. In early 1971, she had launched a special rural family planning project at the Allahabad Agricultural Institute. This project covered 499 villages in economically backward area, and was planned to establish linkages between agricultural and health programmes and mobilizing resources in the Development Block and the Agricultural Institute, animal husbandry, sanitation, immunization, health and family welfare programme. The focus was on development approach suited to local needs, and through such an approach promote family planning among target couples. In May 1973, FPAI had started an extensive project in Belgaum Gulbarga divisions of the Karnataka State. The notable feature of the project was that all the programmes were organised through local institutions and agencies with continuous involvement of the local population in all its activities. Mobile intensive educational teams reactivated dormant social, educational, cultural and other agencies in the community and in places where there were no such institutions FPAI helped to establish them. When the FPAI was requested to undertake the project in Karnataka as a part of Population Project India, it had rich experience of improving family welfare performance in many rural areas including some in Karnataka.

The FPAI selected Malur taluka in Kolar District for experimentation. The Malur Primary Health Centre covers an area of 47.5 sq. km. The population at that time was 1,29,000 distributed in 334 villages under 51 Panchayats. A 24-bedded sterilization-cum-maternity ward was in the process of being completed at the Head-quarter Primary Health Centre. In addition to the Primary Health Centre in Malur Taluka there were four local fund dispensaries, one medical sub-centre, one health type dispensary and an Ayurvedic dispensary.

The Government of Karnataka State issued orders to be effective from 1 March, 1976, handing over to FPAI technical control of family planning and MCH activities in Malur. Another Government order effective 1 April 1976 was issued delegating complete control over the staff in all administrative and financial matters to FPAI*. FPAI could make changes in the staff pattern and adopt programme approach considered appropriate. They did make changes. For ensuring mobility of the staff, a jeep was provided by the Government. The salary of the driver and expenditure for petrol, oil and lubricant had to be met out of FPAI funds. A resident Project Director with a small supporting staff, was appointed by the FPAI. The Project Director worked under overall guidance of FPAI Liaison Committee established in January 1976. The FPAI Bangalore Branch was closely associated with the Project ; their voluntary workers (lady members) frequently visited Malur, contacted local leaders, participated in the programme. The Government constituted in August 1976 a Coordinating Committee including representatives of FPAI, the Department

*First such pragmatic action in the country in health delivery system of a State Government.

of Health and Family Welfare, the Implementing wing of Population Project India and the Population Centre

The local liaison Committee at Bangalore, besides giving guidance and support to the Project and Project Director, periodically reviewed the implementation of the project and reported to the Project Committee at Headquarters in Bombay.

The strategy adopted included a package of ten activities, *viz.*, reallocating areas on the basis of population to health visitors and auxilliary nurse midwives ; reorientation of health visitors and auxilliary nurse midwives ; improving the quality of services ; intensive educational work through increased use of audio-visual material; updating the target couple register; training rural doctors in family planning methods particularly for their involvement in the oral contraceptive (pill) programme : orientation and involvement of teachers in population education programmes ; development of local leadership and involvement of local leaders ; and conducting population related development activities in villages such as voluntary labour (*Shramdan*), improving health practices, sanitation, local communication, etc.

The very striking aspects of the project were : the focus on people and their organisations ; enrolment of volunteers from among the local communities to work for family planning ; involvement of youth clubs ; individual and repeat contacts with the community clubs, Panchayat Boards, Mahila Mandals and other local organisations ; community development activities ; training and retraining ; monitoring ; and development of a vibrant organisation for project activities.

The percentage of the eligible couples following family planning method increased from 8.4 (1976-77) to 35.2 (1979-80). The MCH programme in the Project registered 86 per cent of all ante-natal and 79.9 per cent of all post-natal cases. The number of deliveries conducted by untrained Dais showed appreciable decline. During 1979-80, after withdrawal of the FPAI as a part of Population Project, the performance of Malur Primary Health Centres (PHC) continued to be higher than the Control PHC, Malur record in IUD pill and conventional contraceptive use was the highest in 1979 among all the Primary Health Centres in the District. Six Youth Clubs and six Women's Clubs, with support of the FPAI and the Karnataka State Council of Child Welfare established II Balwadis. A Taluk Youth Federation emerged to coordinate village development activities of Youth Clubs and Women's Clubs. In a single year (1979-80) the Federation activities included the digging of 76 soak pits in 60 villages, 21 compost pits in 10 villages, cleaning of wells in 45 villages, 78 voluntary labour activities (*Shramdan*) for road repairs. A community based distribution of contraceptives included some Youth Clubs besides individuals from the community.

The project promoted cultural activities like Bhajan Mandals 'which composed religious songs with population theme as the focal point'.

Falicitation programmes to honour publicly families who had accepted sterilization as a method of family planning were arranged.

The sensitive indices developed by the Population Centre Bangalore indicated that the performance in Malur was far better than the control Primary Health Centre Kamasundram. This has been mainly attributed to maximum interaction between 'community effect' and 'organisation effect'.[172] The success was really due to leadership, skilled management free from bureaucratic control, programme approach and its operation based on integration of family planning with development and effective peoples participation.

16

Gandhigram

Mahatma Gandhi inspired people all over the country and beyond Indian frontiers to serve weaker sections of society especially in villages. He inspired a number of persons who could endure the discipline, sacrifice and hard work required for such work. Soundram Ramchandran was one of the outstanding among them. Late in her life she qualified as a physician with specific purpose to serve the rural people. Her husband Ramachandran, equally dedicated Gandhian devoted his energies for rural uplift. The husband and wife team started social and economic programmes in a rural area in Madurai District of Tamil Nadu and called the area of their operation as Gandhigram.

Soundram Ramchandran devoted her major attention to health and family welfare programmes. Her pioneering work soon attracted National attention. When Central Family Planning Board was formed in the Health Ministry, Government of India in the 1950s, she was invited to become a member of the Board. She strongly advocated integrated maternity and child health and family planning programme and promotion of these activities through community action. Over the years she provided institutional base for her activities. She established institutions related to sanitation, rural health and family planning. Gandhigram was recognised as National Centre for research and training of workers in rural areas. Gandhigram Institute of Rural Health and Family Planning was formed around October 1969. It was staffed by committed and high quality professionals in a number of disciplines-health, sociology, anthropology, psychology, social services, education, demography, statistics, and health education. The leadership of Soundram Ramachandran generated a high level of team spirit and dedication among all ranks of workers. She received spontaneous respect and love from people in Gandhigram. They generally called her '*Amma*' (mother). The parallel rural development activities managed by G. Ramachandran also blossomed.

Gandhigram pioneered several studies, which had impact on National Family Planning Programme development, such as on identification of natural leaders, methodology for effective implementation of public health and family planning programme, job description of personnel under the reorganised family planning programme with extension approach.

The experimental activities received support from Central and State Governments and the Ford Foundation. The Ford Foundation interest in Gandhigram is traceable to a meeting of Ford Foundation representative in India, Douglas Ensminger and G. Ramchandran in the middle of 1950, at a community development conference in Gandhigram. The Ford Foundation was at that time exploring feasibility of supporting (upgrading) rural institutes in India modelled on Mahatma Gandhi's teaching on rural development work. A team of consultants strongly recommended issuing of Ford Foundation grants to upgrade the institutes and raise them to the status of Rural High Institutes. The Gandhigram was one of them. Food Foundation made the funds available. The Gandhigram Rural Institute alongwith two others in the country overtime were recognised as "being deemed University".

It appears that Ensminger's interest in supporting a family planning project in Gandhigram was influenced by two considerations, *viz.*, a family planning institute in Gandhigram might neutralise the resistance of those Gandhians who were opposed to family planning and a family planning institute as an integral part of Gandhigram (a non-Governmental organisation) would develop speedily as a strong institute. The Ford Foundation had already given two grants to Gandhigram ; one for training women and another for training men for village extension work. The financial support was further extended for developing the Gandhigram Institute of Rural Health and Family Planning.

An action—research project was also launched in Athoor Block in 1962, in seven villages. This was extended to fifty-nine villages by 1965. The methodology for promotion of community based family planning programme was developed. This included identification, selection, training for field activities, supervision and continuous professional guidance of natural local leaders. Communication barriers were identified and measures to overcome them were explored. The results were very encouraging. The use of condoms and persons volunteering for vasectomy increased. The birth rate from 40 per thousand population in 1962 declined to 36.3 in 1965. Several other contributions were made such as job description of each category of worker in the reorganised programme launched in 1960s was developed, based on field experiences, and various first steps in the implementation of family planning programme at the peripheral level were defined. The birth rate in Athoor Block continued to show continuous decline. By 1976, birth rate was reported to be 26 per 1000 population, much below the National average.

Several special features are descernible in Athoor Block such as : social and economic measures to improve the quality of life of people initiated since 1950s, the level of professional support close to the people, the additional in-put in personnel at village level (one auxilliary midwife per 500 population instead for 1000 population as provided in sanctioned staff by the Government) ; the focus on community action through local leadership ; freedom of voluntary organisation in recruitment of suitable staff, their training, continuous guidance in the field ; monitoring and feed back of experience ; personal contact with each eligible couple and rendering advice suited to each of them coupled with appreciating the priorities among felt needs of villagers and attempting to meet them promptly and dedication of workers at all levels.

The prompt fulfillment of the expressed need of the community may be illustrated by the observation of two visitors to a village mainly populated by weaker section of the community in 1978. The project Staff-member accompanying the visitors took the opportunity to discuss the difficulties with the villagers. The villagers expressed great difficulty in looking after their children's health and requested for a female worker (like a *Bal Sewaka*) who could help them. They were prepared for making other arrangements from their own resources. A quick decision had to be made. The Project Staff-member appreciated the fact that the Project activities had brought the villagers to the level of implementing the programme to improve the child care themselves. All they wanted was marginal support (provision of a trained worker), the rest of the inputs they were ready to provide themselves. An immediate promise was given to provide a worker. The same day, a retired lady living in Gandhigram was approached. She provided financial resources. Search for and recruitment of suitable worker and planning for her training commenced. Such prompt action could be taken only by a voluntary organisation.

There is no doubt that the programme approach in Gandhigram has been mainly responsible for its success. Soundram Ramchandran wrote in 1976 : "If we could get good results in Athoor Block, it was because in every hamlet and village we have village leaders, women and men, whether with little education, good education or no education. Auxilliary midwives are deeply involved. All the family planning leaders in the villages, Panchayat members, Panchayat Union members and the President of Panchayat plus devoted work by Primary Health centre doctors in taking up welfare programme like immunization, etc., can deliver the goods".[173]

17

Jamkhed

In 1970s, a great deal of interest in community based health and family planning programme is seen throughout the developing countries. By 1982, about seventy such projects were undertaken in at least 40 countries. "They involve village leaders, women's clubs, traditional midwives or local retailers. Local workers distribute condoms, oral contraceptives, and sometime other items, either free of charge or for a small fee, sometime on a household-to-household basis, sometimes through convenient community points. An objective they all share, however, is to improve access to family planning services by removing some of the geographic, financial, bureaucratic, cultural and communication barriers".[174] The family planning services are generally integrated with health services in these projects. The project areas selected appear to be those where effective health services are available. The focus is on common health problems like maternal and child health. In some projects, family planning is not only integrated with health, but also with the socio-economic development of the community.

Conceptually the community based approach was not entirely new in India. This was implied in the various Five Year Plans. It was explicitly stated in the re-organised programme 1962-63. Projects like those in Gandhigram and Malur had demonstrated encouraging results of such an approach.

Several projects in India had integrated medical and birth control services such as Narangwal (1969-74), Miraj (1973-77), Padgha (1976-77), Vadu (1977-), Hyderabad District (1969-85), Varanasi (1980-) and Jamkhed (1971-) projects. The Jamkhed Project has received special national and international attention.

The project was started by Mabelle and Rajnikant Arole with initial support from the Christian Medical Commission. The project began in 30 villages (population 40,000). By 1983, it extended to 70 villages (population 100,000). The health services included ante-natal and post natal care, deliveries, nutrition education, child weighing, iron and vitamin pills to pregnant women, coordination with mass immunization (against small pox, pertussis, diphtheria, tetanus, poliomyelitis and tuberculosis), diagnosis and treatment of major illnesses in the community, control of chronic illnesses such as leprosy and tuberculosis, hospital care for medical, surgical obstetric emergencies, and provision of safe drinking water. The focus on birth control methods was on resupply of oral contraceptives and condoms.

The social and economic activities covered the felt needs of the people mainly food and water. The activities included : borrowing food and distributing them ; community kitchens ; stimulating the community to dig wells ; land donations ; improvement in animal husbandry and farming methods (replacement of animals by tractors), growing food for nutrition programme, building houses for landless. By 1983, 264 houses were built, 5000 hectares of land was reclaimed, 88 wells were dug, 158 drains were made, 60 handpumps were installed and 14,000 saplings were planted.

The infant mortality declined from 150 per 1000 live births in 1971 to 30 per 1000 live births in 1983. The incidence of malnutrition among children declined from 30 per cent to 5 per cent. The prevalence of birth control practice increased from 3 per cent in 1971 among married women in reproductive age to 51 per cent in 1976. A remarkable achievement.

The success of the project is essentially due to leadership and approach. The local needs were identified. The community was mobilised to plan and implement programmes to meet their urgent needs including health, family planning and development programmes. The delivery of services was geared to achieve easy accessibility of condoms and pills at the door step, referal services, improved physical facilities and free flow of supplies. Great health awareness was generated by educational process. The survival of children was attained through immunization and improved nutrition.

The out-reach services, essential for success, centred round village health workers, mostly middle-aged women, with no household responsibilities. Like Gandhigram literacy was not the criteria for their selection. It was found that even illiterate suitably selected persons given training, supervision and guidance could be trained in child care, nutrition, basic treatment of health problems, family planning, collection and relaying vital statistics, and practicing and promoting health education. By 1983, 150 such workers, generally illiterates were working in the field and had soon earned for themselves a respected position in the community by virtue of their knowledge, dedication and service.[176]

18

Family Planning Through Hospital Care & Maternity Centred Programme

The Family Planning Research and Programme Committee in 1953 had recommended that "family planning services should form an integral part of health services". The Committee considered that "reasonably rapid expansion of family planning services" could be achieved by establishing family planning centres in "existing hospitals, dispensaries and maternity and child welfare clinics". An attempt was made to implement this recommendation. It was especially emphasised that ante-natal period is the period of preparation for the care of the mother and the children and spacing and limiting births and post-natal period for decision to limit the number of births to 2-3 children. In practice the success in this direction, was not being achieved to the desired extent. There appeared to be no simple method to integrate family planning with hospitals and maternity homes.

In 1966, there were about 14,600 hospitals and dispensaries and 4920 Primary Health Centres. It was estimated that there were about 240100 beds with over 8 million indoor patients. About 41.3 million patients were attending out-patients, and another 50 million persons accompanied them. Thus hospital setting offered opportunities for family planning education and services for about 100 million persons yearly. In some maternity and paediatric hospitals family planning education and services were being provided. But such places were few, and depended mainly on the interest of an individual or individuals or the hospital administration. This was mainly due to the pre-occupation with curative services and lack of clear cut simple methodology to integrate family planning with normal hospital and maternity care. This problem was therefore identified as a one of the priority areas for Action-Research. D. Anand and his team made valuable contribution to this important subject.

Anand started a study on raising effectiveness of hospitals in promoting family planning at Lady Hardinge Medical College and Hospital New Delhi. The baseline studies were carried out during March 1962—August 1963 and evaluation during January 1966—September 1966. The information emerging from this study related to the situation in a hospital in New Delhi. In order to relate the finding from this study with experience in other parts of the country, the results from this study were discussed at the workshops on Family Planning Communication Action—Research at Lucknow in 1966 and in Delhi in 1967. The experience in other places, although not quantifiable as in Lady Hardinge Medical College and Hospital study, appeared to be almost similar. After the discussions at the 1966 and 1967 workshops, Anand and his associates formulated their recommendations. The recommendations included :

(*i*) Creation of a climate conducive to providing family planning education and services by (*a*) making the medical superintendent, the heads of clinical departments and the nursing superintendent or heads of hospital, medical and nursing staff appreciate the importance and complexity of the population problem and orienting them in educational approaches, various methods of contraception and research in progress in the field through holding scientific discussion sessions and providing relevant literature ; (*b*) appointing a committee to share joint responsibility for implementation, periodical review of the progress and evaluation ; the committee to include medical superintendent or head of the hospital as chairman, medical officer-in-charge of the family planning centre as secretary and heads of departments of obstetrics and gynaecology paediatrics and social and preventive medicine among others as members ;

(*ii*) training of medical and para-medical personnel in educational programmes, delivery of services and contraceptive techniques and issuing a technical hand book to each of them ;

(*iii*) providing services in a manner suitable to local situation, *e.g.*, locating in one place services in department of obstetrics and gynaecology, or in the department of social and preventive medicine or in still another situation in a separate service centre but working in close co-operation with other concerned departments ; and

(*iv*) locating services relating to family planning (contraceptive guidance and supplies, loop insertions, sterilization operations, semen examination, pregnancy tests, management of infertility and sterility cases and other related services) in a single central place, in close proximity preferably near the maternity block with adequate privacy without undue waiting time.

Anand's report covered a wide field such as roles of senior doctors, house surgeons, and nurses, patients, knowledge, attitude, and behaviour, orientation programme for nurses ; interview with women with unwanted pregnancy ; expected role of nurses in the family planning education programme ; changes in the record system and hospital records, family planning in under-graduate curriculum, health education of the patients.

The study in a hospital attached to a medical college 'provided additional opportunities to identify factors influencing the teaching and learning of medical and nursing students in relation to family planning' and to develop guidelines for upgrading teaching, learning, educational and delivery of services related to family planning. Concepts were translated into feasible programme operation. For example, in the recording system, introduction of separate record sheet was ruled out and stamping of existing records was recommended. The stamp solicited information on : Practicing contraception Yes/No ; Family Planning advice given ; age, marital status, income, parity, number of living children, clinical 'diagnosis, social diagnosis of the attending doctor to provide necessary advice or referal of the patient to appropriate person. Such a stamp could be used both on out-patient and in-patient existing forms including cardiac, diabetic and tuberculosis clinics.[176]

It is difficult to assess the extent of implementation of these recommendations. In some places many of them were adopted. In at least one Mission hospital a stamp (a simple histogram) based on Anand's report was used. In many places basic concepts emerging out of this study appear to have been followed, but not to the extent their adoption was anticipated. The adoption of suggested methodology depended on the interest taken in its implementation by local authority. Perhaps the focus on maternity centered family planning (post-partum) programme diverted the attention from family planning in hospital care of all patients indoor and outdoor and also those accompanying them.

A study for assessing the present situation regarding family planning through hospital care will be useful for taking further effective measures.

MATERNITY CENTRED FAMILY PLANNING PROGRAMME

The Maternity Centred Family Planning Programme took a distinctive form after two demonstration projects were launched under the Population Council International Post-partum programme. In early 1966, one project was started at the Safdarjung Hospital New Delhi under Leila V. Phatak, and another at the S.A.T. Hospital Trivandrum under M. Thangvelu. The International Post-Partum programme operation was based on the assumption that a large number of women could be motivated and actually persuaded to adopt family planning methods in maternity centred family planning programme.

Gerald I. Zutachni, the Director of the international programme summarised the four facets of the programme in his following statement :

"(1) each participating hospital has undertaken to inform each delivery and abortion case to its public services via individual and/or group talks, visual aid and other means that family planning is possible, safe and effective, that family planning services are available through the hospital's post-partum services, that a range of contraceptive devices are available and that any woman who does not wish another child within the next year or two should consider utilizing available services ;

(2) those women who do not return for the post-partum check-up and particularly those who had expressed an interest in family planning are followed up by mail, phone and/or personal visit as appropriate by social worker or equivalent person ;

(3) the services including such supplies as pills, creams, diaphragm and IUDs as well as the indicated follow-up are provided at whatever charge the hospital was accustomed to making for such services, in most cases free ; and

(4) since any such programme would almost surely set up an informal word of mouth network that would bring others who are not recently delivered to the clinic-friends, relatives, neighbours and acquantances—these would be accommodated and the women in the delivery wards would be informed to that effect".[177]

The maternity centred family planning programme, called post-partum programme, gradually expanded In 1986-1987, post-partum family planning services were available from 554 medical institutions at National, State and District levels, including 10+ medical colleges and 2 post-graduate medical institutions, 375 District and other hospitals, 30 local bodies and 43 voluntary organisations. In the begining, post-partum PAP smear testing facilities for early detection of cancer, were provided in 25 Medical Colleges'. The post partum family planning services are being extended further to sub-district level. The number of approved sub-divisional/sub-district/Taluka/Cottage level hospitals for extension of post-partum programme is reported to be 829. The demands appear to be increasing. The reports show 893718 accepters under post-partum programme during 1986-87.[178] The 10th Joint Conference of the Central Health Council and Central Family Welfare Council had recommended provision of post-partum family planning services at a sub-district hospitals covering a population of about 4-5 lakhs and strengthening the existing centres to meet growing demand. These are encouraging developments. Continuous monitoring is required. One of the important area, which may require attention is to develop further, the post-partum contact service. It will be helpful for those who guide the programme to explore answers to question like : Is the quality of service good ? Is programme progressing well if not in some places why ? How can those not yet availing the services (the so-called post-partum contact drop-outs or defaulters) be motivated to avail of the facilities ? How can the post-partum contact service extended to cover cases in private sector ? Are all the expectant mothers adequately prepared in suitable environment to accept family planning during ante-natal period and adequately motivated to take action during post-natal period ? Has sufficient attention been given to details at every step such as preparation of list of questions, normally asked by the persons attending ante-natal and post-natal clinics, while in hospital to deliver the baby and during contacts in their home, through actually noting them down and then carefully preparing the answers in consultation with communication experts for use to resolve their doubts and problems ? What are the number of contracts, places, duration of contact with those who stay in hospital for less than 72 hours and for those who stay more than 72 hours ? What are the main subject discussed during these contacts ? It is obvious that the person soon after delivery is receptive to advice on the care of the child and her own health rather than on controlling births and the subject on family planning should be brought when she is ready for fruitful discussion on planning her family. Have the workers been provided suitable educational aids for their use and also other educational kits to give to their patients and are they in good condition ? Is sufficient time given at each contact ; or the workers are in hurry to contact all cases before their discharge and fulfill the targets ? Are those who do not report for post-natal care followed up in their homes if so how effectively ? Is the husband contacted when he visits hospital and at the time of discharge from the hospital ? Has the attending doctor introduced the medical auxilliary engaged in post-partum service to the patient during the 'rounds in the ward', as an important functionary to create confidence and respect for their advice in the mind of the patients ? Such questions can be multiplied. The post-partum contact service is an important source of recruitment of new accepters. In some place the work-load may be heavy. Part-time voluntary workers, after training may supplement the whole time workers. Efforts should be directed towards post-partum contact service becoming maternal and child health contact service. Such a development is not only desirable but also cost effective.

19

Health of Mothers and Children

In 1940s, only a few States had any organisation for the care of mothers and children. The MCH activities were carried out mainly by voluntary organisations such as the Indian Red Cross, the Bombay Mother and Children's Welfare Society, the Bihar Maternity and Child Welfare Committee. Even in 1950s, when Ministry of Health initiated active measures, the activities were mostly limited to care during pregnancy and delivery. Sufficient attention was not paid tc health of the mother before conception and care of infants and older children. Although the Health Survey and Development committee underlined, among the essential services, "adequate health protection of children from birth through successive stages of infancy and early and later period of child life", the advances in maternal and child care especially preventive pediatrics were often neglected. The important early step taken to improve maternal and child health included establishment of a special MCH section in the Directorate General Health Services Ministry of Health at the Centre and Maternity and Child Welfare Bureau in States. This spurred programmes of training of personnel, increase in centres for delivery of services, provision of materials and technical assistance. The UNICEF and WHO gave valuable support in these developments.

Besides acceleration of efforts by Health Ministry at the

Centre and Health Departments in States, the pioneering efforts were made by the Social Welfare programmes. The prime mover of these efforts was Durgabai Deshmukh. The First Five Year Plan in the section on Social Welfare stated : "the principal social welfare problem relate to women, children, youth, the family, under-priviledged groups and social vice. The social health of any community will depend a great deal upon status, functions and responsibilities of the women in the family and in the community—...Organised efforts are needed to stimulate activities at the community level, both in rural and urban areas .. ...Groups could be organised as 'mothers' clubs or unions' in all ante-natal and post-natal clinics, milk centres, cooperatives and as a part of trade union activities. Such groups could especially be organised in slum areas and backward areas and among working women and women of backward classes in general...– There is need to give general information to adults about subjects like family relationships, family planning, marital hygiene, domestic economy, mother craft and home craft—...Community welfare programmes embody four inter-linked ideas, namely (1) self-help and mutual service, (2) maximum use and development of local resources through organised community life, (3) economic betterment and cultural development through social participation in cooperative effort, and (4) achievement of community objectives through minimum amount of assistance from the State".[179]

In 1954, welfare extension projects were established each covering 25 villages each with a Gram Sewaka. Maternity and child health services, craft classes, social education for women supplementary feeding, recreation, and care of children were major activities. Child welfare workers (*Balsewakas*) in child welfare centres (*balwadis*) provided the much needed care to children in villages. The *Balwadi* was the place for imparting informal education to young mothers on child care, nutrition, hygiene and family planning and the centre for total child development. Soon after *Balsewakas* were trained to provide pre-school education. *Mahila mandals* were formed. In pursuance of the goal of making it people's own activity welfare extension projects were handed over to *Mahila Mandals* (womens club). In 1967, Family and Child Welfare Project with Child Development Centre and Women's Welfare Centre at the Block and Taluk level with sub-centres in key villages were established.

In the health organisation, Primary Health Centres and Sub-centres provided care for mothers (mainly ante-natal, natal and post-natal) and children, immunization, nutritional support, supply of drugs and vitamins and other services.

Since early 1970s Special Nutrition programme also saught reduction in morbidity and mortality through improving nutrition status of children and nursing and pregnant mothers. There were other related nutrition programmes such as Mid-Day Meal programme, Tamil Nadu Nutrition Project supported by the World Bank in which health services were combined with nutrition inputs and informal health and nutrition education and the Applied Nutrition Programme in which local production of food required was encouraged.

A survey conducted on the needs of children had shown that their needs and needs of the family and community and the total environment were closely inter-related. This re-inforced the concept that to improve MCH programme the focus should be on the family and community rather than only children.

In mid-1950s, Leona Baumgartner and Frank Notestein Mission had recommended specific steps required for rapid development of maternal and child welfare goals including : continuing to strengthen professional staff in the Central and State Governments by addition of well-qualified personnel, particularly those oriented to care of children and preventive measures ; setting specific goals and devising programmes for training the staff necessary to man hospitals......and adding enriched inservice training for those already in service ; establishing paediatric departments and child health institutes in medical schools .....and adding more substantive material relating to child health in all courses for doctors; nurses, social workers, health visitors, mid-wives and others, working towards a closer integration of maternal and child welfare and general health services ; searching out and recruiting for government programmes younger physicians with some training in pediatrics and interest in preventive pediatrics and social medicine ; stimulating the use of opportunities for training and service in preventive pediatrics afforded by the many creches and nurseries operated for children of industrial workers and other establishments caring for children.[180]

Programme in 1960s and 1970s were geared to take above steps. Actual implementation continued to be slow. The major constraints appear to be insufficient financial resources in health sector, placement of maternal and child health section at the Centre and in States at administrative level which did not commensurate with their importance, and continuing maternal and child health* separate from general health services with the result in practice the integration between them continued to be weak. There seems to be no lack of expertise. The major weaknesses were in available resources, health structure and implementation of the programme.

In 1972, the Planning Commission appointed expert teams. The teams recommended involvement of local communities to the extent possible, provision of supplementary feeding and pre-school education services to the poorer section of the population and establishment of a non-formal pre-school infra-structure as an entry point for health and nutrition services. In fact such activities were advocated for a long time and mentioned in the First Five Year Plan. A working group comprising representatives of Ministries of Health and Social Welfare formulated a scheme based on the recommendations of the teams. The outcome was the Integrated Child Development Scheme (ICDS) in 1975.

INTEGRATED CHILD DEVELOPMENT SCHEME

The major objectives of ICDS are : to reduce malnutrition, morbidity and mortality of children in the age group 0-6 years ;

---

*MCH and Nutrition were placed in the Family Welfare Department, initially called Family Planning Department.

improve health and nutritional status; provide the environmental conditions necessary for their psychological, social and physical development; enhance the ability of mothers to provide proper care to their children; and achieve effective co-ordination among various departments providing development services to children. The goals are to be achieved through supplementary nutrition; immunization; health check-up; referal services; nutrition and health education and non-formal pre-school education. The budgetary control, administration and coordination with the Ministries of Education, Health and Family Welfare, and Rural Development, are vested in the Ministry of Social Welfare.

At State level the Department of Social Welfare and in some States other Departments such as Tribal Welfare, Women and Child Welfare, Health, Rural Development are responsible for the programme. At the Block level, the Block Development Officer has over-all responsibility for the programme. At this level there are two parallel organisations the Primary Health Centre personnel and ICDS Staff headed by the Child Development Project Officer.

The focal point of ICDS at village level is Anganwadi (meaning neighbourhood, round a courtyard) and key worker at the village level is Anganwadi worker (AWW).

Major tasks of AWW are: to survey the community and identify child and mother beneficiaries; to monitor the growth of children using weight for age and identify children suffering from malnutrition; to maintain growth charts and a record of attendance, immunization, births and deaths, etc., at Anganwadi; to provide supplementary feeding to children; to assist the LHV* in distributing Vitamin A to children and iron and folic acid supplement to pregnant and lactating women and refer patients to local health services; to teach non-formal pre-school education to 3-6 year old children and functional literacy classes for adult women; to make home visits in order to

*Lady Health Visitor.

enlist community and beneficiary support to various activities ; and to organise women's clubs (*Mahila Mandals*) as a forum for health nutrition education and centres for income-generating activities.

The ICDS has been an outstanding success story for example ; an assessment in May 1983 by Krishnamurthy and Nadkarni showed that the immunization coverage increased from 10-20 per cent to above 50 per cent. It was expected that by the end of March 1985, ICDS would "provide 10.30 million children with immunization and health check-ups ; 6.1 million children and 1.1 million women with supplementary nutrition and 3.4 million mothers with non-formal education. "The assessment also identified some weaknesses. The peoples' participation and contribution was stated to be "rather slow".[181] This is not surprising, as the community was not involved during the planning of the scheme and during implementation their association with the scheme was marginal. It is reported that ICDS will cover 2000 community development blocks by 1990. It may be noted that one of the major objectives of ICDS is to reduce malnutrition, morbidity and mortality of children in the age group 0-6 years. Director National Institute of Public Cooperation and Child Development D. Paul Chowdhry in a workshop observed that all the children under three years were not given the care originally envisaged. This is a serious weakness in the implementation of the scheme which requires immediate attention, as mortality among children is highest in the age group 0-4 years and a large number die before they reach the age of 1 year. There are also other schemes for children.*

It may be added that several organisations are making valuable contribution to development of children such as Indian Council of Child Welfare, Children Need Institute Calcutta,

---

*In 1985, Ministry of Welfare, in collaboration with UNICEF and the National Institute of Disability & Rehabilitation Research Education Deptt., U.S.A., launched District Rehabilitation Centre Scheme to work with health and ICDS worker.

SEWA in Gujarat, Jamkhed Child Development Project Ahmednagar (Maharashtra).

There is every justification for extending ICDS Nation-wide after making modification to remove its present weaknesses. Promotion of ICDS should be considered as a matter of expediency. Ultimately (sooner than later) it should form an integral part of health, education and community development activities.

IMMUNIZATION

The expanded programme of immunization was started in the country in 1978 with the objectives of reducing the morbidity and mortality due to six diseases, *e.g.*, diphtheria, whooping cough, tetanus, poliomyelitis, tuberculosis and typhoid fever by making vaccination services available to eligible children and pregnant women.

The immunization programme is being expanded in a phased manner so as to achieve Universal Immunization of all eligible children and pregnant women by 1990. Immunization against 'Measles' has also been included. To achieve this objective during Seventh Five Year Plan, besides making efforts to be self sufficient in production of vaccines, various inputs like trained manpower, 'cold chain' equipment, transport facilities and other essential supplies and equipment are proposed to be augmented. The Seventh Plan document observes that the performance of the MCH during Seventh Plan period, particularly in the field of immunization and ante-natal care was far from satisfactory. High priority would therefore be given to MCH programme and implemented vigorously by strengthening infrastructure, organising special IEC* camps to educate women, involving voluntary organisations and village health committees, women's organisations, etc.

The achievement (in lakhs) during 1986-87 reported is as shown below :

*Information, education, communication.

Vaccine	*Achievement*
TT	116.64
DPT	115.64
Polio	102.63
B.CG	111.23
Measles	37.12
D.T.	107.96
Typhoid	78.42
T.T. (10 years)	52.75
T.T. (16 years)	34.75[182]

The UNICEF, WHO and UNESCO in partnership with many world's leading medical and children's organization have published *Facts for Life* to achieve the first level of primary health care a well informed community. The contents of the publication should be widely disseminated. The chapter on immunization is reproduced below.

"What every family and community has a right to know about immunization :

Without immunization, an average of three out of every hundred children born will die from measles. Another two will die from whooping cough. One more will die from tetanus. And of every two hundred children, one will be disabled polio. The four prime health messages....can help to prevent these tragedies.

Children can be protected against these diseases by vaccines.

But even when the service is available, many of the infants who need it are not brought for the full course of immunizations.

It is therefore essential that all parents know why, when, where, and how many times their infants should be immunized.

If the health service does not provide immunization, parents should ask for it through their community organizations.

1. Immunization protects against several dangerous diseases.

A child who is not immunized is more likely to become undernourished, to become disabled, and to die.

* Immunization protects children against some of the most dangerous disease of childhood. A child is immunized by vaccines which are injected or given by mouth. The vaccines work by building up the child's defences. If the diseases strikes before a child is immunized, immunization is too late.

* A child who is not immunized is very likely to get measles and whooping cough. These diseases can kill. But even children who survive these diseases are weakened by them and may die later from malnutrition or other illnesses.

* Measles is also an important cause of malnutrition, and blindness.

* An unimmunized child will almost certainly be infected with the polio virus. And for every 200 children who are infected, one will be crippled for life.

* Tetanus germs grow in dirty cuts and kill most of the people who become infected—if they are not immunized.

* Breastfeeding is a kind of natural immunization against several diseases. Some of the mother's resistance to disease is passed to the child in her breastmilk, and especially in the thick yellow milk (called colostrum) which is produced during the first few days after the birth.

2. **Immunization is urgent. All primary immunizations should be completed in the first year of the child's life.**

* It is vital to immunize children early in life. Half of all deaths from whooping cough, one third of all cases of polio, and a quarter of all deaths from measles, occur before the age of one year.

* **It is vital for infants to complete the full course of immunizations, otherwise the vaccines may not work. Some vaccines need to be given only once. Others have to be given three times, with a gap of at least four weeks between each dose.**

* The important thing for parents to know is that a child should be taken for immunization five times in the first year of the child's life.

* At birth, or as soon as possible afterwards, babies should be immunized against tuberculosis with BCG. A first dose of polio vaccine can also be given at this time.

* At the age of six weeks, parents should bring their babies for a first immunization against diphtheria, whooping cough, and tetanus. These three vaccines are given together in a single injection called 'DPT'.

* At the ages of 10 and 14 weeks, parents should return for their infants to have two more doses of DPT vaccine. A dose of polio vaccine should also be given on each of these visits.

* As soon as possible after the age of nine months, parents should bring their babies for immunization against measles.

* Measles is one of the most dangerous of all childhood diseases. For the first few months of life, the child has some natural protection against measles, inherited from the mother. But after about nine months, natural protection comes to an end. The child is now at risk from measles and can and should be immunized. So it is vital to take a child for measles vaccination as soon as possible after the age of nine months.

* If for any reason a child has not had all the vaccine doses in the first year of life, it is vital to have the child immunized as soon as possible thereafter. A booster dose of DPT and polio vaccine should be given at one and a half years of age and a dose of DT (diphtheria, tetanus) at five years.

Immunization Schedule for Children

Age	*Vaccine*	*Diseases to be Immunized Against*
Birth	BCG, Polio	Tuberculosis, polio
6 weeks	DPT, Polio	Diphtheria-whooping cough-tetanus, polio
10 weeks	DPT, Polio	Diphtheria-whooping cough-tetanus. polio
14 weeks	DPT, Polio	Diphtheria-whooping cough-tetanus, polio
9 months	Measles	Measles
1½ years	DPT, Polio	Diphtheria-whooping cough-tetanus, polio
5 years	DT	Diphtheria-tetanus.

3. **It is safe to immunize a sick child.**

* One of the main reasons why parents do not bring their children for immunization is that the child has a fever, a cough, a cold, diarrhoea, or some other mild illness on the day the child is to be immunized. Even if the child with a case of mild illness or malnutrition is brought for immunization, health workers may advise against giving the injections. This is wrong advice. It is now known that it is safe to immunize a child who is suffering from a minor illness or malnutrition, and, where diseases such as measles or whooping cough remain dangerous, every opportunity should be taken to do so.

* After an injection the child may cry, develop a fever, a rash or swelling at the site of injection. As with any illness, a child should be given plenty of food and liquids. Breastfeeding is especially helpful. If the problem seems serious or lasts more than three days, the child should be

taken to a health centre. A pimple or a sore develops at the BCG site after about a month. This dries up in 2 4 weeks by itself and needs no treatment.

4. **Every women between the ages of 15 and 44 should be fully immunized against Tetanus.**

* Many mothers give birth in unhygienic conditions. This puts both mother and child at risk from tetanus, a major killer of the new-born. If the mother is not immunized against tetanus, then one baby in every hundred will die from the disease.

* Tetanus germs grow in dirty cuts. This can happen, for example, if an unclean knife is used to cut the umbilical cord or if anything unclean is put on the stump of the cord. (Anything used to cut the cord should first be cleaned and then boiled or heated in a flame and allowed to cool).

* If the tetanus germs enter the mother's body, and if she is not immunized against tetanus, then her life will also be at risk.

* Mothers can protect themselves—and their new-born babies—against tetanus by making sure that they are immunized before or during pregnancy. All women of child-bearing age should be immunized against tetanus, and every woman who becomes pregnant should make sure she is immunized.

* If a woman is not already immunized, a first dose of tetanus vaccine should be given as soon as pregnancy is known. The second dose can be given four weeks after the first, and should be given before the last two weeks of the pregnancy.

A third dose should be given 6 to 12 months after the second dose, or during the next pregnancy.

* These three tetanus vaccinations protect the mother, and her new-born babies, for five years. All infants should be

immunized against tetanus (which is included in DPT) during the first year of life and given a booster dose at 1½ year and 5 years".[183]

It is well recognised that high infant mortality results in high fertility as the parents want to ensure that minimum number of children survive. High fertility in its turn influence adversely health of the mother.

ORAL Re-hydration

About one million children die each year of diarrhoea. This can be avoided by adequate rehydration at an early stage. The present programme of distributing packets of oral re-hydration salts (ORS) seems to be inadequate when we look at the large number of deaths of children due to dehydration. There is urgent need for disseminating information on diarrhoea and simple ways to combat it. The extracts from chapter on Diarrhoea from *Facts for Life* is reproduced below :

"What every family and community has a right to know about diarrhoea :

Diarrhoea causes dehydration, which kills approximately 1 million (10 lakh) children every year in India. Diarrhoea is also a major cause of child malnutrition.

The seven health messages can help parents and communities to prevent almost all of these deaths and most of the malnutrition caused by diarrhoea.

The main causes of diarrhoea are poor hygiene and lack of clean drinking water. It is the responsibility of government to support the community in tackling these basic problems.

1. **Diarrhoea can kill children by draining too much liquid from the body. So it is essential to give a child with diarrhoea plenty of liquids to drink.**

* Diarrhoea is dangerous. Roughly one in every two hundred children who get diarrhoea will die from it.

* Most often, diarrhoea kills by dehydration, which means that too much liquid has been drained out of the child's body. So as soon as diarrhoea starts, it is essential to to give the child extra drinks to replace the liquid being lost.

* Suitable drinks to prevent a child from losing too much liquid during diarrhoea are :

  * Breastmilk

  * Dal water, water from *khichri*, buttermilk or lemon water with salt and sugar.

* In almost all countries, special drinks for children with diarrhoea are available in pharmacies, shops, or health centres. Usually, these come in the form of packets of oral rehydration salts (ORS) to be mixed with the recommended amount of clean water. Although these 'salts' are specially made for the treatment of dehydration, they can also be used to prevent dehydration.

* Do not add ORS to liquids such as milk, soup or soft drinks.

* An effective drink for diarrhoea can also be made by using eight level teaspoons of sugar and one of salt disolved in one litre of clean water.

* If none of these drinks is available, other alternative are :

  * Weak tea

  * Green coconut water.

* If nothing else is available, give water from the cleanest possible source.

* To prevent too much liquid being lost from the child's body, one of these drinks should be given to the child every time a watery stool is passed :

* Between a quarter and a half of a large cup for a child under the age of two
* Between a half and a whole large cup for older children.

* The drink should be given from a cup or a spoon (feeding bottles are difficult to clean properly). If the child vomits, wait for ten minutes and then begin again, giving the drink to the child slowly, small sips at a time.
* Extra liquids should be given until the diarrhoea has stopped. This will usually take between three and five days.

ORS—A Special Drink

A special drink for diarrhoea can be made by using a packet of oral rehydration salts (ORS). This drink is used by doctors and health workers to treat dehydrated children. But it can also be used in the home to prevent dehydration. To make the drink :

* Dissolve the contents of the packet in the amount of water indicated on the packet. If you use too little water. the drink, could make the diarrhoea worse. If you use too much water, the drink will be less effective.
* Stir well, and give to the child to drink in a cup or a spoon.

2. **When a breastfed child has diarrhoea, it is important to continue breastfeeding.**

* When a breastfed child has diarrhoea, breastfeeding should continue, and if possible increase. If the child cannot suck, it is best to squeeze out the breastmilk and feed it to the child with a clean cup and a spoon.
* If the child is being fed on milk solutions or cow's or buffalo's milk, more liquid should be given by adding twice the usual amount of clean water to the child's normal feed. The extra dilution should be stopped as soon as diarrhoea stops.

3. A child with diarrhoea needs food.

* It is often said that a child with diarrhoea should not be given any food or drink while the diarrhoea lasts. This advice is wrong. Food can help to stop the diarrhoea. Also diarrhoea can lead to serious malnutrition unless parents make a special effort to keep feeding the child during and after the illness.

* A child with diarrhoea usually has less appetite, so feeding may be difficult at first. But the child should be tempted to eat frequently, by offering small amounts of his or her favourite food.

* Children who eat solids should be given soft, well-mashed mixes of cereal and pulses, vegetables, etc. Add one or two teaspoonfuls of oil to vegetable mixes if possible. Also good for the child are yoghurt and fruits (espcially brightly coloured fruits such as bananas and mangoes). Foods should be freshly prepared and given to the child five or six times a day.

4. Trained help is needed if diarrhoea is more serious than usual.

* Parents should seek help from a health worker without delay if the child :

  * Becomes dehydrated. Some signs of dehydration are :
    Sunken eyes
    Extreme thirst
    No tears when the child cries

  * Has a fever

  * Will not eat or drink normally and vomits frequently

  * Passes several watery stools in one or two hours

  * Passes blood in the stool (a sign of dysentery)

* If a child has any of these signs, qualified medical help is needed quickly. The doctor or health worker will give the child a drink made with special oral rehydration salts. In the meantime, keep trying to make the child drink liquids.

5. **A child who is recovering from diarrhoea needs an extra meal every day for at least a week.**

    * Extra feeding after the diarrhoea stops is vital for a full recovery. At this time, the child has more appetite and can eat at extra meal a day for at least week. This will help child to catch up on the food 'lost' while the child was ill and the appetite was low. A child is not fully recovered from diarrhoea until he or she is at least the same weight as when the illness began, and plays about as before.
    * Breastfeeding more frequently than usual also helps to speed up recovery.

6. **Medicines should not be used for diarrhoea, except on medical advice.**

    * Most medicines for diarrhoea are either useless or harmful. The diarrhoea will usually cure itself in a few days. The real danger is usually not the diarrhoea but the loss of liquids from the child's body.
    * Do not give a child tablets or other medicines for diarrhoea unless these have been prescribed by a trained health worker.

7. **Diarrhoea can be prevented by breastfeeding, by immunizing all children against measles, by using latrines, by keeping food and water clean, and by washing hands before touching food.**

    * Diarrhoea is caused by germs from faeces entering the mouth. These germs can be spread in water, in food, on hands, on eating and drinking utensils, by flies, and by dirt under fingernails. To prevent diarrhoea, the germs must be stopped from entering the child's mouth.
    * Poverty and lack of basic services such as clean drinking water mean that many families find it difficult to prevent diarrhoea. But the most effective ways are :
    * Give breastmilk alone for the first four-to-six months of a baby's life (breastmilk helps to protect babies against diarrhoea and other illnesses).

- At the age of four-to-six months, introduce clean, nutritious, well-mashed, semi-solid foods and continue to breastfeed.

- If milk-powder solution or fresh animal milk has to be used, give it to the child from a cup and a spoon rather than a bottle.

- Use the cleanest water available for drinking (water from shallow ponds, wells, or rivers should be boiled for five minutes and cooled before use).

- Always use latrines to dispose of faeces, and be sure to put children's faeces in a latrine, or bury them, immediately (children's faeces are even more dangerous than those of adults).

- Wash hands with soap and water immediately after using the latrine and before preparing or eating food.

- Cover food and drinking water to protect it from germs.

- If possible, food should be thoroughly cooked, and prepared just before eating. It should not be left standing, or it will collect germs.

- Bury or burn all refuse to stop flies spreading disease.

- Measles frequently results in serious diarrhoea. Immunization against measles therefore also protects a child against this cause of diarrhoea. There is no vaccine to prevent ordinary diarrhoea".[184]

During the seventh plan, oral rehydration therapy and appropriate feeding practices to prevent a large number of infant and child deaths and growth interruptions resulting from childhood diarrhoea would be promoted through massive educational programme along with production and easy provisioning of oral rehydration salt (ORS) packets.

Improvement in MCH Programme

It is proposed to maximise the use of the ICDS infrastructure for enhancement of MCH programmes during the Seventh

Five Year Plan. It is also proposed to develop National Institute of Maternal and Child Health Prophylaxis against anaemia in mothers and children, and against blindness is being promoted.

Efforts are being made to improve further MCH programme such as World Health Organisation Project strengthening MCH services ; Demonstration of integrated MCH/Family Planning curriculum ; Demonstration of integrated paediatric curriculum workshops on perinatology ; District Public Health Nurses, and State level MCH officers ; Inservices training of PHC officers with UNICEF support ; assistance to medical colleges, Paediatric Unit of District Headquarters Hospitals, Urban Family Welfare Centres and MCH Centres ; Supply of sets of drugs, diet and Supplements ; Curriculum on Management of the Problems of Breast Feeding ; circulating recommendations on peri-natal care to various institutions and State Governments and Union Territories.

The achievement of National MCH goals will rest on approach and priorities. The approach should have focus on family and community with due emphasis on mothers and children. Priorities should include :

(*i*) Translation of Declared policy into financial and other inputs ;

(*ii*) An effective organisations. This implies on organisation with highly competent persons, particularly those oriented to care of mothers and children and promotive and preventive measures, at the Central and State Headquarters. The MCH should be placed at a level in the health administration hierarchy from where their voice can be heard and respected. The organization should be staffed not only with well trained persons but also with commitment to community health and family welfare ;

(*iii*) Real peoples participation ;

(*iv*) Integration of MCH in health system ;

(*v*) The programme should be directed to have a well

informed community on primary health care, through well developed information, education, communication, training and research systems and institutions.

"The following are the top ten messages distilled from *FACTS FOR LIFE*:

1. The health of both women and children can be significantly improved by spacing births at least two years apart, by avoiding pregnancies before the age of 18, and by limiting the total number of pregnancies to two or less.*
2. To reduce the dangers of childbearing, all pregnant women should go to a health worker for pre-natal care and all births should be assisted by a trained person.
3. For the first few months of a baby's life, breastmilk alone is the best possible food and drink. Infants need other foods, in addition to breastmilk, when they are four-to-six months old.
4. Children under three have special feeding needs. They need to eat five or six times a day and their food should be specially enriched by adding mashed vegetables and small amounts of fats or oils.
5. Diarrhoea can kill by draining too much liquid from a child's body. So the liquid lost each time the child passes a watery stool must be replaced by giving the child plenty of the right liquids to drink—breastmilk, home-based fluids such as dal water, rice water, buttermilk, etc., or a special drink called ORS. If the illness is more serious than usual, the child needs help from a health worker—and the special ORS drink. A child with diarrhoea also needs food to make a good recovery.
6. Immunization protects against several diseases which can cause poor growth, disability, and death. All Immunizations should be completed in the first year of the

*In the original text the number given is three or less.

child's life and a booster given at one and a half years. Every woman of child-bearing age should be immunized against tetanus.

7. Most coughs and colds will get better on their own. But if a child with a cough is breathing much more rapidly than normal, then the child is seriously ill and it is essential to go to a health centre quickly. A child with a cough or cold should be helped to eat and to drink plenty of liquids.

8. Many illnesses are caused because germs enter the mouth. This can be prevented by using latrines ; by washing hands with soap and water after using the latrine and before handling food ; by keeping food and water clean ; and by boiling drinking water if it is not from a safe piped supply.

9. Illnesses hold back a child's growth. After an illness, a child needs an extra meal every day for a few days to make up the growth lost.

10. Children from birth to three years should be weighed regularly every month for the first year and at least every alternate month thereafter. If there is no gain in weight for two months, something is wrong".[185]

Goals for Children and Development in the 1990's

A very notable recent events has been the Convention on the Rights of the Child. It is hoped that India will soon sign this convention

"[The World Summit for Children endorsed the following goals for the well-being of children in the 1990s. Achievement of these goals is essential to full implementation of the Convention on the Rights of the Child, which is the ultimate objective of programmes for children and development.]

The following goals have been formulated through extensive consultation in various international fora attended by virtually all Governments, the relevant UN agencies including WHO;

UNICEF, UNFPA, UNESCO, UNDP and IBRD, and a large number of non-governmental organisations. These goals are recommended for implementation by all countries where they are applicable, with appropriate adaptation to the specific situation of each country in terms of phasing, standards, priorities and availability of resources, with respect for cultural, religious and social traditions. Additional goals that are particularly relevant to a country's specific situation should be added in its national plan of action.

I. Major Goals for Child Survival, Development and Protection

—Between 1990 and the year 2000, reduction of infant and under 5 child mortality rate by one-third or to 50 and 70 per 1000 live births respectively, whichever is less.

—Between 1990 and the year 2000, reduction of maternal mortality rate by half.

—Between 1990 and the year 2000, reduction of severe and moderate malnutrition among under-5 children by half.

—Universal access to safe drinking water and to sanitary means of excreta disposal.

—By the year 2000, universal access to basic education and completion of primary education by at least 80% of primary school age children.

—Reduction of the adult illiteracy rate (the appropriate age group to be determined in each country) to at least half its 1990 level with emphasis on female literacy.

—Improved protection of children in especially difficult circumstances.

II. Supporting/Sectoral Goals

1. Women's Health and Education

—Special attention to the health and nutrition of the female child, and pregnant and lactating women.

—Access by all couples to information and services to

prevent pregnancies which are too early, too closely spaced, too late or too many.

—Access by all pregnant women to pre-natal care, trained attendants during child birth and referral facilities for high risk pregnancies and obstetric emergencies.

—Universal access to primary education with special emphasis for girls, and accelerated literacy programmes for women.

2. *Nutrition*

—Reduction in severe as well as moderate malnutrition among under-5 children by half of 1990 levels.

—Reduction of the rate of low birth weight (2.5 kg. or less) to less than 10%.

—Reduction of iron deficiency anaemia in women by one-third of 1990 levels.

—Virtual elimination of iodine deficiency disorders.

—Virtual elimination of vitamin A deficiency and its consequences, including blindness.

—Empowerment of all women to exclusively breast-feed their child for four to six months and to continue breast-feeding with complementary food well into the second year.

—Growth promotion and its regular monitoring to be institutionalised in all countries by the end of the 1990s.

—Dissemination of knowledge and supporting services to increase food production to ensure household food security.

3. *Child Health*

—Global eradication of poliomyelitis by the year 2000.

—Elimination of neonatal tetanus by 1995.

—Reduction by 95 per cent in measles deaths and reduction

by 90 per cent of measles cases compared to pre-immunization levels by 1995, as a major step to the global eradication of measles in the longer run.

—Maintenance of a high level of immunization coverage (at least 90% of children under one year of age by the year 2000) against diphtheria, pertussis, tetanus, measles, poliomyelitis, tuberculosis and against tetanus for women of child bearing age.

—Reduction by 50 per cent in the deaths due to diarrhoea in children under the age of five years ; and 25 per cent reduction in the diarrhoea incidence rate.

—Reduction by one-third in the deaths due to acute respiratory infections in children under five years.

4. Water and Sanitation

—Universal access to safe drinking water.

—Universal access to sanitary means of excreta disposal.

—Elimination of guinea-worm disease (dracunculiasis) by the year 2000.

5. Basic Education

—Expansion of early childhood development activities including appropriate low-cost family and community based interventions.

—Universal access to basic education, and achievement of primary education by at least 80 per cent of primary school age children through formal schooling or non-formal education of comparable learning standard, with emphasis on reducing the current disparities between boys and girls.

—Reduction of the adult illiteracy rate (the appropriate age group to be determined in each country) to at least half its 1990 level, with emphasis on female literacy.

—Increased acquisition by individuals and families of the knowledge, skills and values required for better living, made available through all educational channels, including the mass media, other forms of modern and traditional communication, and social action, with effectiveness measured in terms of behavioural change.

6. *Children in Difficult Circumstances*

—Provide improved protection of children in especially difficult circumstances and tackle the root causes leading to such situations".

[*Source* : UNICEF]

Comprehensive Primary Health Care

The specific references to immunization, re-hydration, maternal and child health schemes may not be considered as support only to disease and treatment specific health programmes, often called selective approach. The selective approach has its own value. But the comprehensive primary health care should receive the highest priority. In words of D. Banerjee, "the primary health care is based on people, rather than predetermined system. It emphasises social control over health services, involving people at all stages of health service development, namely problem identification, programme formulation, programme implementation and evaluation. Selective primary health care...adopts an authoritarian or paternalistic approach in selecting for others a number of limited vertical health programmes and leaves the other causes of ill health untouched". The achievements of health goals will depend on fulfilling commitments made at Alma-Ata in 1978.

20

Indian Railways

The interest of officials of the railways in family planning is traceable to late 1930s. Lt. Colonel S.A. Wilkinson, the Chief Medical Officer Bombay, Baroda and Central India Railways was a great supporter of birth control movement. He called birth control 'regulated family sex hygiene' according to the usage at that time. He observed : "Every where in the world today intelligent and far seeing people are beginning to realise the importance of this subject. Arrayed against them are the potent forces of religious superstition, ignorance and people with the Hun or Cannon fodder mentality, but necessity for scientifically controlled and properly regulated family sex hygiene teaching in India is being realised more and more every day".[186] Such a statement of a senior official of the Railways in 1930s was considered a very bold one. It is difficult to surmise the extent of provision of family planning services to railway employees, at that time. It is safe to assume that family planning services were almost non-existent for the railway employees.

The first well organised family planning services for railway employees were organised in Bombay in 1950s. The initiative came from the Family Planning Association of India. The newly formed Family Planning Association was franticly looking for a suitable place for their family planning clinic. The

General Manager Western Railways, Kamta Prashad Mushran, had built a Welfare Centre for railway workers. He readily agreed with Lady Dhanvanthi Rama Rao the President of the newly formed Family Planning Association of India to provide accommodation for establishment for a family welfare centre (Kutumbh Sudhar Kendra) by the Family Planning Association of India with the stipulation that services to railway employees would be free. The Kutumb Sudhar Kendra, was thus opened in 1949.[187] Sushila Gore, a physician deeply committed to family planning movement and wife of a senior officer working in the Railways, mobilised support of railway officials and their wives in Bombay. She greatly contributed to the development of the family welfare activities of the Kutumb Sudhar Kendra in its formative years in the railway colony. Individual medical officers took initiative in other places and started giving birth control advice. But it was not till late 1950s and early 1960s that the programme on widescale was launched. In early days Dr. Lal and later Dr. S.S. Verma in the Ministry of Railways put the programme on sound foundations.

The Indian Railways is the largest public sector undertaking. About one crore persons travel daily in the Indian Railway. An innovative activity associated with railways was launched by Dr. Pai at the Victoria Railway Station Bombay through education programme among commuters and providing on the spot vasectomy facilities with cooperation of the Railway authorities.

In 1978, the number of employees in the Indian Railways was 2.15 million (including 0.7 million temporary and casual worker). The population is dispersed as the railway runs (criss-crosses) over 60,000 route kilometers and passess through about 7,083 railway stations. 'Only 40 per cent of the total railway employees live in larger stations and only half of these are housed in railway colonies. Twenty per cent of the total population lives in small wayside stations or along the track in rural conditions and 60 per cent outside the railway premises'.

The family planning programme had to be deviced to suit the dispersed nature of the railway population and conform with the general administrative system and within the administrative system integrated with the health system. Ministry of Railways has a Railway Board as an Executive Body with a number of technical departments including health directorate with a health professional as its head later designated as Director General and Ex-officio Additional Secretary. There are nine zones and three production units each under General Manager with a Chief Medical Officer. The Zones have Divisions, a senior medical officer is head of the Divisional health services. The Railway health organisation in 1978 had 99 well equipped hospitals, 567 Health Units and 247 Maternity and Child Welfare Centres, 62 Family Welfare centres and 29 sub-centres. The health services were manned by about 2300 doctors and 53,000 para-medical personnel, including 625 personnel financed by the Ministry of Health and Family Welfare.

The family planning organisation in the Indian Railways included :

(*i*) At Railway Board : a Dy. Director Family Planning, a Health Education Officer, two publicity officer, two statistical assistants and supporting secretarial personnel.

(*ii*) In each zonal Headquarters : Senior Medical Officer F P., one Extension educator, one statistical assistant, Projectionist and supporting staff.

(*iii*) Family welfare centres about 6? : each with Asstt. Medical Officer, extension educator, field worker one male and one female, ANM or Lady Health Visitor or Public Health Nurse and supporting staff.

(*iv*) Family Planning Sub-centres 29 : each with Field worker male or ANM.

The railway health service being integrated service, all health personnel were required to provide family planning services as a part of health care. As some staff was financed by Ministry of Health and Family Planning it was arranged that railway health staff would spend about 20 per cent of their time on family planning and the family planning staff 20 per cent of their time on general medical and health services. The diverting of family planning staff to other work appeared to have been objected by Ministry of Health. Ultimately saner advice prevailed and deployment of staff according needs was accepted.

The family planning programme was integrated with maternal and child health programme. The general programme activities of family planning workers began with immunization and nutrition programme (during first two or three visits no reference was made to birth control). The subject of birth control was discussed only after the rapport was established.

The Railways adopted 'a Four Step' and 'Star Scoring' system. As the minimum age of employment was 18 years and retirement 58 years education programme was geared to 'Four Steps', *viz.* : (1) bachelor ; sex education : (2) just married condom and or other convenient contraceptive, to delay the first child by about three years ; (3) IUD or oral contraceptive to delay the second child by about three years ; and (4) when second child two years old : sterilization.

The star scoring "system" was included in the Target Couple Register. The number of stars indicated level of motivation (*contacted : **no impression ; ***using conventional contraceptive irregularly motivated for IUD or sterilization ; ****IUD inserted or regular pill user ; and sterilization (vasectomy or tubectomy) or oral pill user successfully for three years).

The results reported showed an increase of sterilizations from 13,284 (in 1955-65 ten years) to 27,407 in 1975-76 (in a single year) and a record figure of 8,751 in 1976-77. IUD insertions, like rest of India in early years (1965-66 and 1966-67) began well around 12-13 thousand insertions than gradually decreased to about 3000 in 1971-72 and slightly picked up in 1975-76 and 1976-77. The conventional contraceptives gradually increased and reached the figure of ,24,829 in 1976-77. The cumulative achievement, in the railways has been of high order. The notable feature has been that the acceptors of both sterilization and IUD acceptors were mostly, around 90-92 per cent, with wives in the age group 29-30 years. The cost analysis for 1975-76 shows that cost per unit equivalent sterilization was Rs. 133.00 as compared to All India Rs. 259. The Railway had adopted extension approach. The incentives (compensation) were introduced as part of all Indian programme. Verma observes, it will be very difficult to say in retrospect what success we would have achieved in case compensation money was not paid, but one can only guess that perhaps it would not have made much of a difference.[188]

21

Christian Medical Association

The Christian Missions in India has a long history of dedicated service in the field of health and education. There are other Missions like Ramakrishna Mission, but their share in health care services, in resources and extent of services provided to the people are not comparable to the Christian Missions. The hospitals, affiliated to the Christian Medical Association of India established in 1926, support the National Family Planning Programme.

The Christian Medical Association of India (CMAI) is a voluntary health agency and is the medical wing of the National Council of Churches in India. The three teaching institutions at Vellore, Ludhiana and Miraj are affiliated to the Christian Medical Association. Sixty per cent of the institutions are in rural areas, twenty per cent in semi-urban areas and the rest in urban areas The main function of the Association is to provide advisory services to its institutions in their work and development. The institutions under the Association offer also formal training in : 3 institutions involved in formal training in medical education ; 80 in nursing education ; 30 in laboratory technology ; 6 in radiography technology ; 3 in medical record technology ; 1 in rural health guide and 1 in hospital auxilliary (leprosy). The Hospital Auxilliary (leprosy) is a programme that has been recently commenced with a view to prepare personnel for work in leprosy control. It is now recognised that personnel for work in leprosy control areas require specific preparation. The course is well accepted and many agencies, both in the country and others from neighbouring countries, are taking advantage of this programme. CMAI has 400 institutions affiliated to it and of which 286 are under a programme for health and family planning promotion in areas, each of these institutions cover.

The Association had established a section for preventive medicine about 30 years ago. In 1966 the Association commenced a project for establishing family planning services in their institutions with a view to promote family planning in the community. Initially, is was intended to help the institutions to offer family planning services for which they were given monetary incentives by covering their expenditure incurred in establishing and providing such services. Training of personnel in the institutions was necessary if the family planning services were to be augmented. The training to be persued required an infrastructure. Regional training teams were instituted. Each regional team consisted of a social scientist, (often graduate at the master level in social work) and a nurse educator. The social scientist was involved to work out motivational techniques, prepare the community for acceptance of family planning and bring about change in the attitude of people for the acceptance of small family norm. While some of the social scientists working in the project were effective in this regard, others were totally found to be inappropriate. In the beginning the teams were given, each year, a briefing for a week. This was not found adequate. Four week training sessions were commenced from April/May 1984. The briefing/training sessions were to strengthen their existing knowledge, provide new knowledge and develop skills. Some posts of social scientists are now being filled with nutritionist. The social science support required by the teams is now being covered through contract service with local experts as and when necessary.

In the early part of 1977, the preventive medicine section of the Christian Medical Association of India was amalgamated with the Project, to ensure that family planning service is a component of the primary health care service.

The Association studied the health services provided by its member institutions and prepared a health care delivery pattern. It has advocated to its institutions a three tier delivery procedure. The first tier is the community service and is community based. The second tier is the family service. This includes such services as family planning, nutrition, control of tuberculosis, leprosy and other aspects that require care in the family context. The third tier is individual personalised service that will meet the individual need which often is curative in character. The institutions have adopted this health care delivery pattern and established primary health care services.

Initially the primary health care services provided by the institutions were confined to maternal and child health and family planning gradually other components were added and thus widening the spectrum of their services. This comprehensive approach to the provision of family planning services has been found to be useful in reaching many among the eligible couples in the community. Thus diversification of services at the community level, incorporating the family planning services in it, was a phase the institutions had gone through.

In order to understand further the regional variations in the adoption of small family norm, action-cum-research programmes were introduced initially in selected hospitals. Regional spread of the institutions was ensured and 4 institutions with schools of nursing and 4 others without such schools were selected. The intent of the programme was to ascertain if on the assurance of the survival of the off springs, the couples would opt for family planning. The hypothesis tested in the field was found to be valid. Some of the institutions in the scheme after the action-cum-research programme was over have continued it as they found that family planning programme was carried out better if family centered approach was adopted. Gaining, some experience from the initial action-cum-research scheme, another scheme covering 22 hospitals was introduced with a post-partum approach. The scheme envisaged the augmentation of family planning in rural communities where small hospitals exist and where the community presented potential for family planning practices.

The action-cum-research schemes were to identify the determinants for augmenting family planning work and to bring the member hospitals (including some that were involved in research) in partnership with the Christian Medical Association for the scrutiny of the prevailing situation, regionally, to accelerate further demand for family planning services.

At the community level, health promotion alone carried out was found gradually insufficient. It required to be linked with other aspects of community development. Therefore, in August 1979, the Governing Body of the Christian Medical Association of India took the decision to tie up health and family planning programme with other aspects of development of the community and persuing non-formal education. The scheme is a package offered to the member institutions. The package includes : health and family planning promotion ; socio-economic development of the community ; agricultural improvement, for correlation exists between good agriculture, good yield in the wake of it and possibly better nutrition among people resulting from it, and the provision of knowledge on nutrition, population and community awareness in a non-formal manner. Some of the member institutions have implemented this package programme.

While the above activities were persued, in early 1980s three factors were identified as essential ingredients for development of the programme, *viz.*, the need for strengthening the infrastructure of the Association for training, improving the nutrition components of primary health services of the member institutions ; and augmenting health education. There are at present 12 regional teams located in the different parts of India, each team covers on an average, 25 member institutions. It is planned to develop 12 regional training centres. These training centres will be attached to member institutions that have schools of nursing. The purpose of locating them in such institutions, where schools of nursing exist, is to pool the available manpower and utilise them for training. A centre will be governed by a local board made up of medical superintendents of member institutions in the region. The training will be based on the needs of the region and will be assisted by local experts. Such decentralised, need-based training will be given in a non-formal manner to groups of professionals (doctors and nurses), para-medicals in the institutions, the para-professionals (community health workers) and the community (mothers, youths, teachers, etc.) and the community group and the local officials at the community level. The stream-lining of the procedures of nutrition component is being done. For augmentation of health education a suitable health education programme is being prepared, based on a survey carried out to assess the pattern and pace of health education in each of the member institutions and to learn if scope existed for further augmenting it in the community that each of the hospitals cover.

The project has been subjected to the scrutiny of three evaluation teams, since its inception. The first was provided, on request by the Association, by Ministry of Health and Family Planning in December 1968, including H. Banerjee Assistant Commissioner Family Planning, M.G. McGovern Ford Foundation Consultant National Institute of Health Administration and Education (NIHAE), M.I.D. Sharma Professor Programme Evaluation NIHAE, and E.B. Sundaram Superintendent Clara Swain Hospital Baraillev. The second evaluation team was composed of Professor of Research and Evaluation NIHAE, the Director of the Central Institute of Social Sciences Bangalore and Professor of Community Nursing, College of Nursing Vellore. The last evaluation was done by the Institute of Management Ahmedabad.

Since inception of the Project cumulative total family planning acceptors till December 1983, reported in Association member-institutions were 8,81,507 (tubectomy 6,40,221, vasectomy 70,485, IUD & Cu-T I, 17,136, and orals 48,665).

Further efforts were directed to : strengthen the family planning services in member institutions by improving quality of the procedures adopted, revised documentation procedure giving both person users and method users ; briefing the medical and nursing superintendent member institutions, regionally, for three days to help them to understand how well they can further reduce morbidity, mortality and fertility in their respective communities ; and convening the meeting of the church leaders, regionally, so that they become aware of the need to promote family planning through the church communities.[189]

22

Indian Tea Association

The tea in India has a long and fascinating story. The estates present a refreshing rural scene and are appropriately called 'tea gardens'. Health and welfare services in them are equally of interest. On February 1, 1834, the East India Company appointed a Committee on cultivation and manufacture of tea on a commercial scale. On December 24, 1835, the committee reported to Lord William Bentinck, the Governor General that "the tea shrub is beyond doubt indigenous in Upper Assam" and that "this discovery is by far the most important and valuable that has ever been made on matters connected with the agricultural or commercial resources of this empire". This was important to the East India Company, as the tea was being imported by them from China and the Company's monopoly of China tea had ended in 1833. Thus started the long march of commercial production of tea in India. Whether the Indian tea is indigenous or a foreign crop, has been a subject of controversy. It seems that 80,000 seeds of China tea arrived in India : of these 42,000 seed germinated in the Botanical gardens and were distributed in Assam, Western Himalayas and Nilgiris in the South. The Chinese seed grew in the Kangra Valley only and is still produced there in small quantity as green tea. In the rest of tea plantations the tea grown is indigenous and not the Chinese plant. "George Williamson took over management of the estates belonging to Assam Company, the first company to be floated (1839) in London with manufacture of Indian tea as its main business and Dwarkanath Tagore and Moti Lal Seal among its directors in Calcutta. "Around mid 19th century there was only one large tea plantation near Dibrugarh. The tea production centres gradually increased-Darjeling and Cachar in 1856, the Terai in 1862, the Dooars in 1874 in North India ; and Nilgiris, Travancore-Wynaad and Annamalais in the South India during the last one-third of 19th century. The United Kingdom was the world's principal 'consumption and transit market'. The China remained the major supplier to the United Kingdom market. The position changed after 1879, for example in 1964 the United Kingdom consumed 150 million lbs of Indian tea and 15 million lbs of Chinese tea. India now is worlds largest producer and exporter of tea, export earning for 1983 were Rs. 520 crores, 6% of India's total earnings. The contribution of tea to GNP is estimated to be Rs. 1000 crores annually.

The story of tea plantation workers and their living conditions, in early days, is very depressing. The indentured labour (almost slaves), lived in poverty and squalor. There were however some enlightened employers. But their number was very limited. The indentured labour was abolished in 1926. But the exploitation of labour continued. The situation now has changed. In October 1951, the plantation Labour Act was enacted by the Parliament and brought into force on April 1, 1954. The actual enforcement was delayed due to severe recession in tea industry. It was enforced by 1956 in all the important tea estates except Kerala. The enforcement in Kerala was done in 1959. The tea plantation workers, in addition get benefits of almost all the labour laws such as : Contract Labour (Regulation & Abolition) Act 1970 ; Equal Remuneration Act 1976 ; Industrial Disputes Act 1976 ; Industrial Employment (Standing Orders) Act 1945 ; Minimum Wages Act 1948 ; Maternity Benefit Act 1961 ; Payment of Bonus Act 1965 ; Payment of Gratuity Act 1972 ; Payment of Wages Act 1936 ; the employees provident funds and miscellaneous provision Act 1952 ; workmen's compensation Act 1923.

The initial interest of employers in health of workers, generally, appears to have been generated by their self-interest. Malaria and other health hazards caused high mortality and morbidity. Getting labour and retaining them became difficult. Group practice and medical and health advisers were employed. Gradually well organised medical and health services emerged in plantations. Although services provided to workers in plantations were better than they would get in the villages from where they were recruited, they remained for long far from satisfactory, as is seen from reports of the Health Survey and Development Committee 1943, and Lloyds Jones Technical Report 1947. Lloyd Jones observed that "vast bulk of morbidity and mortality were due to conditions arising from poor diet, poor sanitation, untreated or inadequately treated water supply and ignorance of workers". The Labour Conference held in Delhi in January 1947 recommended that "the Government should prescribe the standards and enforce them, the actual provision of medical services being left to employers. Large gardens would run their own services while small gardens would combine and share expenses". The Plantation Labour Act 1951, included free housing, wholesome drinking water, medical aid, education of children, canteen, creche and appointment of Labour Welfare Officer.

The number of plantation workers in 1950s was estimated to be about one million. There are two special characteristics about plantation labour : the large number of female labour and the labour recruited over the year from different parts of India, an appreciable number in Assam are of tribal origin (the Mundas, Santhals, Urangs). Different languages, traditions and customs are thus found in plantations and yet they have developed some common behaviour patterns and even common dialect, the so-called 'garden *Bat*'. In many ways their living conditions are now better than in the villages they come from. The wages necessarily are not uniformly high, but as in appreciable number of cases the whole family works the situation is eased. Further the fringe benefits provide relief. There is wide variation in health and family planning facilities provided. Some employers more than fulfill the statutory obligations and provide high standards of health and medical care. There are also plantations where conditions are often below standard. There are small plantations scattered, which by their very nature, cannot provide adequate facilities. One important feature from the very beginning has been the support of both employers and workers to family planning. The family planning activities promoted by two associations are of special interest, *viz.*, the Indian Tea Association and the United Planters Association of Southern India.

INDIAN TEA ASSOCIATION

In 1950s the Indian Tea Association (ITA) had a membership of about 700 tea estates of varying sizes (from large agency house to small 'proprietorship' gardens), scattered in Assam (Darang, Goalpara, Kamrup, Lakhimpur, Nowgong, Sibsagar and Cachar) and West Bengal (Darjeeling, Terai and Dooars). The large agencies have a very well developed health and medical services : a Chief Medical Officer, well staffed dispensaries, garden hospitals, a central hospital, a central laboratory. The Labour Welfare Committee found that the hospital beds and medical and para-medical staff provided by members of the ITA were far more than required under the Plantation Labour rules.

One important feature was the Ross Institute for Tropical Hygiene Indian Branch, which served as the Chief technical resource for all plantations. The Ross Institute was formed in London as a memorial to Sir Roland Ross, who discovered in his small laboratory in Hyderabad that mosquitoes carry malaria. Sickness and deaths caused by malaria had assumed serious proportions in India especially in Assam, and caused anxiety among tea planters. In 1930, the Indian Branch of Ross Institute was opened in Cinnamara. In 1934, the Ross Institute was incorporated with the London School of Hygiene and Tropical Medicine. This development had important bearing on future activities of the Institute's Indian Branch. As malaria began to loose its previous lethal impact the activities extended to cover social and preventive medicine including hygiene sanitation, and water supply and in the 1950s family planning. Several associations and industries became members of the institute by paying subscription based on area under plantation or amount of product produced or ad hoc payment depending on the size and location. In 1965 the Committee of control of the Ross Institute Indian Branch included the Indian Tea Association, the United Planters Association of Southern India, Imperial Chemical Industries (India) Pvt. Ltd. Indian Jute Mills Association, Duncan Brothers, Indian Mining Association, Sarwar (India) Ltd., and Bengal Chamber of Commerce and Industries. In 1966-67 there were 34 subscribers to the Institute. The Institute conducted training courses for medical officers, orientation courses for managers, collected vital statistics, to some extent monitored the health and family planning activity and initiated new activities and served as chief technical resource to its members. The Ross Institute illustrates the very fruitful cooperative mechanism through which several agencies contributed to one institute of excellence in hygiene and tropical medicine to meet the needs for training of both management and medical personnel, educational programme both of employers and labour, monitoring collecting much needed information on progress of programme especially vital statistics on regional basis and providing technical advice.

The initiation of family planning activities in the ITA associated units can be traced to 1950s, when the tea estate doctors undergoing training or refresher courses at the Ross Institute in Cinnamara were given instructions on family planning in addition to the other normal subjects on hygiene and tropical medicine. It is difficult to assess the extent of impact till late 1950s of this training on implementation of family planning programme. But it seems many doctors after training did give birth control advice in their respective places of work. In 1957, the Indian Tea Association requested the Family Planning Association of India (FPAI) for assistance. The FPAI made available the services of Devikrishna Rao to work with the Principal of the Ross Institute. The family planning programme in tea plantations was thus launched by stages-beginning with training, on more extensive scale than before, both at the Institute and hospitals for medical staff; provision of supplies after completion of initial training and development of educational programme.

By 1959 about 75 per cent of medical officers were trained and arrangement for supplies in almost all hospitals was made. A whole-time social worker was engaged for educational programme. Before educational programme was launched a sample survey was undertaken. The survey showed that 20% of workers were willing to use contraceptives, another 20% were willing after having one or more children and very few were opposed to controlling birth. A fertility survey was also done. It was observed that average tea garden woman worker gave birth to 7.5 live babies and for every 1000 children born 764 were among woman in the age group 20-34 years.

In early 1963, the methods used were condom, foam tablets and sterilizations. The ITA carried out a field trial in 1963 with oral contraceptives. It was found that large scale use of oral contraceptives was not feasible in plantations. Among factors like cost and side-effects it was observed that in the absence of regular supervision tea garden women could not be relied upon for continued and uninterrupted use of pills. In 1965, the regular IUD programme was introduced in plantations. The methods used at this stage were condom, IUDs and sterilization operations. Besides the incentives offered by the Government, the ITA offered additional cash incentives on sliding scale-parents having two children Rs. 100, parents having three children Rs. 70 and parents having more than three children Rs. 50 for sterilization cases.

By 1968, the family planning programme of ITA was considered as a success story. These developments were mainly due to the commitment and drive of the Chairman of ITA Morris at that time and the drive of Allan Gilroy the Principal of the Ross Institute in Cennamara. The female sterilizations were mainly confined to the tea estates in upper Assam and male sterilizations to around Jorhat and depended on the interest of the medical officers in the Garden Hospital (one surgeon near Cennamara was a great vasectomy enthusiast).

The record of vital statistics in tea estates was reliable for several reasons. For every birth the worker was given maternity benefit which was a strong motivating factor for reporting births. Miscarriages were also entitled to a partial maternity benefit. Every resident on an estate was entitled rations at subsidised rates. This implied that a person dying had to be taken off the ration strength. Besides, the plantations labour being a well knit community, every case of death came to the notice of the garden manager concerned and usually the manager had to issue the death certificate permitting burial or cremation. Gilroy meticulously collected the information and computed according to area and not according to the number of estates as some were very small and others very large. Nearly all estates reported the information on births and deaths. In 1960 the birth rate was 43 4, dropped to 32.3 in 1966 and in 1968 to 22.7, per thousand population, much below National average.

There has been some comment on infant mortality in the tea plantations. The infant mortality reported increased from 78.9 in 1960 to 93.0 in 1966. Higher figures were reported by some observers. The reasons may be non-utilisation of the maternity benefits for care of maternal and child care or wrong reporting or both. Gilroy comments that one doctor told him that 'the infant mortality rate was computed on the number of babies dying before reaching their second birthday'. In other words the person reporting did not know that infant mortality rate is computed for 1000 live births under one year of age registered in the calender year. The need for training of concerned field staff in bio-statistics was obvious.

The momentum of pace of development of family planning programme among members of ITA appeared to come to a virtual halt in 1969. The interest of the association seemed to wane. The Indian Branch of Ross Institute was closed without replacing it with another organisation with similar function.

With the closure of the Institute Gilroy left. One of the reason given for the declining interest and inputs in family planning programme is stated to be that 'the deteriorating economic condition of the Tea Industry'. Another reason given is that outside parties started interfering with work of medical staff engaged in family planning work with the result that social worker and some estate medical staff left their services. 'The prominent feature seems to be the lack of commitment of employers to family planning and of leadership provided by the Chairman Indian Tea Association and the non-replacement of the Ross Institute by a similar mechanism to provide technical guidance and support. The inevitable result was rise in birth rates.

The rising trend in birth rate, led ITA to take serious notice of family planning programme again. K.N. Sircar, Adviser Indian Tea Association picked up old threads and recommended appointment of two medical officers one in Assam and another in West Bengal to fill the gap created by the closure of the Ross Institute in Cennamara. The training and education programme was restarted. The existing status of programme in each estate was resurveyed. The plans for all membar estate were reformulated. The collection of demographic information was improved. It was possible to carry out periodical appraisal of the programme and oversee the execution of the programme of member estates, and bring about greater co-ordination with the Government family planning programme.[190]

On 31-12-83, the birth rates reported were : Assam Valley 47.50 ; Surma Valley 31.9? ; Dooars 31.00 and Terai 37.44. These figures relate to resident population of 9,94,037 and total population (including dependents) of 16,0?, 93 in 433 gardens in North East India (The number of reporting garden was 394).[191]

A notable activity launched in 1980s was ILO/UNFPA/ITA Projects. Some of the important aspects of the Project are :

(*i*) Central Branch and Plantation level Committees ;

(*ii*) A Population Cell at Dooars Branch ITA (DBITA) Headquarters ;

(*iii*) A mobile Education Unit headed by a Social worker/ educator ;

(*iv*) Worker/Motivators ;

(*v*) Orientation of Managers and Assistant Managers and Medical Officers and training of social worker educator and Para medical staff ;

(*vi*) Provision of training material ;

(*vii*) Base line survey in each individual tea estate, development of information system providing monthly information on vital statistics and family planning acceptors, and mid-term and final evaluation.

The Central Coordinating Committee was made responsible for the appointment of the Project Coordinator and Project Director. The Adviser ITA based in Calcutta was made the Project Coordinator. The Project Director was made responsible for directing the work of Population Cell, arranging visits of the mobile unit to tea estates, visiting member estates to check on the work of the mobile unit and worker-motivators, the progress of the programme ensuring availability of contraceptives, collecting and collating the figures of acceptors and coverage of the persons exposed to the programme, arranging and conducting orientation and training and keeping the Committees at different levels informed of the progress of the project.

Two aspects of the Project are of special interest, *viz.*, Composition of Branch level and plantation level Committees and the Worker-motivator. The Branch level Committee had two members each of employers (Executive Committee of DBITA) and workers organisation (nominees of the Coordinating Committee of Tea Plantation workers), besides the Vice-Chairman of DBITA, General Secretary and Adviser DBITA, a member of the District Health Department and Project Director. The Plantation level labour – Management Committee on selected Plantations included the Manager and Assistant Manager, the Estate Medical Officer, two workers representative and two worker-motivators. The Project Work Plan laid down that worker-motivators will be selected from amongst the union leaders and other influential estate workers, and provided training at the Health and Welfare Training Centre at Jalpaiguri. After their training their task was to provide information on matters connected with family welfare to their fellow workers ; and information where services were to be obtained ; to educate and motivate fellow workers through formal and informal meetings and inter-personnel communication ; and to liaise with medical and para-medical staff and estate management in furtherance of family welfare activities. The Worker-motivators and representation of labour and management on Committees were two important aspects of programme operation. It is reported that the plan to form Labour-Management Committee in each garden was eventually discarded. It was considered that informal meetings held periodically, between the managerial staff, medical officers, worker-motivators and workers representatives would serve the purpose. There may have been some valid reasons for adopting such an alternative in a specific situation. But in principle, the full and intimate workers participation at grass-roots is difficult in the absence of Labour-Management Committee assuming full responsibility for a programme. A review of the situation about mid 1984 showed that the number acceptors increased, and there was greater awareness of the need for family planning in younger age group, irrespective of their literacy status, than the older generation. But still about 60 per cent to 65 per cent of the workers want to have 3-4 children. This does not appear to be based on high infant mortality, if the reported rates are correct. In Dooars the infant mortality reported in December 1983 was 51.27, much below the National average. A deeper look is required in programme operation especially : (*i*) extension education ; (*ii*) selection of worker-motivators and their training, the methods used in Gandhigram may be helpful both for selection and training worker-motivators who are really local leaders ; (*iii*) orientation of management to reconsider adoption of original work plan and to resist the temptation of relentless persuit of sterilization targets ; (*iv*) guidance of worker in the field, refresher courses for orientation and training ; (*v*) innovative approachs to information, education and communication ; (*vi*) promotion of comprehensive Labour Welfare as in Southern India* ; (*vii*) development of the programme as workers own programme. The workers' own programme means that in each tea garden workers form their own health and welfare committee and management and professionals (medical officers, health educators and others) give the requisite support.

23

The United Planters Association of South India

Plantations basically refer to agricultural operations including tea, coffee, rubber, cardomom and pepper. Besides Assam and West Bengal, they are located in Kerala, Tamil Nadu and Karnataka. Tea is also grown in Bihar, Himachal Pradesh, Tripura and Uttar Pradesh, but in small quantity. There are large and small plantations (tea, coffee, rubber, cardamom and other minor products) in Kerala, Tamil Nadu and Karnataka. The United Planters Association of Southern India (UPASI) established in 1893, represents plantation industry in Southern India.

According to popular belief, the first seven seeds of coffee were brought by Haji Baba Budan from Arabian Red Sea port of Mocha to Chikmaglur in Karnataka on his return journey from Mecca to India, and coffee was generally used as euphoric drink by Sufi saints. The earliest reference to coffee is made in a letter written by Abbe Dubois to Colonel Miller the British Resident in Mysore State, in 1803. It appears that the East India Company in 1799, established an experimental station for cultivation of coffee at Anjar near Tellichary, and in 1825 the coffee cultivation started in North Wynad. Now coffee is grown on large areas on the slopes of the Western Ghats, at heights varying from 500 to 1500 metres. In India, coffee forms a very small proportion of the quantity grown in the world (about 2.5%). But the quality of Indian coffee beans is rated very high, as they have unique flavour and colour. Indian coffee beans are in demand in foreign markets for marrying with other seeds, hence a foreign exchange earner. Rubber is a late comer. It was in 1902, that rubber plantations started in Thattaked (Periyar estate) in Travancore (now part of Kerala). The cardomom and pepper cultivation on small scale appears to be prevalent from ancient times.

In 1977, there were about 48,000 coffee plantations and over 1,10,000 small rubber holdings. Large units were 30,000 only. The estimated labour force, at that time, in tea, rubber and coffee was 591950. The small units generally were not able to employ resident labour or regular labour. Of the 591950 estimated labour about 320400 only were covered by the Plantation Labour Act. The number of resident population was over a million. Large units and a few small holdings were members of the UPASI. Health and welfare services in the plantations in Southern India passed through the similar phases as the plantations in rest of the country. The interest of the UPASI in family planning emerged later than the ITA. Initially the larger companies took an interest in population programmes, when the Government of India took a lead. The planters who were faced with large families of workers, whom they had to house and secure foodgrains to feed and to provide medical care free of charge, found the family planning programme an attractive idea. There were senior medical men like R. Mahadevan in the High Ranges of South India who took a great deal of interest and made valuable contribution in the promotion of family planning programme.

The UPASI was increasingly becoming aware of the population problem on the remote estates where there was no alternative opening for employment for the large number of workers' dependents. The UPASI had the advantage of ITA experience of family planning programme in tea gardens. The first important step taken by the UPASI was to carry out a survey to explore the population situation in the estates. In 1968, V.I. Chacko the Secretary and Adviser UPASI, initiated a district wide study in the estates. Ronald-Ridker of the USAID in New Delhi came to know about this study. In 1970, Ridker put forward a scheme for experiment in the estates on a deferred incentive scheme which came to be known as No birth Bonus scheme. Chako was very sensitive to innovative approaches. The UPASI consequently agreed to try this scheme in five estates in the neighbourhood of Coonor in Nilgiris. The No-birth Bonus scheme was later combined with the comprehensive Labour Welfare Scheme which extended to six districts.

NO-BIRTH BONUS SCHEME (NBBS)

The NBBS was financed by the USAID from 1971 to 1973. The Federation of Indian Chamber of Commerce and Industries and Family Planning Foundations, New Delhi gave financial support in the following year. The NBBS was basically simple. Under the scheme, Rupees Five per month were credited to the account of each eligible female on the plantation roll who volunteered to enrol in the scheme, with the stipulation that she will forfeit amounts on graduated scale in case the woman had the third child or more ; Rs. 50 to be forfeited in case the women had a third child after three years of having the second child ; Rs. 100 if she had the third child within three years of the second child ; Rs. 200 if she had the fourth child ; and the total amount deposited if she had the fifth child. The woman, who forfeited the entire amount deposited, could rejoin the scheme, if either the woman or husband accepted sterilization.

A pilot project was started in three estates, *viz.*, Ben Gorm, Parkside and Glendale. The consolidated figures upto June 1977 show that the number of woman under NBBS varied from 580 in 1971-72 to 521 in 1976-77. The percentage of women who did not forfeit the amounts deposited was 79.1 in 1971-72 and as high as 92.7 in 1974-75. Of the women who forfeited all the amount deposited 26 re-entered the scheme during 1971-77.*

COMPREHENSIVE LABOUR WELFARE SCHEME

The genesis of this scheme can be traced to the perception of the Secretary and Adviser UPASI, V.I. Chacko. In a paper 'Facing the Future' in 1971 he observed that "An association could be a vital and creative force if it is alive to something more than the grievance aspect of producing community. It would be a catalyst for developmental action, an instrument for the generation of new wealth and could provide leadership for the whole community within a free and democratic framework". The assessment of UPASI, based on ad-hoc surveys and experience in some of their estates, reinforced the feeling that some alternative strategy was needed to deal with the population problem. The major concern of the workers in the estates appeared to be the health of their family and their own.

Many estates offering Rs. 100 as incentive for sterilization since 1966, even after doubling the amount were not getting the expected results. The introduction of IUD and pills did not make material difference.

Some of the ways to energise the programme, like health and extension education and integrating family planning with maternal and child care, and the new suggestion on deferred incentive inherent in No-Birth Bonus, were known. The Govern-

*A bill on "no-birth bonus" is reported to have been introduced in the Philippines Congress which provides for couples who have no more than two children : tax exemption of 12,000 pesos or double the present tax allowance ; 50 per cent discount on real e tate tax ; free school supplies and priority in admission to school for their children ; a personal exemption of 15,000 pesos also double the present amount allowed to Heads of two child families ; and also that the couples shall be divested of the privileges under the bill immediately the couples become parents of the third child (Popline September-October 1990 cited in *Planned Parenthood Bulletin*, Family Planning Association of India, November, 1990)

ment over the years was conveying to the industry to take a more effective role. The managements in the estates generally were hesitant to add additional inputs. The one way to convince them was through actual results of a pilot demonstration project.

The conceptualisation of such projects involved a series of discussions. Its implementation took a long time mainly due to difficulties in getting financial resources, and after the resources were assured building up of the organisation, recruiting personnel and their training.

"It took over four years" from initial discussion of proposal to actual receipt of the grant.* The six districts in the pilot projects were : Anamallais, Coorg, Central Travencore, Nilgri-Wynnad, Kanan Devan and Chikmaglur. The actual work in Districts commenced on different dates extending from June 1972 in Annamallais to March 1973 in Chikmaglur. The methodology developed in the NBBS in Nilgiris was helpful in developing the six pilot projects.

The Comprehensive Welfare Scheme was a nine pointed programme, *viz.*, care and training of the youth ; nutritional support ; social education ; population dynamics ; environmental and personal hygiene ; craft training ; planning for leisure, preventive medicine and family planning. The integration of family planning with not only health but total welfare of the worker and family of the worker was attempted. It was felt that the family planning programme has a better chance of success if total welfare of the worker within a family was given due emphasis. The apprehension of misinterpreting** the

*The 1973 annual report of the UPASI Comprehensive Labour Welfare Scheme Six District Project lists the following steps that were taken : Conceptual Origin : Meeting with B.L. Raina and H. Krishna Rao end of 1967 ; Application to Government of India December 1967 ; visit A.P. Mathur March, 1971 ; Government grant order issued November 1971 , Contact with Principals and Districts, UPASI Committees approval, contact with D.P.A. Trade Union Leaders and Government officials ; (Government) grant received Feb' 1972.

**The employer promoting family planning for his own benefit like saving on the maternity benefits.

intentions of the employers in promoting family planning could also be avoided in such a comprehensive approach. The Headquarters of the Project at Coonor and field organisation was developed. Chacko himself became the Hony. Director of the Projects, indicating the importance given to the Projects by UPASI. V. Rahmathulla joined the Project as Medical Adviser and M.S. Cherian as Campaign leader. The service support in and around Coonor was provided by Marie Buck Chairman Family Planning Association of India Nilgiris Branch Coonor, ably assisted by S. Thyagarajanan UPASI medical officer.

The Headquarters activities included planning and administration, recruitment and training, preparation of schedules, establishment of reporting system and further contacts, analysis of data, feedback to the district and evaluation. It may be seen that the functions of the Ross Institute relating to ITA were performed by the Headquarters of the UPASI Project.

The NBBS continued as a part of the package of CLWS in the three estates. It will be of interest to examine the trend of birth rate in six project districts in two groups, *viz.*, those with CLWS with NBBS and those with CLWS only and also in non-project districts which could be considered as control districts for such an examination. The limited data available shows that there was decline in birth rates in all the three groups, during 1969-74; slightly greater decline in the estates where CLWS was in operation and still greater decline in estates under CLWS+NBBS. The rates reported were : a decline in birth rates in Control from 39.2 in 1969-70 to 33.0 in 1973-74 ; in areas under CLWS only from 49.49 in 1969-70 to 32.00 in 1973-74 ; and in areas under both CLWS+NBBS from 40.40 in 1969-70 to 25.40 in 1973-74. It will be seen that the birth rate in the CLWS estates in the base year (1969-70) was higher than the other two.* No information was available on the actual number of eligible couples protected in the three groups

* The year mentioned refer to 1 July to 30 June of the succeeding year.

and comparable figures on infant mortality. Some doubts were also expressed on the reporting system. Still certain trends are noticeable in infant mortality in the District as whole and selected estates, *e.g.*, in 1973-74 in the Annamallais the infant mortality was 90.57 where as in selected estates 76.62. In Kanan Devan there was great difference—reported figures for District and selected estates were 84.40 and 28.27 respectively. In the three estates with CLWS+NBBS there was marked decline in infant mortality from 89 in 1969-70 to 48 in 1973-74. The figures in the Project areas for both general health as measured by infant mortality rate; and birth rates were far lower than National figures. It may difficult to assess all the causes for such results, but there is no doubt that comprehensive labour welfare scheme including deferred incentives played a major or significant part in achievement of these results.

The impact of the programme in estate associated with UPASI continue to be encouraging. The reports for 1981 show a decline in crude birth rate from 40.1 in 1971 to 23.0 in 1981. The infant mortality shows a decline from 119.3 in 1971 to 52.1 in 1981. In 1981, 12792 had voluntarily got themselves sterilized 128 males and 12664 females, *i.e.*, eligible couples protected by sterilizations alone were 42 per cent. There may be others among them following methods to space their births. There is not sufficient information to estimate their number. But it may be safe to assume that the percentage of eligible couples protected in 1981 was over 42.0 ; a remarkable achievement.[192]

The Link Worker

The details of the various schemes, which formed an integral part of the Comprehensive Labour Welfare Project can be found in the annual reports of the Project and other UPASI reports. But one scheme requires special attention, *viz.*, 'the Link Worker Scheme'. The title link worker was used for persons selected from the community to carry out health and welfare programme in the estates—a link between programme managers and workers in the plantation. Preference in the selection of Link Workers was given to middle aged men and women (in the age group 30-40 years) who had completed their family size preferably users of birth control method, who were cheerful in disposition, who had considerable patience and understanding of their fellow workers ; and above all who had gained confidence of the community ; in other words informal local leaders-designated in the 1963 reorganised family planning programme as *Pariwar Kalyan Sahayak* and *Sahayakas*.

Generally one man and one woman was appointed in each colony, but larger number in large colonies. After assessing the workload, it was so arranged that a female "Link Worker" should not have to visit more than three families in one day and should be able to cover each family twice a month at the rate of 4 working days in a week. The role of Link Worker was "to bridge the gap in culture and communication between the health department management and workers ; to bring about participation by the workers in health and welfare programme ; and to establish a two way communication channel between the Health Department management on one side and workers on the other. There was no difficulty in identifying formal leaders as they were well known. For identifying informal leaders two methods followed in Gandhigram were suggested by UPASI Project HQ, *viz.*, the selective group method and systematic sampling method.

A training manual for Link Workers was prepared and circulated. There are no available records of the progress and evaluation of this scheme. It may be assumed that wherever this scheme was implemented the programme appeared to have taken the form of "Plantation Workers own programme".

The marked decline in birth rates in the UPASI Projects was achieved not by laying out targets or giving incentives. The success was achieved through integration of family planning with total welfare of plantation labour, health education, workers participation and strong commitment of the UPASI leadership. The organisation and the management with its central training and multi-disciplinary professional group, regular periodical assessment of programme operation, flexibility of operation, and sensitivity of management to professional advice contributed a great deal to the success of the programme.

24

Industrial Sector

There were about 222 million workers in the labour force. Of these 25.3 million workers were employed in the organised sector, *i.e.*, about 11 per cent of the labour force of the country.* "If cooperative and semi-organised sectors are also added to the organised sector, then this group will form about 15 to 20 per cent of total labour force population".[193] Some images of developments in family planning programme in industrial sector are given below.

The Employees State Insurance Corporation (ESIC)

The industrial worker is specially vulnerable to injury, disease and invalidity. The Employee's State Insurance Act 1948 thus came into being. The Act was amended from time to time, to enlarge the benefits under the Act. Further protection was provided through other measures like Workers' Compensation Act, and the Maternity Benefit Act. The Employees' State Insurance Act applied in the first instance to factories using power and employing 20 or more persons, and covered all employees who were in receipt of remuneration not exceeding Rs. 400 per month. It covers risks of sickness, maternity and employment injury. In addition to the medical care to which an insured person is entitled, cash payment are given equal to

*1988.

about half of the average wages. The scheme framed under the Employees' State Insurance Act was introduced first in Delhi and Kanpur in 1952". Since several developments have taken place both in the Employees' State Insurance Corporation (formed under the Act) organisation and beneficiaries. A Medical Benefit Council advises the Standing Committee (the Executive Body of the Employees State Insurance Corporation). There are regional offices in each State and local offices within a State. One of the four principal officer of the Chief Executive (the Director General ESIC) is the Medical Commissioner. The ceiling of income per month of beneficiaries has been increased and has been extended to establishments not using power, factories with ten or more persons using power shops and establishments employing 20 or more persons, hotels, restaurants, cinemas, road motor transport undertakings, newspaper establishments. Members of workers' families entitled for medical care varies from out patient care to full medical care.

In 1950s, in response to the request of Ministry of Health, the Employees' State Insurance Corporation Ministry of Labour and Employment recommended the implementation of family planning programme in association with medical benefit scheme. Under this expanded scheme, the medical officer of the State ESIC dispensaries were required to give family planning advice as a part of their normal activity. In 'panel areas', where such dispensaries were not available, arrangements for pre-natal and post-natal care were made for workers or their families, through institutions providing the maternal care services. There were several limitations in the beginning in the provision of family planning services to all workers through ESIC, such as : full comprehensive medical care was not available to all families of the workers ; development of maternal and child health services were not fully developed in ESIC institutions ; the absence of a person specifically responsible or an administrative cell in the State Family Planning Bureau for the family planning programme in the organised sector. The problems were overcome to some extent by providing family planning services through labour welfare centres which were being formed in many labour colonies. The progress in development of the programme depended largely on the interest taken by individual employers. Some employers, generally in large industries, made pioneering contribution.

The strategies for promotion of family planning among industrial workers, in the beginning, were not very clear There were not many studies on the subject, except the notable experience reported from Japan. In Japan at the request of the employers in the iron and steel industry the family planning programme was organised in 1953. In 1954, dissemination of family planning information was launched as a part of "New Life Movement" in Tokyo and Yokohama. A special committee of the New Life Guidance was composed of about 100 persons including representatives of Government, financial and industrial circles and the Trade Unions. By 1958, 82 companies participated in the movement. The plan of action generally included : a Governing Body of the project with representatives of the employers, the Trade Unions and health insurance society and sometime wives of workers : a task force (called the secretariate) to implement the programme, headed by the Chief of the Welfare Section with a special official on whole-time basis ; housewives were organised in units of 5-10 members, one of them acting as "stewardess to arrange meetings, maintaining liaison with the secretariate and instructors ; and joining the small units in larger group. When a unit was formed and when small units joined larger group a ceremony was held at which members of Governing Body and Secretariate were present. The work in a unit began with lecture-discussions, question and answer sessions ; collecting basic data about members (marital history, the number of births. the experience of induced abortion and use of birth control past and present, the desired number of children), and group and individual guidance by instructors. The impact of the programme showed decrease in incidence of induced abortion, increase in birth control practice, reduction in birth rates, stable family life and decrease in industrial accidents.[194]

The Japanese experience gave valuable leads for development of family planning programme in industrial sector. Gradually an outline of an effective organisation started taking shape at three levels, *viz.* : (*i*) planning development of the programme, implementation and evaluation at the enterprise level by a task force/committee including representatives of health and welfare staff, workers and workers' families, management organisations and professionals groups ; (*ii*) intermediate State level co-ordinating committee for planning, co-ordination, pooling of resources, guidance, selected direct programmes, evaluation, consisting of representatives of the Government, employers' and workers organisations, and supporting professional and voluntary groups ; and (*iii*) national level organisation in the Ministry of Health and Family Planning/Ministry of Labour (in either case both working in close co-ordination) for policy, support, national and international, co-ordination, evaluation, with close involvement of employers and workers organisations, concerned voluntary organisation and professional groups. In the early stages Surjit Pannu (Sandhu) at the Central Family Planning Institute New Delhi and her team made valuable contribution in developing of methodologies for family planning programme in the organised sector. The Family Planning Association of India pioneered family planning activities among industrial workers. The programme gradually extended to both public and private sector.

A notable step was taken in January 1976, when a Family Welfare Project was started, sponsored by the International Labour Organisation with financial assistance of the United Nations Fund for Population Activities. "The immediate objectives were : (1) establishment of Family Welfare Centres with extension education staff in the existing ESIC dispensaries and hospitals in a phased manner ; (2) organisation of educational and motivational programme through interpersonal communication during their visit to dispensaries and hospitals and through home visits ; (3) provision of services for prevention of conception including IUD insertions and sterilization operations (both vasectomy and tubectomy) for the beneficiaries of the scheme ; (4) ensuring regular and continuous supply to insured ; (5) establishing tubectomy beds for wives of insured men and women workers : and (6) achieving acceptance in the form of regular practice of one or other contraceptive method among 40% of the target couples covered by the project at the end of its duration. This included 17,500 tubectomies by the end of the third year. In 1976, the use of oral pills and in 1977 the services for medical termination of pregnancies were introduced in the Project. From August 1976, the ESIC had also doubled the sickness benefits for vasectomy (7 days) and tubectomy (14 days). The number of tubectomies reported in the Project during the first two years was 21228 (3728 more than the expected number during the entire period of three years).[195] Originally the plan of operation was mainly based on extension approach of the reorganised programme of 1960s, which led to the appointment of extension educators. Later there was some change in the original plan. The performance of extension educators was measured in terms of actual number of cases motivated directly by them. This led to the decision to discontinue appointment of extension educators. Obviously, there was lack of understanding of the role of extension educators or weakness is in the training of extension educators. The Project gave many valuable leads and demonstrated that workers and their families in industry can be readily, and effectively motivated through ths ESI Medical Benefit Scheme with marginal inputs to the extensive network of dispensaries and hospitals and showed the need of a small cell in the State Family Planning Bureau for family planning programme in the organised sector. The project also appeared to show that the debate on 'work-place centred' and 'home centred' programme is not the question of either/or but the desired results can be achieved through a proper mix of the two, suited to local needs.

PUBLIC SECTOR ENTERPRISES

Over one hundred enterprises were in Public Sector like Bharat Heavy Electricals Limited, Bhopal, Ranipur and Trichurapalli, Bhilai Steel Plants, Heavy Engineering Corporation Ltd. Ranchi, Antibiotic Plant at Rishikesh, Bharat Electronics Bangalore, Hindustan Photo Film Manufacturing Co., Ootacamund. Ministry of Health gave them grants for maintenance of urban Family Planning (Welfares) Centre. It was, visualised that overtime the Public Sector enterprises should have family planning programme maintained from their own resources. The rationale for such an approach was that the enterprises concerned should view it as their own programme as a part of their normal activities, Ministry of Health and Family Welfare could provide technical advice. Besides the grants from the Ministry of Health and Family Welfare the enterprises did provide additional aid from their own resources. For example the Bharat Heavy Electricals were providing additional staff and additional incentives (Rs. 200/- for male sterilization operation and Rs. 400/- in case of women with two children offering for sterilization operation). The Family Planning Association of India also assisted in several cases. In some cases results achieved were notable such as Bharat Heavy Electrical Township the birth rate was reported around 20 per 1000 by 1978.

PRIVATE SECTOR ENTERPRISES

Initially the employers, in general, did not show much interest in making active contribution to family planning programme. It seems that with the introduction of the Employees State Insurance Act some employers felt that after paying their share of contribution to ESIC their responsibility for investment in health including family planning care had ceased. Some were vociferous in stopping the maternity benefits to workers with more than two children. There were exceptions. The outstanding among them in private rector is J.R.D. Tata. His interest in population issues is traceable even before the Government of India launched the family planning programme. When President Family Planning Association of India approached him for help in arranging the First International Conference in 1952, he readily gave adequate office space in the Greens Hotel free of cost, and also helped financially. In 1957, when the FPAI was in difficulties to move to a suitable building on Hornby Road (Dadaji Nowroji Road) he immediately gave a cheque to enable the FPAI to meet the financial commitment He viewed population in a broad perspective, which is well illustrated in his address to the Annual General Meeting of the Tata Iron and Steel Company on August 22, 1955. He said : "There has been in the past, an extraordinary reluctance to consider the population problem at all or equally dangerous tendency to over simplify it by relating it only to food production. Even if the latter could be made to keep pace with the rise of population, which seems impossible in the long run, the problem will be solved only in part because people in our country are not likely to be satisfied for long with sufficiency of food. Awakened to the higher standards prevailing in western countries, they will rightly demand improved standards also in clothing, shelter, education, health, security, etc. To build up such standards, within reasonable time, from pitifully low level to-day. it would be a prodigious task even if population remained at the present level". He suggested that "the first step that the Government should take without delay was to constitute a high power commission consisting of eminent scientists, economists and sociologists to investigate the problem in all its aspects. A clear and authoritative statement of facts underlying the problem and of the remedies to which they point would provide an effective starting point for education of public opinion and formulation of the necessary legislative and administrative action".[196] It is not surprising that Tata Group of Industries pioneered family planning programme for their workers as early as 1951. The industrial group who initiated family planning programme before Tata group appears to be TVS—Lucas.

Among family planning programmes for industrial workers, in 1930s a family planning clinic was opened in Parel Bombay by Pillai and Seth Lal Chand Sethi an industrialist in Ujjain provided free accomodation to Matra Sewa Sangh—a voluntary organisation providing integrated health and family planning service.

Gradually, other employers of large groups of workers started taking interest in family planning programme. The Tatas were closely followed by Godrej (1957) and the Hindustan Spinning and Weaving Coy in 1958, (again through personal interest of Godrej and Vijay Merchant). Kohinoor Century Bombay Dying, Bata Shoe Coy., Escorts, Swedeshi Mills, Century Mills and others launched family planning programme.

Small industrial units found difficulties in initiating action. Their structure, and resources put serious limitations to develop programme on their own. Other strategies like co-operative effort, linkages with organisations with health and family planning programme and mobile units were suggested.

It took sometime to persuade all the employers' organisations in the country to take part actively in the programme. The Government offered 100% assistance for specified components of the programme, and made the expenditure on family planning free of income tax. Ultimately the employer associations took measures to extend the programme, *e.g.*, the Federation of Indian Chambers of Commerce and Industry agreed to consider family planning as a major sphere of activity and attempted to persuade its constituent employers' association to activate industrial units. The Federation also instituted an award for family planning performance. In Calcutta, Bhanwar Mal Singhi, a freedom fighter, a superb Hindi writer, a social activist and ardent promoter of theatre movement, (along with his wife Sushila an equally distinguished social worker) got interested in the family planning movement. He contributed to generating interest of Indian Chamber of Commerce. In or around 1968, with cooperation of the Indian Chamber of Commeree he launched family planning programme in Labour areas of Calcutta. The programme has since considerably developed and Singhi is now a recognised pioneer of family planning movement. One of the notable activity started by him was publishing in simple Hindi messages on family planning welcomed by readers, which was considered very difficult at that time. The Indian Chamber of Commerce in Calcutta and Indian Merchant Chamber Bombay established an institutional mechanism to promote family planning. Several employers established links with professional institutions such as the TVS Madras with the Institutions of Rural Health and Family Planning Gandhigram, Faridabad Industries and several others with Family Planning Association of India. The Employers' Association of Northern India and the Indian Junior Chamber members and others took notable interest.

Despite the declared support to family planning by the employers and their organisations and Government assistance financial and otherwise, the pace of actual programme was generally slow. For example in a survey carried out by the Family Planning Association of India for the Co-ordinating Committee of the Indian Merchants Chamber Bombay in 1967, showed that out of 230 industrial units surveyed 61 only were offering family planning services ; in a survey in Kanpur, also by the Family Planning Association of India, during December 1969—April 1970, showed that out of 227 industrial units surveyed 19 units only had undertaken family planning activity (two units of the 160 small units and the rest in large units). The encouraging observation made during these surveys was that most employers were interested in starting family planning activities. This underlined the need of expert team in each State. Family Planning Bureau devoted their attention to the programme in organised sector especially information, education and communication programme among employers and workers, provision of services for workers especially in small units, training and organisation at different level suited to the local situation which could help in planning, implementation, monitoring and evaluation.

Main Factors in Successful Programmes

The importance of the programme in the organised sector and strategies likely to give the desired results was emphasised in a number of discussions in the country and international workshops in Asia, the Carribeans and Africa arranged by the International Labour Organisation,[196] initiated by Kailash Doctor. The full realisation that workers come from villages and continue to have rural links and are important channels of communication and that can have multiplier effect on rural population, came very slowly.

There is now a wealth of experience and expertise developed in organising family planning in organised sector. There are several industrial establishments which can be identified as doing outstanding work with encouraging results. Some observers tend to classify successful units in different types or models and attribute success to approach adopted in them, such as high incentives in Tata Group of Industries, and linking number of children with facilities for housing and children admission to school in Godrej and Boyce Man. Co. Pvt. Ltd. Such a typology for a successful programme is over-simplification of a complex issue. The factors that can be identified in successful programmes are : interest and commitment of top employer ; existence of well developed health, maternal and child health, medical and welfare services in the industrial unit, high quality of services within easy reach with personalised attention ; credibility of measures taken by the employer among workers and full support and involvement of the worker in the programme ; and good organisation and management developed to implement the programme at various levels especially with focus on health education and extension education.

Special efforts were made to mobilise support of trade union bodies and provide population education facilities among workers. In 1979-80 of the six ILO projects with financial support of UNFA one was taken up with the India National Trade Union Congress and one with Hind Mazdoor Sabha. (The remaining four included one each to be implemented by the Employers, Federation of India, All India Organisation of Employers, the Employers State Insurance Corporation and Coal Mines Welfare Organization). The ILO/UNFPA projects by the Textile Labour Association Calcutta continued during 1983-84.

MINES AND MINERALS

The terms mines and minerals are defined* as all substances which can be obtained from the earth by : mining, digging, drilling, dredging, hydraulicing, quarrying or by other operations and including mineral oil (which in turn include natural gas and petroleum) ; any excavation where any operation for the porpose of searching for or obtaining minerals has been or is being carried on.

A detailed examination of labour covered in the Mines Act showed that the problem of providing family planning services

*The Mines Act 1952.

to them was far from simple. They widely varied in size. A number of provisions had been made for welfare of labour under the Mines Act 1952, the Mines Rules 1955, the Maternity Benefit Act 1961, the Mines creche Rules 1966, the Pithead Bath Rules 1963, etc. In some, the labour was employed in large groups, in other in small clusters spread over large areas. A number of non-statutory health, family planning and welfare measures were provided in a number of places. Some had a well-organised medical, health and welfare services like in coal mines. In other places the situation was very un-satisfactory. The major problem was to provide adequate family planning services to the entire labour force in mines. Initial action was taken in respect of those workers where there was already organised health and welfare services.

The Coal Mines Labour Ordinance 1944, had been replaced by the Coal Mines Labour Welfare Fund Act 1947, A coal cess and interest from the amount collected as cess provided funds for the welfare of coal mines labour. In 1966-67, this amount was over Rs. 40,000,00. Ministry of Labour administered this fund. The coal Mines Labour Commissioner was head of the organisation. A tripartite advisory committee including an equal number of representatives of Government, workers and employers periodically met to suggest welfare measures. The coal fields were located in Jharia. Mugma, Bokaro, Karanpura Ramgarh, Korba, Raniganj, Sambalpur, Talchar, Vindya Pradesh, Chanda, Korea, Madhya Pradesh, Assam and Rajasthan. Sub-committees also tripartite in composition were operating as advisory bodies for coal fields two in Bihar, and one each in West Bengal, Madhya Pradesh, Assam, Orissa and Andhra Pradesh. The general medical and health services included a dispensary at the colliery, regional and central hostals. The Labour Welfare Fund had developed a well organised medical and health services with two well equipped central hospitals (one each in Asansol and Dhanbad) nine regional hospitals (one each at Katras, Tisra, Choral, Jamai, Dhanpuri, Naiserai, Phusro, Kuisia and Bhuli), maternity and child welfare centres and dispensaries. There were mobile medical units and health promotion centres in some places. Thus the coal mines welfare fund organisation provided a good infra-structure through which family planning programmes could be promoted. This was facilitated by the deep insight in Labour Welfare of V.K.B. Pillai, Secretary, Ministry of Health. In 1950s Ministry Health requested Ministry of Labour to promote family planning programme. Direct contact with the Labour Welfare Fund was later established. Ministry of Labour sanctioned ; (*i*) one family planning unit and one fully equipped mobile unit for each of the hospitals at Dhanbad and Asansol ; (*ii*) one family planning unit each at regional hospitals at Naisarai Hazaribag, Jamai District Chindwara, Dhanpur, Burhar, Sanctori—a Hospital of M/s. Bengal Coal Coy. Ltd., Disergarh, Sri Laxmi Narain Deo Trust Hospital Jharia (not by Labour Welfare Fund but by colliery) ; (*iii*) one mobile unit for regional hospital Bhuli Bihar ; (*iv*) a mobile education unit and 39 extension educators.

The family planning programme in coal mines started in 1957 extended rapidly and was intensified in 1966-67. The result in some areas were impressive such as in Singarani colleries in Andhra Pradesh.

There were Welfare Funds in Iron Ore and Mica Mines providing health cover. The health and medical facilities varied in them, some had maternity and child welfare centres. The gold mines had medical department with a central hospital, two dispensaries and four maternity clinics in the Kolar Gold Field and a hospital in the Hathi Gold Mine. The family planning services were started in them. In 1987, the Labour Welfare Fund Laws (Amendment) Bill was passed. The Bill provides for undertaking family welfare activities out of funds created for the welfare of workers in mica, limestone, dolomite, iron ore and other mines.

The oil establishment likewise had health infra-structure. The Assam Oil Company at Digboi had a very well equipped and staffed hospital with 220 bed. The Oil and Natural Gas

Commission in Ahmedabad, Baroda, Ankleshwar, Cambay, Sibsagar, Lakwa, Hoshiarpur, Jwalamukhi, Karikal, Port Canning and Rajasthan had gradually developed health and medical services. The family planning services were provided by the medical personnel. In the beginning there were no facilities for sterilization operations, IUD insertion and distribution of contraceptives. The family planning services were restricted to providing information, and the actual services were provided by Government run clinics.

The lime stone mines, unlike others mines, posed difficulties in providing family planning services. A small proportion of them were covered by ESIC scheme. The medical facilities provided generally were meagre. In several place the population was scattered in small groups, in some multiple agencies were operating, *e.g.*, in Satna District there were six major establishments (Birla Cement Works and Universal Cables. Sana Lime Stone Co., Lime Klinsalso Red and Yellow Ochere, Hindusthan Steels Ltd.). The family planning programme was under the civil surgeon. He arranged, as best as he could, field workers in the labour areas. The District Family Planning Officer and other family planning staff visited the area periodically. The progress in some places was notable and services in District hospital were of high standard.

There were other group of workers like in stone querries. The Labour Welfare Committee noted that the arrangements for health and family planning in them were far from satisfactory. It was suggested that family planning should be included as a statutory provision and become an integral part of maternal and child health services. The need for extensive survey of the areas where the labour was being employed was emphasised. The available resources could then be mobilised and programme developed suited to the local situation in consultation with the representatives of the employers, workers, Governmental and non-Governmental agencies. Suggestions were also made for developing organisation dealing with organised labour at various levels. It seems that no such survey was done till 1978.

R.M. Kapoor pleaded for almost similar survey at the GOI/ILO National Seminar in February 1978.[198]

The ILO Projects with financial assistance of UNFPA in 1970s included the family planning programme in mica, Iron Ore, and limestone mines.

The Kerala Story

Kerala is unique in many ways. A visitor to this beautiful land is impressed immediately on arrival, with lush green environment, cleanliness of its land and cheerful people ; the rural and urban areas merging with each other, houses in villages surrounded with coconut trees; a number of people in villages reading newspapers and a large groups of children on the road in the morning going to school.

Kerala has been formed from two States, previously ruled by Maharajas (Travancore State and Cochin State), and Malabar region of the former British India Madras State (now Tamil Nadu). Sixty per cent of the population is from former two Princely States.

The State, a narrow strip of land, has the Arabian Sea in the West and Western Ghats in the east. The influence of various cultures and religions is evident—the Dravadian, the Arayan, the Arabian, the European (Portugese, Dutch, French and British), Islam, Christianity and Judaism from the West Asia. Christianity (Syrian Christians) came to Kerala before it reached Europe. The religious composition in Kerala is now more or less homogenous. The Aryans who came to Kerala, several centuries (2-3 centuries) before others, introduced their own cultural practices. A social organisation developed over the years among a group in which mother is head of the family and the inheritance is through female child (matriarchal system).

EDUCATION

The Princely States of Travancore and Cochin had the distinction of having enlightened rulers and Diwans (Prime Ministers). This contributed to high levels of inputs in education and health services and overall good management. Rani Gwori Parwati, in 1817 ordered : "the State shall defray the entire cost of education of the people". The educational policy developed gave great attention to equitable distribution of educational facilities. The Christian Missionaries further supplemented the State efforts to serve the large number of Christian Community. The benefit of their efforts over-flowed to other communties. The net result was that by the end of the nineteenth century every village in Kerala had a Primary School and through out the State there was a network of institutions for pre-school, primary, secondary and higher education and education in various professions. The education was provided free or at nominal cost, to both males and females. The 1981 Census showed that the percentage of literates in Kerala was 70.42 as against 36.23 in India (excluding Assam). The female literacy* in Kerala was 65.73 as against 24.82 in India.

HEALTH

Similarly Kerala has an old history of wide distribution of health services especially for promotion of health and prevention of diseases. Maharaja of Travancore is reported to have stated at the inauguration of a civil hospital : "I take this opportunity earnestly to impress this fact on the minds of all my native subjects and to urge them to seek for themselves, for their children, for their friends and for their servants the great protection of vaccination...there is no member of my family who has not had this protection conferred at an early age". The

*Average age at marriage is highest among women with 10+schooling, then gradually declines to lowest among women with no schooling. Average number of children in 10+, 2.1 and no schooling.

tradition of evenly distributed health services, within easy reach, is old in Kerala. Besides the modern system of medicine the Ayurvedic system of medicine has been common in Kerala. The pace of provision of primary health care and specialised medical care has been accelerated since 1950s. Provision of such care in Kerala at present is more than the rest of India. For example there is a Primary Health Centre within 232 sq. km. (the figure for India is 563 sq. kms.) ; a sub centre within 21 sq. kilometer (the figure for India is 63 Kilometers) ; there are 458 hospital beds in urban areas and 107 hospital beds in rural areas per 100,000 population in Kerala (1979-80), as against 263 hospital beds in urban areas and 12 hospital beds in rural areas per 100,000 population in India as a whole.

Young girls from Kerala have made valuable contribution to health services not only in Kerala, but throughout India. A large number of nurses from Kerala are working throughout India. Maternal and child health services and nutritional programmes are now well advanced. The number Pre-school feeding centres and school mid-day meal programme are spread through out the state and are increasing. The impact of health services especially for mothers and children are reflected in : the life expectancy at birth (1976-80) in Kerala 65.5 years ; 13.2 years higher than India as a whole.

Crude Death Rate Kerala 6.1 (rural 6.0 ; urban 6.9), India 11.1 (rural 12.1 ; urban 7.6) (1986).

Infant Mortality Kerala 27 (rural 28 ; urban 20) ; India 96 (rural 105 ; urban 62) (1986).

The crude birth rate in Kerala has been declining from 1950s. It has been consistently lower than rest of India. In 1986 it was 22.5 (Rural 22.4 ; Urban 23.0), as against India 32.4 (Rural 34.1 ; Urban 27.0).

Age at Marriage. Family Planning Practice.

The age at marriage and education, both female and male, in Kerala are remarkable. Although marriage is almost universal as in rest of India, but in Kerala women marry late. In 1981.

the average age at marriage of females was 21.85 years,* as against 18.33 years in India ; and the age at marriage is on the increase. The number of desired number of children in Kerala, are reported to be 3.25 (the average children actually born is reported as 3.48 of these 3.02 survive). The level of knowledge of family planning methods in Kerala is high (nearly 90% of married women have knowledge of family planning methods) and the level of family planning practice (as on 31st March, 1985 couples protected by sterilization were 1,508,165), (37 2% of all eligible couples) : by IUD 89,154 (2.2%), and other methods 70,853 (1.7%), *i.e.*, 41.1% couples were effectively protected.

The Paradox

Per capita income in Kerala is below the National average. Yet Kerala has been able to achieve remarkable decline in fertility.

Inter-action of Several Factors

Several questions arise, such as : Why with almost similar financial inputs as other parts of India, Kerala is a success story ? Who makes the decisions about the age at marriage ? What considerations influence this decision ? What factors influence the attitude on desired number of children and the birth control practice ? What are the lessons of Kerala that can be applied to rest of the country ?

The decision on marriage is still largely made by parents (90% of cases by parents uncles, brothers and others ; 7% by both parents and couples ; and only 3% by couples alone). The parents do consult the daughter or son. Most marriages are delayed for economic reasons. Many factors operate and inter-act in determining age at marriage such as education, employment prospects of the groom, housing problem, dowry, changes in values placed on inherited and acquired

---

*Median age of marriage ; high in Alleppy and Ernakulam districts (with old and new industrial activities), and low in Palaghat (predominently agricultural, often called rice bowl of Kerala).

status. Land reforms, agrarian reforms and other related policies, brought weaker sections of society in the mainstream of social and economic life and devalued inherited status. Parents started placing main weightage, in selecting the prospective bridegroom, to education, employment or prospects of employment, Age at marriage of girls seems to have been effected by education of both boys and girls. The long time spent by boys in education and attaining skills required for employment inevitably moved forward the age of marriage of boys, consequently age at marriage of girls.

The spread of education among girls also contributed to selection of prospective bridegroom. Education is seen as the most important determinant of age at marriage, as on it (among other things) rests the prospect of employment and on employment and economic status depends the marriage. Most women are married to men in Kerala who are employed or have other means to support a family at the time of marriage. The influence of education is carried forward after marriage in building the family and family life. Housing does not yet appear to be determining factor in getting married, most continue to live in parents household after marriage. In cases, when place of work, is in another town, the newly wed have to live separately from parents. But this does not appear to influence postponement of marriage.

Dowry has been, sometime, mentioned to prolong marriage negotiations and/or contribute to lag between employment and decision to marry, and consequently influencing age at marriage. The evidence does not appear to be convincing. It is a fact that despite making dowry illegal about thirty years back (in 1961), the practice persists. The proportion of women not married or delayed marriages in Kerala on account of inability of parents to give the needed dowry appears to be very small.

Education, health and land, agrarian and other reforms have contributed to the demand for family planning services and to the use of the services for birth control and consequently to the small family norm.

PROGRAMME IMPACT

Has the family planning programme in Kerala influenced the demand for and acceptance of birth control ? The answer is "Yes".

Among various reasons for such influence are : the programme management ; the ready accessibility to services facilitated by the wide network of road and river communication ; continuous activation of administrative machinery ; and decentralisation.

SOCIAL AND ECONOMIC FACTORS

The example of Kerala is often cited to underline that the fertility decline can be achieved, despite the low level of economic development. The Kerala story no doubt has demonstrated that the higher level of education especially of females, the higher age at marriage, low infant fertility, accessibility to good health and family planning services and their management and peoples participation are very important determinants of fertility decline. But this is not the full story. With education and health levels along with accessible services to meet the needs, it seems that larger number of couples than at present could have been using effective methods of birth control and the Kerala population growth could have reached very close to replacement level. The reason for Kerala not reaching yet the replacement level may be due to children still remaining a source of economic return in weaker sections of society and anxiety for old age security. Within Kerala the birth control acceptance rate is higher in districts with higher level of socio-economic development.[199] Parents depend on their children in old age. Such dependence for old age security influences the parents desired-family-size and to have at least one son if not two. The decline in child and infant mortality has to be reinforced by further social and economic development. Such developments may be anticipated in Kerala. There is already a great concern about Harijan and Girijan welfare. This concern is being translated in vigorous programme activities. The weaker sections of society in both urban and rural areas are being given the rightful place in society. The steps have been taken that benefits of social and economic development actually reach the people especially weaker sections. Measures to prevent exploitation of the weaker sections are being taken, for example, village level societies have been formed in fishing villages. Housing facilities, drinking water scheme, health care and educational facilities are being further expanded and public distribution system further strengthened.

Kerala has ingredients with powerful influence on fertility. The pace of fertility decline will be accelerated by increasing opportunities for employment of young men and women; adequate old age security measures; and economic development throughout Kerala.

This pace can be further accelerated by use of new generation of contraceptives, development of a simple, safe, without any side-effects, effective, acceptable, reversible and accessible contraceptive (s), and greater understanding of human reproduction and human behaviour.

Kerala story, in detail and depth, should be studied by other States as a guide for upgrading their performance.

Besides the factors mentioned during the discussion on fertility decline in Kerala (like education of women, age at marriage, infant mortality), other factors operating and interacting should also be given serious attention such as quality and accessibility of health and family planning services, health management, the commitment to community participation, the various factors responsible for age at marriage, differences in fertility behaviour within the State, the measures which can further accelerate the fertility decline in Kerala. The quest for a small family must go on. The success is within reach.*

---

*Some images of Kerala are given in this chapter. For details see: Zachariah, K.C., *The Anomaly of the Fertility Decline in India's Kerala State—A Field Investigation*, World Bank, Washington, 1984.

Notes and References

1. Himes, Norman, E., *Medical History of Contraception*, Gamut Press Inc., New York, 1963.

2. Singh, S.P. and Singh L.P., "Folklore claims by Tribals and Experimental Evaluation of Some Medicinal Plants with Special Reference to Contraception" in *Tribal Health*, ed., Buddha De Chaudhuri, Inter India Publication, New Delhi.

3. Chaudhury, Ranjit Roy, *Plants with Possible Antifertility Activity*, Indian Council of Medical Research, Special Report Series No. 55, New Delhi, 1966.

4. Himes, Norman E., *Medical History of Contraception*.

5. Baker John (with a chapter by Carlton, H.M.), *The Chemical Control of Contraception*, Chapman & Hall Ltd., London, 1935.

6. The birth control movement virtually began in 1822, when Francis Place published, *Illustrations and Proofs of the Principles of Population*. Among his followers Richard Carlile in 1825 wrote, *What is Love*, which a year later was published with the title *Every Woman's Book or What is Love?* Robert Dale Owen and Dr. Charles Knowlton in USA were influenced by work of Place and Carlile in England. In 1830 Robert Dale Owen published, *Moral Philosophy* and in 1832 Charles Knowlton wrote a more detailed book *Fruits of Philosophy*. "One Henry Cook of Bristol, who it is alleged, interleaved obscene pictures with Charles Watts edition

of Knowlton's pamphlet, was as a consequence sentenced to two years imprisonment of hard labour". This set in motion the trial of Charles Bradlaugh and Anie Besant. They maintained that Knowlton's pamphlet was useful and not obscene and had organised the Free thaught Publishing Company with specific purpose of printing and selling the pamphlet. They had informed the time and place from where the distribution was to take place. They were consequently arrested. Lord Chief Justice Cockurn gave judgement in favour of Bradlaugh and Besant and legitimised the publication of Knowlton's pamphlet, and set the stage for worldwide dissemination of information on birth control methods. See Himes, Norman E., *Medical History of Contraception.*

7. Karve, R.D., "Experiences of Birth Control Work During Thirty Years", *Report of the First All India Conference on Family Planning*, The Family Planning Association of India, Bombay, 1951.

8. Raina, B.L., *Planning Family in India Prevedic Times to Early 1950s*, Commonwealth Publishers, New Delhi, 1990.

9. *Proceeding of the First Meeting Family Planning Research and Programme Committee 13-18 July, 1953*, Ministry of Health Government of India, Manager Publication Delhi, 1963.

10. Raina, B.L., *Family Planning Why, When and How*, New Book Company Private Ltd., Bombay, 1951. The book was first published in 1939 with the title, *Birth Control Why, When and How.* The methods recommended in the book may be considered to represent the advice generally given in Europe and USA, as the manuscript was technically scrutinised by Dr. Helena Wright of Family Planning Association London and the Foreword was written by the Lord Horder.

11. Israel, Sarah, and Kamat, Melba, "The Acceptability and

Effectiveness of Two Methods of Birth Control : An Evaluation of 352 Cases", *Journal of Family Welfare*, Bombay, September, 1958.

Israel, Sarah and Kamat, Melba, "A Study of the Effectiveness of Contraceptive Methods in Family Planning Clinics in India", *Journal of Family Welfare*, 5.3, Bombay, March, 1959.

Also see Gopal Rao, Kamla (with Mullick, Saroj Project Associate), "Contraceptive Use and Experience" in *Studies in Family Planning : India*, Abhinav Publications, New Delhi, 1974.

12. Wyon. Jhon B., and Gordon, John E., *The Khanna Study*, Population Problems in the Rural Punjab, Harvard University Press, Cambridge, Massachusetts, 1971.

13. Baumgartner, Leona and Notestein, Frank W. Suggestions for a Practical Programme of Family Planning and Child Care. Submitted to Rajkumari Amrit Kuar, December, 1955.

    For the background of Baumgartner and Notestein Mission and the other recommendation of the Mission see Raina, B.L., *Population Policy*, B.R. Publishing Corporation (Division of D.K. Publishers Distributors, (P) Ltd., Delhi, 1988.

14. Wyon, John B. and Gordon, John E., *The Khanna Study*.

15. Haupt, Arthur, *Population Today*, Vol. 18, No. 7/8, Population Reference Bureau Inc. Washington, July/August, 1990.

16. Gabelnick, H. (National Institute of Child Development, Personal Communication cited in "New Developments in Vaginal Contraception", *Population Reports*. Sr. H. No. 7, Population Information Programme, The John Hopkins University, Baltimore Maryland, January-February, 1984.

17. Prupes, K., "Custom Cervical Cap rentering Clinical

Trials", *Journal of American Medical Association* 250 (15) 1946-47, 1951, October 21, 1983, cited in New Developments in Vaginal Contraception", *Population Reports*.

For an earlier review on The Diapnragm and other Intravaginal Barriers see *Population Reports*, Series H. Number, 4 January, 1976.

18. New Developments in Vaginal Contraception, *Population Reports*, Sr. H. No. 7.

19. Vorhauer, B.W., Edelman D.A., North, B. and Soderstrom, R.M., Today Vaginal Contraceptive Sponge : A Technical Review Report Irivine, California VLI Corporation, June, 1983, cited in "New Developments in Vaginal Contraception, *Population Reports*.

For an earlier review on spermicides see *Population Reports*, Series H. No. 5, September, 1979.

20. "New Developments in Vaginal Contraception", *Population Reports*, Series H. Number 7, January-February, 1984.

21. "New Development in Vaginal Contraception", *Population Reports*, Series No. 7, January-February, 1984.

See also Morris, L., Lewis, G., Powell, D.L., Anderson, J., Way, A., Cushing, J., and Lawless, G. Contraceptive Prevalence Surveys : A New Source of Family Planning Data, *Population Reports*, Series H. No. 5, John Hopkins University Population Information Programme, Baltimore, May-June, 1981.

Ebanks, G.E. and Gilkes, L., *Country Profile Barbados*, Population Council, New York, December, 1973.

Canada, *Report of the Committee on the Operation of the Abortion Law*, Ministry of Supply and Services Canada, Ottawa, 1977, Mosher, W.D. Contraceptive utilization United States, 1976, *Health Statistics Series - 23*, Data from National Survey of family growth No. 7, March, 1981.

Bone, M., *Family Services in England and Wales*, Her Majesty's Stationary Office, London, 1973.

22. "Long-Acting Progestins-Promise and Prospects", *Population Reports*, Series K. No. 2, May, 1983.

The Population Council Annual Report 1989.

Diczfalusy, E., Landgren, B.M., New Delivery Systems Vaginal Devices in : Chag, C.F., Griffith, D., and Woolman, A., eds., *Recent Advances in Fertility regulations, Proceedings of a Symposium Organized by the Ministry of Public Health of the People's Republic of China ana the World Health Organisation's Special Programme of Research, Development and Research Training in Human Reproduction*, Beijing September 2-5, 1980. Atar Geneva, 1981.

Nuttal, I.D., and Elstein, M., Steroid Releasing Vaginal Rings, *Acta Europaea Fertilitatis*, 11.3, September, 1980.

Toivonen J., Lahteenmki, P., and Luukkainen, T., The use of Contraceptive Vaginal ring governed by pattern of individual uterine bleeding, *Contraception*, 19.4, April, 1979.

Victor, A., and Johansson, E.D.B., Contraceptive Rings self administered treatment governed by bleeding, *Contraception*, 16.2, August, 1977.

Sivin, I., Mishell, D.R., Jr. Victor, A., Diaz, S., Alvarez-Sanchez, F., Nielsen, N.C., Akinla, O., Pyorala, T., Coutinho, E., Faudes, A., Roy, S., Brenner, P.F., Abren, T., Pavez, M., Brache, V., Giwa-Osage, O.F., Fasan, M.O., Zausner-Guelman, B., Darze, E. Silva, I.C.G., Da Diaz, J., Jackanicz, T.M., Stern, I., and Nash, H.A., A multicentre study of levonorgestrel-estradiol contraceptive vaginal ring, International comparative trial, *Contraception*, 24.4, October, 1981.

Das, R.P., *Contraceptive Technology, Past, Present and Future* in : Gupta, J.P. and Kapoor, S.D. eds. *Status Report Series, I*, National Institute of Health and Family Welfare, New Delhi, 1989.

23. For Rhythm Study see *Final Report on Pilot Studies in Family Planning*, WHO Regional Office, New Delhi, September, 1954, Chandrasekharan, C. and Murthy, DVR, "Pilot Studies on the Rhythm Method of Family Planning".

    Studies in Family Planning, Directorate General Health Services Government of India, New Delhi, 1960.

    The chapter is mainly based on *The Report of Pilot Studies on the Rhythm*, (Photostat Courtesy D.V.R. Murthy).

24. Rama Rau, Dhanvanthi, *Personal Communication.*

25. Desai, Morarji, *Personal Communication.*

26. Rama Rau, Dhanvanthi, *Personal Communication.*

27. Population Growth and Family Planning Committee, *Report*, Planning Commission, New Delhi, 1959.

28. Ogino, K., 'ovolutionstermin and Konzeption strmin', (ovulation day and conception day), *Zentralblatt Fur Gynaklogie*, 54 (8), Feb., 1930.

29. Knaus, H., 'Du periodesche Frket-und Unfucfitbarket des weibes.' (Periodic fertility and infertility in women), *Zentralblatt fur Gynaekologie*, 57 (24) June, 1933.

30. In April, 1951, Prime Minister Nehru, during a discussion with Dr. Abraham Stone said : "I am entirely in favour of limiting the growth of population by institution of various methods including birth control". Stone, Abraham, "Present day International trends in Family Planning", *Annals of the New York Academy of Sciences*, 54(5), May, 1952.

31. Stone, Abraham, "Fertility Problem in India", *Fertility And Sterility*, 4(3), May-June, 1953.

A paper presented by him at the eighth Annual Meeting of the American Society for Study of Sterility. Chicago Illinois, June 9, 1952.

32. Collins, W.P., "The physiological basis for natural family planning" in *International Seminar on Natural Methods of Family Planning*, (organised by the Department of Health, Dublin, Ireland in collaboration with the World Health Organisation), Dublin, October, 1979.

33. *Population Reports*, 1, 3 Periodic Abstenance, The John Hopkins University, Baltimore, Sept., 1981.

34. Ogino, K., "Ovulation Day and Conception Day".

35. Stone, Abraham, "*Report to the World Health Organisation on Family Planning in India*, (mimeo).

36. Chandrasekharan, C. and Murthy, D.V.R., *Report on Pilot Studies on the Rhythm Method of Family Planning in India.*

37. *as above.*

38. Letter of Abrahm Stone to Ministry of Health.

39. Stone, Abraham, Fertility Problems in India.

40. Symonds, Richards and Carder, Michael, *The United Nations and The Population Question*, Chatto & Windus for Sussex University Press, 1973.

41. *Population Reports Series 1, Number 3, Periodic Abstenance*, September, 1981.

Population Information Programme the Jhon Hopkins University Baltimore Maryland USA.

42. *Population Reports Series 1, Number 3, Periodic Abstenance*. Dorairaj, K., 'Fertility Control in India, Natural Family Planning an alternate strategy', Indian Social Institute, New Delhi, 1981.

43. Herman, C.B., *et. al.*, *Periodic Abstenance in Developing Countries and Policy Options*, Institute for Resource

Development at Westinghouse, Columbia, May & June, 1986.

44. See also International Federation of Family Life Promotion Fourth International Congress, Ottawa, Canada, June-July, 1986.

45. *Population Reports Ser. 1, No. 3, Periodic Abstenance*, World Health Organisation Special Programme of Research Development and Research Training in Human Reproduction, Ninth Annual Report, WHO, Geneva, Dec., 1980.

46. Missionaries of Charity Natural Family Planning, Calcutta, Missionaries of Charity, July, 1976 (unpub.), cited in *Population Reports, Sr. 1, No. 3, Periodic Abstenance.*

47. *Population Reports, Series 1, No. 3, Periodic Abstenance.*

48. Himes, Norman E., *Medical History of Contraception.*

49. *as above.*

50. Mukhopadhyaya, Girindranath, *History of Indian Medicine*, Vol. I, University of Calcutta, Calcutta, 1923.

51. Himes, Norman E., *Medical History of Contraception.*

52. "Update on Condoms, Products, Protection, Promotion", *Population Reports*, Series H, No. 6, Population Information Programme, The Jhon Hopkins University, Baltimore September-October, 1982.

53. Sakondhavat, C. and Potter, L., "Further Testing of Female Condoms & Letters", *British Journal of Family Planning*, Vol. 15, No. 4, 1990.

54. Chitre, K.T., "Acceptability of Contraceptives in Maharashtra State", *Family Planning News*, 4.7, July, 1963. Other findings reported by Chitre included : decline in foam tablets from 69.74 (1958) to 31.4 per cent (1962) in rural areas, and from 51.74 (1958) to 23.3 per cent in urban areas ; the acceptibility of diaphragm and

and jelly rose and then declined in urban areas, but showed little change in rural areas ; the acceptibility of jelly in urban areas increased from 9.91 (1958) to 13.5 per cent (1962).

55. *Family Welfare Programme In India Year Book 1986-87*, Department of Family Welfare, Ministry of Health and Family Welfare, New Delhi, 1988.

56. *Manufacture of Male Contraceptive in India : Report of Technical Consultants to Ford Foundation*, Mar. 20, 1964.

57. HLL Presents Rs. 44 lakh Dividend to Minister State for Health and Family Welfare Shri Rasheed Masood, Press Information Bureau Government of India, New Delhi, October, 1990.

58. "Social Marketing of Contraceptives" Press Information Bureau Government of India, New Delhi, October 23, 1990.

59. Bhatia, B.B.S., Dubey, D.C., and Devgan, A.K., *A Study in Family Planning Communication—Direct Mailing*, Central Family Planning Institute, New Delhi, 1966.

60. Raina, B.L., Blake, R.R., and Weiss, E.H., *A Study in Family Planning Communication : Meerut Direct*, Central Family Planning Institute, New Delhi, 1967.

61. "Update on Condoms, Products, Protection and Promotion", *Population Reports*, No. 6, Sept.-Oct., 1982.

62. *Population Reports*, Series H, No. 6, September-October, 1982.

63. Israel, Sarah and Kamat, Melba, *The Journal of Family Welfare*, 5.3, March, 1959.

Virkar, Katayan, "Evaluation of Condom Method", *The Journal of Family Welfare*, 11.1, September, 1964.

The All India Institute of Hygiene and Public Health Calcutta. Follow-up Study of Contraceptive Users. Paper presented at the Fifth Communication—Action—

Research Workshop Central Family Planning Institute, New Delhi, April, 1976, Mimeo.

Bhardwaj, K.S. and Mullick, S., "Experience of men about Condom", *The Maharashtra Medical Journal*, 18.6., September, 1971, Bhardwaj and Mullick observed that over 82 per cent of respondents (707 male condom users of different groups) were successful in avoiding pregnancies.

See also Gopal Rao, Kamla (Mullick Saroj Project Assistant), "Conventional Contraceptives", *Studies in Family Planning in India*, Abhinav Publication, New Delhi, 1974.

64. IPPF Open File, August 24, 1990, Cited in *Planned Parenthood Bulletin*, Vol. 38, No. 2, Family Planning Association of India, Bombay, August, 1990.

65. Gopalaswami, R.A., *Planned Development and Population Growth*, Institute of Applied Manpower Research, New Delhi, 1963.

66. Bravery, V. Bravery, Court of Appeal, 26 July 1954. All England Law Reports 59, 1954, cited in Legal Trends and Issues in Voluntary Sterilization cited in *Population Reports*, Series E, No. 6, Mar.-April, 1981.

67. Ministry of Health letter to All States, No. 23-3/58/FP dt. 20th Apr., 1960.

68. Krishenkumar, S., *The Story of Ernakulum Experiment in Family Planning*, Government of Kerala, 1971.

69. Rakshit, B., "Experiments on tubal blocking for sterilisation without laprotomy", *Journal of Obstetric And Gynaecology of India*, 18(2), 1968.

70. Rakshit, B., "Attempts at chemical blocking of the fallopian tubes for female sterilization", *Journal of* Obstetrics and Gynaecology of India, 1970.

71. "Minilaprotomy and Laproscopy Safe Effectively widely used, *Population Reports*, Series C, No. 9, May, 1985.

72. Family Welfare Programme in India, Year Book, 1986-87.

73. Jhaver, P.S., Davis, J.E., Lee, H., Hulka, J.F. and Light, G., "Reversibility of Sterilization by vas occlusion clip Fertility and Sterility 22.4, April, 1971.

74. 'Reversing Female Sterilization", *Population Reports*, Series C, No. 8, Sept., 1980.

75. *Population Today*, 14(9), The Population Reference Bureau Inc., Washington, Sept., 1985.

76. Annual Meeting of the Indian Council of Medical Research (Aurangabad 1965) and Advisory Committee on Scientific Aspect of Family Planning recommended : "(1) From the data presented at this meeting, reports of the Second International Conference on Intra-uterine Contraception held in New York, October 2-3, 1964 and the data presented from clinical studies conducted in India, it has been demonstrated that IUCD is safe, effective and acceptable and should be made available through all medical and health centres having requisite facilities. No para medical person should be permitted to insert the intra-uterine device, only the physicians may do the insertions for the present. (2) the IUCD may continue to be evaluated as is being done at present, but with a few more well-controlled studies added under the Director General Indian Council of Medical Research. (3) For the present Lippes Loop may be IUCD of choice. (4) Immediate manufacture of the IUCD should be undertaken in India"

77. Roy, Somnath, ed., *Intra-uterine Contraceptive Device*, 1966, Central Family Planning Institute, New Delhi, 1970.

78. Laumas, K.R., ed., *Review of Research Work in India on Intra-uterine Contraceptive Devices*, 1968, Indian Council of Medical Research, New Delhi.

79. "Basic and Clinical Aspects of Intra-Uterine Devicee",

World Health Organisation Technical Report No. 332, World Health Organisation, Geneva, 1966, See also "Intra-Uterine Devices. Physiological and Clinical Aspects", *World Health Organisation Technical Series No. 397*, World Health Organisation, Geneva, 1968.

80. Mohapatra, P.S., Sugathan, T.N., Prakash, V., and Roy, Somnath, *A Four Year Follow-up Study of Intra-uterine Contraceptive Device Acceptors*, National Institute of Family Planning, New Delhi, 1973, *See also* : Phatak, L.V., and Jain, Anrudh K., *Post-insertion Contraceptive and Fertility Behaviour of IUCD Acceptors*, National Family Planning, Institute, New Delhi, 1973.

81. IUDs—Update on Safety, Effectiveness and Research", *Population Reports*, Series B, No. 3, May, 1979.

82. The Population Council Annual Report, 1989.

83. Sivin, I, "IUDs are Contraceptives not abortificents ; a comment on research and belief", *Studies in Family Planning*, 20.6, 1989.

84. Sivin, I. and Schmidt, F., Effectiveness of IUDs. : A Review : *Contraception*, 361, 1, July, 1987.

85. "IUDs—A New Look", Population Reports, Series B, No. 5, March, 1988.

86. *as above.*

87. *as above.*

88. *Family Planning in India*, Directorate General Health Services Ministry of Health, New Delhi, 1959, see also, Sanyal, S.N., "Oral Contraceptive for Use of both Males and Females", and observations during discussion by C. Chandrasekaran and Warren O. Nelson, *International Conference on Planned Parenthood*, New Delhi, 14-21, Feb., 1959.

89. Roy Chaudhury, *Plants with Possible Antifertility Activity*, ICMR Special Report, Series No. 55, Indian Council of Medical Research, New Delhi, 1966.

90. Raina, B.L., "March of Conception Control Research", Address at the Conference of The Indian Society of Reproduction and Endocrinology Bombay, 24 February, 1970.

Das, R.P., *Contraceptive Technology, Past, Present and Future*, National Institute of Health and Family Welfare New Delhi, 1969.

Pincus, G., "Some Effects of progestrone and related compounds upon reproduction and early developments in mammals in : Pincus, G., ed., *Proceedings of the Fifth International Conference Planned Parenthood, Tokyo, October, 1955*, International Planned Parenthood Federation, 1955.

Pincus, G., Rock, J., Garcia, C.R., Ricewray, E., Paniagua, M, and Rodriguez, I., "Fertility Control with oral Medication", *American Journal of Obstetrics and Gynaecology*, 75.6, June, 1958.

Pincus, G., Rock, J., and Garica, C.R., "Effects of certain 19-nor steroids upon reproductive process", *Annals of the New York Academy of Sciences* 71, July 30, 1958.

91. Rock, John, Garcia, Celso-Ramon, and Pincus, Gregory, "Clinical Studies with Potential Oral Contraceptives", Pincus, Gregory, Rock, John and Garica, Celso R., "Field Trials with Norethynodrel as an Oral Contraceptive", in *The Sixth International Conference on Planned Parenthood*. The paper on the field trial was based on the analysis of various data over a 30 month period of 830 women in Puerto Rico (including San Juan and two others more rural than San Juan) and Haiti.

92. Oral Contraceptives in the 1980s, *Population Reports*, Series A, No. 6, May-June, 1982, See also : OCs-Update on Usage, Safety and Side Effects, *Population Reports*, Series A, No. 5, Jan., 1979.

Mechanism of Action of Sex Harmones and Analogous Substances, W.H.O. Tech., Report Series, 303, World Health Organisation, Geneva, 1965.

Clinical Aspects of Oral Gestogens, W.H.O. Tech. Report Series 326, 1966.

Harmonal Steroids in Contraception, W.H.O., Tech, Report, Series 386, 1968.

Steroid Contraception and the risk of neoplasma, W.H.O., Tech. Report, Series 619, 197c.

The Effect of female sex harmones on fetal development and infant health, W.H.O. Tech. Report, Series 657, 1981.
Mini Pill, A Limited Alternative for Certain Women, Population Report, Series A, No. 3, Sept., 1957, See also Devi, P.K., "Oral Contraceptive", in. *Drugs Bulletine,* 2(1), Department of Pharmacology, Postgraduate Institute of Medical Education and Research, Chandigarh, Jan., 1979.

93. Mohapatra, P.S., Sugathan, T.N. Sharma, B.B.L. and Mehra, Leila, *The Oral Pill Pilot Project in India,* Report of an Acceptor Follow Up Study, National Institute of Family Planning, New Delhi, 1971.

94. Inman, W.H. and Vassey, M.P., "Investigation of deaths from pulmonary, coronary and cerabrol thrombosis in women of child bearing age, *British Medical Journal,* 11, 1968.

"Royal College of General Practitioner's Oral Contraceptive Study.

95. Prasad, R.N.V. and Ratnam, S.S., The Cardio Vascular and Thromboembolic Risks of Oral Contraception—A Review, *Singapore Journal of Obstetric & Gyneocology,* 11.1., 1980.

Fotherby, K., "Oral Contraceptives, Lepoids and Cardeo-Vascular Disease, *Contraception*, 31, 1985.

96. Ratnam, R.R., "Contraceptive Technology of the Future in : Chandrasekaran, C., ed., *Three Contributions,* Applied Population Research Trust, Banglore, 1989. Das, R.P., *Contraceptive Technology Past, Present and Future.*

97. *Family Welfare Programme in India, Year Book 1986-87.*

98. Kapoor, M. and Ghosh, A.K., "Attituditional and Motivational Determinants of Birth Planning Behaviour", *Journal of Family Welfare*, Vol. 35, No. 5, Family Planning Association of India, Bombay, 1989.

99. *Family Welfare Programme in India, Year Book 1986-87.*

100. Ministry of Health, Government of India, No. F-4-38/64, F.P. II, 29 September, 1964.

The Terms of reference of this were to examine the question of legalisation of abortion in all its aspects—medical, social, legal and moral and to make recommendations.

101. *Report of the Committee to Study the Question of Legalisation of Abortion*, Ministry of Health and Family Planning, New Delhi, Dec., 1966.

102. *The Medical Termination of Pregnancy Act*, 1971. The Act became effective from 1st Apr., 1972.

103. *Family Welfare Programme in India, Year Book 1986-87.*

104. Franklin, R.R., and Dukes, C.D., "Antispermatozoal Anti-body and Unexplained Infertility", *American Journal of Obstetrics and Gynaecology*, 89.1, May 1, 1964, also see "Update on Condoms-Products, Protection and Promotion", *Population Reports*, Series H, Number 6, September-October, 1982.

105. Ratnam, S.S., "Contraceptive Technology of the Future", *Population Issues, Three Contributions*, Applied Population Research Trust Banglore, 1989.

106. *The Population Council Annual Report, 1989.*

107. Ratnam, S.S., "Contraceptive Technology of the Future".

108. WHO Task Force on Post-Ovulatory Methods of Fertility Regulation. Postcoital contraception with levonorgestrel during the pre-ovulatory phase of Menstrual cycle, *Contraception*, 36, 1987.

109. Lei, H.P. and Hu, Z.Y., The mechanism of Action of vacation pills in : Fen, C.C., Griffen, D., and Woolman,

A., Eds., *Recent Advances in Fertility Regulation*, Atar S.A., Geneva, 1981.

110. Ratnam, S.S., "Contraceptive Technology of the Future". See also Das R.P.. *Contraceptive Technology Past, Present and Future.*

111. *as above.*

112. *as above.*

113. Injectables and Implants, *Population Reports*, Series K, No. 3, March-April, 1987.

114. *The Population Council Annual Report, 1989.*

115. Das, R.P., *Contraceptive Technology, Past, Present and Future.*

116. Ratnam, S.S., Contraceptive Technology of the Future.

117. Das, R.P., *Contraceptive Technology, Past, Present and Future.*

118. Ratnam, S.S., Contraceptive Technology of the Future.

119. Berelson, Bernard and Stiener, Gary A., *Human Behaviour* An Inventory of Scientific Findings, Harcourt, Brace & World Inc., New York/Burlingame, 1961.

120. Press Information Bureau, December 1, 1990.

121. The estimates of the level of support for research in reproduction by Oscar Harkavy and Anna Southam were presented at the meeting in December, 1968 at Paris arranged by the Development Centre of the Organisation for Economic Cooperation and Development Paris.

122. *Report of Small Family Norm Committee*, Ministry of Health, Family Planning and Urban Development, New Delhi, 1968.

123. Dr. D.C. Dubey and his associates Dr. Miss Amita Bardhan, Mrs. S. Mullick and Mr. A.S. Chandoke studied the perception of incentives. Dr. S.D. Kapoor studied the psychological aspects of acceptors. He was

helped by Mr. A.K. Verma and Mrs. Shailbala Dayal, Professor E.I. George, Head of the Department of psychology Kerala University and Professor A.S. Patel, Head of Department of Psychology M.S. University, Baroda also helpd. Mr. B.R. Kohli and his associates Mr. P.K. Jain, Mr. H.B. Channa, Mr. O.P. Goel and Mr. B.B.L. Sharma studied the demographic and socio-economic characteristics of acceptors.

For details see Nanda, A.K., ed., *Vasectomy Camps—A Study*, National Institute of Family Planning, New Delhi, 1973.

124. Karan Singh, *Personal Communication.*

125. Chavan, S.B., "Population Problems a Planner's View" in *Yojna*, 27(1 & 2), Ministry of Information & Broadcasting, New Delhi, 26 June, 1983.

126. Bhatia, P.S, "Demographic Implications of incentives to Central Government Employees for adopting Small Family Norm" revised version of paper presented at the Annual Conference of Indian Association for Study of Population, Calcutta, December, 1980.

127. Satia, J.K. and Maru, Rushikesh, M., "Incentives and Disincentives in the Indian Family Welfare Programme" in *Studies in Family Planning*, 7(3). The Population Council Inc., New York, 1986.

128. *Revised Strategy for National Family Welfare Programme*, Department of Family Welfare, Ministry of Health & Family Welfare, New Delhi (mimeo).

129. Bhatia, P.S, "Planning for Human Resource Development", paper presented at the Annual Conference Indian Association for the Study of Population Jaipur, December, 1983.

130. The definition of education, training, communication and motivation were presented in the Report to the ACC Sub-committee on Population, ad-hoc Group on inter-

Agency Consultations on these and allied terms UNESCO and endorsed by the Working Group on Training of Personnel in Family Planning organised by the Economic Commission for Asia and the Far East (now ESCAP) in collaboration with the United Nations Fund for Population activities. Working Group on Training of Personnel in Family Planning Programmes (ECAFE), Report 1970, ECAPE, Bangkok ; and UNESCO document, May, 1970, EDS/FP/2341/1405.

131. *Meeting of the Family Planning Research and Programmes Committee, 1st July 1953, Proceedings, Meeting of the Family Planning Research and Programmes Committee, 2nd January, 1954.*

132. *Family Planning in India*, Directorate General Health Services, 1959.

133. *Meeting of the Central Family Board, 12th Dec., 1961*, New Delhi, *Summary Proceedings.*

134. Raina, B.L., and Chitkara, I.D., *Role of Hospitals in Family Planning Programme*, Paper presented at the Indian Hospital Association Annual Convention, New Delhi, Oct., 1967.

135. Raina, B.L., *Universities and Studies in the Field of Population*. Address at the Symposium on Population and Family Planning, Nov., 1967, Delhi University, Delhi.

Raina, B.L., *Universities and Studies in the Field of Population*, Central Family Planning Institute, May, 1969, New Delhi.

136. Workshop on Training of Family Planning Personnel, March, 1966, Central Family Planning Institute, New Delhi.

137. Raina, B.L., and Chaudhri, D.N., *Training in Family Planning Programme*, Central Family Planning Institute, Paper prepared for the International Conference on Family Planning held in Dacca, January-February, 1969.

138. Levell Hugh, R : Mayes, William F. and McGavran,

Edward G., *Intensive Health and Family Planning Programe ; Observations and Suggestions on Implementation*, Ford Foundation, New Delhi, 1963.

139. Notestein, Frank W., "Proposal for Demographic Training and Research Centre", mimeo. Princeton University Library, Office of Population Research, Princeton, 1955.

140. Bhende, Asha, Kanitkar, Tara, and Rama Rao, G. eds., *25 Years of IIPS*, International Institute of Population Studies, Bombay, 1981.

141. Raina, B.L., *Social Situation in India*, Commonwealth Publishers, New Delhi, 1990.

142. Dutt, P.R., *Rural Health Services in India*, Central Health Education Bureau, New Delhi, 1965.

143. Stewart, Sara, "Video as a Tool in Training and Organizing : Experience of Video SEWA", *Development 2*, Journal of the Society For International Development Rome, 1990.

144. *Family Planning Education Seminar*, (March 1960), Central Health Education Bureau, Directorate General Health Services, New Delhi, 1961.

145. Nyswander, B. Dorothy, *Dynamics of Planning in Health Education*, A digest of a presentation to the Health Educarion Workshop, Asilomar, 1955 (Mimeo).

146. See Chandrasekharan, C., and Bebarta, P.C., "The Relative Rate of Information Sources in the Dissemination of Knowledge of Family Planning Methods in Bombay City", in *The Journal of Family Welfare*, 9(4), Family Planning Association of India, Bombay, June, 1963.

147. Krishnamurthi, K.G., *Research in Family Planning in India*, Sterling Publishers (Pvt.) Ltd., Delhi, 1968. This was the first attempt in publishing research activities in family planning in India.

A number of reviews were later published such as Dubey, D.C. and Devgan, A.K., *Family Planning Communication Studies in India*, Central Family Planning Institute, New Delhi, 1969. Rao, Kamla Gopal (and project associate, Mullick, Saroj), *Studies in Family Planning : India*, Abhinav Publication, New Delhi, 1974.

Parekh, U., and Rao, T.V., *Behavioural Sciences : A Status Study on Population Research in India*, Vol. I, Tata McGraw-Hill Pub. Coy., New Delhi, 1947.

In 1984 selected studies were reviewed by Bardhan, Amita, Dubey, D.C. and Mullick, S. in "Communication and Family Welfare" during the National Seminar on Communication Research Trends and Priorities in March, 1984. Department of Communication Research, Indian Institute of Mass Communication, New Delhi.

148. Indian Institute of Management, "India : Evaluation of a Publicity Programme on Family Planning (Hooghly Experiment)" in *Studies in Family Planning*, The Population Council, New York, 21 June, 1967.

149. Bogue, Donald and Johnson, W. Burt, "Towards A Master Plan for Family Planning Communication". Paper presented for section 'Communication in Development', Eleventh World Conference of the Society for International Development, New Delhi, 14-17 November, 1969. Many persons trained at Community and Family Study Centre University Chicago made valuable contribution to development of communication strategies.

150. See Frank, Wilder, 'Getting More of the Mass Media : A Modern Guide for Modern Family Planning Programme. Prepared for the Conference on Family Planning and National Development, the International Association, at Bandung June 1 to 7, 1969, gives background of actual development of use of mass media when D.K., Tyagi became Chief of Media.

151. Naik, V.R., *Communication in the Health and Family Welfare Programme in India: Some Observations*, National Institute of Health and Family Welfare, New Delhi, July, 1981.

152. Singh, K.N., *Agricultural Communication*, Paper Presented at the National Seminar on Communication Research Trends and Priorities, Institute of Mass Communication, New Delhi, March, 1984.

153. Narula, Uma, *Development Communication*, Paper presented at the National Seminar on Communication Research Trends and Priorities, Indian Institute of Mass Communication, New Delhi, March, 1984.

154. Rao, Y.V. Lakshmana ;'and Lim u Won Lena, "Research and Practice in Mass Communication in Asia : Doing and Understanding" in *Studies in Broadcasting*, NHK Tokyo, 1979, cited by Yadav, J.S., "Communication Research Some Reflections", paper presented at National Seminar on Communication Research Trends and Priorities, Indian Institute of Mass Communication, New Delhi, March, 1984.

155. Patil, B.R., *Community and Communication*, paper presented at the National Seminar on Communication Research Trends and Priorities, Indian Institute of Mass Communication, New Delhi, March, 1984.

156. Childers, Erskine B., "The New Age of Information—What Kind of Participation ?" *Development*, 2, Rome, 1990.

157. Gupta, P.P., "Application of Information Technology for Development in India", *Development* 2, Rome, 1990.

158. Boulding, Elise, "Building a Global Civic Culture", *Development*, 2, Rome, 1990.

159. Vajrathon, Mallica, "UNFPA Adolescents and Newlywed Couples as New Actors in Population and Development", *Development*, 2, Rome, 1990.

160. Sichalwe, Mann. V., "Reporting the Rural Areas", *COMBROAD*, Commonwealth Broadcasting Association, London, September, 1986.

161. Atkins, George S., "Farm Radio in Developing Countries: A Case Study of the Developing Countries Farm Radio Network", *Development*, 2, Rome, 1990.

162. Schram, Wilbur, *The Mass Media in Family Planning Campaigns*, Paper presented at the International Workshop on Communication Aspects of Family Planning Programme, December 2-14, 1968.

163. Himes, Norman E., *Medical History of Contraception*, Gamut Press, Inc., New York, 1963.

164. Mace, D.R., Bannermann, R.H.O., and Burton, J., *Teaching of Human Sexuality in Schools for Health Professionals*, Public Health Paper 57, World Health Organisation, Geneva, 1974.

165. *Population Participation as a Strategy for Promoting Community-level Action and National Development*, United Nations, New York, 1981.

166. Flavier, J.M., "Gaining Intersectoral Support : The Case of People's School", *Hygie*, 8.1, International Institute of Rural Reconstruction, Silang, Cavite, Philippinres, 1989.

167. Narula, Uma, "Development Communication" in *National Seminar on Communication Research Trends and Priorities*, Indian Institute of Communication, New Delhi, 1981.

168. Ariyaratne. A.T., *Case Study—A People' Movement for Self Reliance in Sri Lanka*, Sarvodaya Shramdan Movement Sri Lanka, 1977, See also by the same author, *A Struggle to Awaken*, 1978.

169. Leavell, Hugh R., Mayes, William F., McGavran, Edwarde G., *Intensive Health and Family Planning Programme Observations on Implementation*, Ford Foundation, New Delhi, February, 1963.

170. Sawhney, Nirmal, *Personal Communication*.

171. Seshagiri Rao, K. Rao, Anasuya N., Yadav, S.S., Potnis, S.K., Sushama, P.N., Bhat, K.P., Kempwadkar, Shashikala V., Chandramouli, A.S., Ashokan, V., and Sampath, K., *Experimentation of Alternative Strategies in Family Planning*. An Evaluation, Population Centre India Population Project, Karnataka, Banglore, 1979.

172. *as above*.

173. Soundram Ramchandran, *Personal Communication*.

174. "Community—Based Health and Family Planning".

Population Reports, Series I, No. 3, Population Information Programme John Hopkins University Baltimore, Nov.-Dec., 1982.

175. Chakravorty, Ujjayant, "A health project that works-progress in Jamkhed", in *World Health Forum*, Vol. 4, No. 1, World Health Organisation, Geneva, 1983.

176. Anand, D., *Family Planning Through Hospital Care*, Central Family Institute, New Delhi, 1969.

177. Zatuchni, Gerald I., "The Post-Partum Programme: A New Approach", in *Family Planning Programmes*, An International Study edited by Bernard Berelson Basic Books Inc., Publishers, New York, London, 1969.

178. Family Welfare Programme in India Year Book 1986-87.

179. *First Five Year Plan*, Planning Commission, New Delhi.

180. Baumgartner, Leona and Notestein, F., "Suggestions for a Practical Programme of Family Planning and Child Care".

181. Krishnamurthy, K.G. and Nadkarni, M.V., *Integrated Child Development Services, An Assessment*, UNICEF, Regional Office, for South Central Asia, New Delhi, May, 1983.

182. Family Welfare Programme in India Year Book, 1986-87.

183. *Facts for Life*, UNICEF, India Country Office 73, Lodi Estate, New Delhi-110003, 1990.

184. *as above.*

185. *as above.*

186. Wilkinson, S.A., "A Commentry" in, *Birth Control Why, When & How*, by B.L. Raina, New Book Coy, Bombay, 1939.

187. Raina B.L., *Planning Family in India.*

188. Verma, S.S., Government of India/ILO, National Seminar on the Management of the Family Welfare Programme in Organised Sector, New Delhi, February, 1978.

189. Isac, D., *Personal Communication.*

190. The account is based on the paper on "Plantations" by B.L. Raina for the Labour Welfare Committee, and reports and information provided by K.N. Sircar and M.K. Chaudhri.

191. Choudhri, M.K., *Personal Correspondence.*

192. Chacko. I.V., *Personal Correspondence* and UPASI Reports and Papers.

193. Talwar, P.P. and Gaba, K.L., "Family Welfare Educational Activities in Industrial Sector-Experiences and An Operational Guideline", in Sen Gupta, B., Guha, A. and Talwar, P.P., Eds., *Corporate Sector and Family Welfare in India, Overview of Problem* Council of Indian Employers, New Delhi, 15 January, 1990.

194. *Caribbean Regional Employers Seminar on Population and Family Welfare Planning Port of Spain 10 14 April, 1973*, International Labour Office, Geneva, 1973.

195. Chitre, K.T., "Family Welfare Programme in the Organised Sector. Employees State Insurance Corporation", Paper presented at the GOL/ILO National Seminar on the Management of the Family Welfare Programme in the Organised Sector, New Delhi, February, 1978.

196. Tata, J.R.D., Address at the Annual General Meeting of Tata Iron and Steel Company, August, 1955. Personal Communication.

197. See reports of Asian seminar on trade unions, workers education and population questions Bangalore 1970 ; Asian employers seminar on population and family planning New Delhi 1971 ; Asian Symposium on Labour and Population Policies Kuala Lumpur 1972 ; Carribbean Regional Seminar on Population and Family Welfare Planning Port of Spain April 1973 : African sub-regional employers seminar on population and family welfare planning Accra 1973 ; MEF/ILO-UNFPA seminar on population and family welfare planning. Port Louis September 1973, International Labour Office, Geneva.

198. Kapoor, R.M., "Programme Development and Management at Unit Level" paper presented at GOI/ILO National Seminar on the Management of the Family Welfare programme in the Organised Sector, New Delhi. February, 1978.

199. Zacharia, K.C., *The Anamoly of the Fertility Decline in India's Kerala State*, A Field Investigation. The World Bank Washington D.C. USA, 1984.

Index